Praise for *Clearance and Copyright*

"Everything you need to know about clearance and copyright is in Michael Donaldson's book, a must for everyone in the film business."
—Barbara Boyle, Producer, *Bottle Rocket, Instinct*;
Chair, UCLA Department of Film, Television and Digital Media

"You can't deliver a film to a distributor or sales agent without having cleared the hurdles discussed in this book. Michael Donaldson helps you clear those hurdles with humor and clarity. Don't try to sell your film without it." —Kathy Morgan, Chairperson, AFMA (formerly the American Film Marketing Association)

"While making *Spellbound*, we found this to be an indispensable resource. The writing is clear and lucid; the advice is thoughtful and practical. In short, this book is the next best thing to having a top-notch lawyer on your production team."
—Jeff Blitz, Director, *Spellbound*

"This book is a godsend for the independent filmmaker! With what it's saving my next production in legal fees, I can afford to hire another grip and rent two more 4Ks. For regional filmmakers, Donaldson's book is indispensable. It gives those of us working in the Heartland easy access to the legal tricks of the trade usually only available on 'the coast.' I'm buying one for myself AND one for my local attorney."
—Glen Pitre, Writer/Director/Producer, *Belizaire the Cajun*, *The Scoundrel's Wife*

"'Let's make a movie.' It's never that simple. Michael Donaldson has written an invaluable book on the A to Z of pitfalls that all independent filmmakers should be aware of before they start to shoot one frame of film. Essential reading." —Piers Handling, Toronto International Film Festival

"Your film can win many festival prizes, but you still have to obtain the proper clearances or your film is undistributable, and sometimes even unshowable at some festivals. Too often the independent filmmaker does not realize how important the issues of clearance, copyright, insurance. and licensing are in the arena of selling your film. This book guides you through all of these areas." —Geoffrey Gilmore, Director of Film Festival, Sundance Institute

CLEARANCE & COPYRIGHT

CLEARANCE

&

COPYRIGHT

verything the Independent Filmmaker Needs to Know

2nd Edition ■ Revised, Updated & Expanded

BY MICHAEL C. DONALDSON

SILMAN-JAMES PRESS ■ LOS ANGELES

Second Edition
10 9 8 7 6 5 4 3 2 1

Library of Congress Cataloging-in-Publication Data

Donaldson, Michael C.
Clearance and copyright : everything the independent
filmmaker needs to know /
by Michael C. Donaldson.—2nd ed., rev., updated,
and expanded.
p.   cm.
Includes index.
1. Copyright—Motion pictures—United States—Popular works.
2. Copyright—United States—Popular works.
3. Copyright clearinghouses—United States—popular works.
I. Title
KF3070.Z9D66 2003   346.7304'82—dc22   2003055926
                         [347.306482]

ISBN: 1-879505-72-X

This book is sold with the understanding that neither the author
nor the publisher is rendering legal advice with regard to any specific
situation or problem. This book is for your general education on
the subject of clearance and copyright. If you need legal advice,
seek the services of an attorney. The publisher and the author cannot
in any way guarantee that the forms in this book are being used
for the purposes intended and, therefore, assume no responsibility for their proper and correct use.

Cover design by Heidi Frieder

Printed and bound in the United States of America

Silman-James Press
1181 Angelo Drive
Beverly Hills, CA 90210

To inquiring clients to whom I have said,
"Buy a book". . . and there was none.

CONTENTS

INTRODUCTION
TO THE SECOND EDITION

This book's first edition was written for independent filmmakers who constantly face copyright and clearance questions as their projects progress. That is still the intent and focus of this second edition.

To my surprise, *Clearance and Copyright* is used in many college classrooms. It also shows up on the desks of a lot of people clearing content for the large film studios and the television networks and cable channels and their various suppliers of content. Its wide acceptance has brought me personal joy and professional satisfaction.

This second edition brings the book up to date with the many changes in statutory law, case law, and some administrative procedures that have occurred during the last seven years. It is a page-one rewrite that includes many new stories, four new forms, and three entirely new chapters: The first is an expansion of the sections on fair use. The second expands my discussion of collaboration. The third addresses copyrights on the Internet.

Organized in the chronological order in which you normally meet various real-world legal issues that come up while nurturing a film to the big or small screen, *Clearance and Copyright* begins with acquiring material, and includes some help with the most baffling question: "Whom do I call, anyway?" It takes you through development, pre-production and production, the registration of the completed work, and the film's release, and includes a chapter that discusses copyright infringement.

Nothing is overly esoteric here. This is not a legal treatise. It's a book filled with timesaving forms, quick answers, and reminders that certain areas are the domain of experienced legal counsel. This book does not take the place of an attorney's advice. For specific advice, be sure to seek out a knowledgeable attorney.

Use this book to save thousands of dollars by gaining a working knowledge of the issues you need to discuss before you employ an attorney. The more you know, the more efficient your conversation is with your lawyer. Lawyers bill by the hour, so a one-person seminar on copyright basics, on copyright infringement, or on filling out a copyright form can be a very expensive proposition. The more knowledgeable and organized you are, the more you get out of the time you spend with your attorney, and the more your attorney will enjoy working with you.

Good luck!

ACKNOWLEDGMENTS

Those who use the book in class or professionally have been enormously helpful in defining the course of this new edition. Ram Bergman and Dana Lustig, who first inspired this book, have been joined by a legion of users and questioners: students and filmmakers and professionals involved with clearing films. All of them have helped to mold and shape the present edition's contents.

Because my work on this book was extensive, there were moments at home that required enormous understanding and support. Special thanks go to my partner, TK. My three daughters, Michelle, Amy, and Wendy have been cheerleaders in all my endeavors. Thanks again.

My editor Jim Fox took on a larger role in this edition than is usually the case. Many thanks to him and to his business partner, Gwen Feldman, who had the wisdom and flexibility to make our relationship work so well.

The following men read the manuscript from cover to cover for architectural integrity, flow, and common-sense comments:

Timothy W. Kittleson

Joseph F. Hart

J. Stephan Sheppard

Dixon Q. Dern

The contracts were reviewed by Frank Lunn.

Individual chapters of the book were critiqued for content by the following:

Doug Irvine - Chapter 13 – E&O Insurance

Bruce Polichar - Chapter 22 – Copyright on the Internet

David Powell - Chapters 15 and 16 concerning music

While Vince Ravine's film producing duties kept him too busy to help with the revision, his influence from the first edition is still present.

Also, many thanks to the technical reviewers of the first edition: Ed Blau, Mitch Block, Eric Feig, Craig Gates, Ron Gertz, Betsy McLane, Lou Petrich, Jerry Philips, Lon Sobel, Larry Sugar, and Tom White. These people gave of their valuable professional time to check the accuracy of this book. Their time and experience added great value to it.

Last, but definitely not least, my law office staff deserves my sincere gratitude. Led by Alexandra Sandmann, Tevis Dick and Van Tran helped in too many ways to mention. They make every workday a pleasure—for me, for each other, and for our clients.

PART I

GATHERING THE RIGHTS

Getting started is always difficult. This section covers everything you need to do to have the right to develop a film project, no matter what the source of your inspiration.

CHAPTER 1

COPYRIGHT AND IDEAS

You have an idea for a film. No script. No rights. Nothing. Just an idea. You think that your idea would make a great film, but how do you get other people interested in your idea without them stealing it? At seminars from Los Angeles to Cannes, filmmakers and those who want to be filmmakers are worried that someone will steal their great ideas—someone will rip them off. Often, they do not even know that they are asking a copyright question.

WHAT IS COPYRIGHT?

Think simple. Copyright, at its simplest, is the right to copy. In fact, when the U.S. passed its first copyright act in 1790, making copies was just about the only right that was protected. Keeping that simple beginning in mind will go a long way toward answering many of your copyright questions. It certainly will remind you how to spell the word: *copyright* = right to copy. The constitution authorizes a monopoly for those who create things. The creator and the creator's heirs have the right to exploit their creation or hide it in a closet, never to be seen or heard by anyone. Congress passed the necessary laws, using the profit motive of absolute monopoly, to encourage the flow of creative juices—you create it, you own it! You own it, you—and you alone—decide the ways in which you will profit from it.

Specifically, here is a partial list of the creations protected by copyright:

Books

Plays

Comic books

Songs

Musical compositions

Recordings of music, even if the music itself is in the public domain

Photographs

Quilts

Choreography

Paintings

Drawings

Sculptures

Jewelry

Fabric designs, but not the clothes made from them

Architectural drawings, but not the buildings created from them

Maps, but only the newly created elements, not the location of things on the map

Computer programs

And, of course, movies and scripts for movies and treatments for scripts for movies.

The Bad News

Copyright law does not protect ideas. Copyright law only protects the "expression of an idea that is fixed in a tangible form." This means that written words are protectable; the ideas behind them aren't. You can't own an idea that's in the air.

You can write up your ideas for movies to your heart's content. The written words can be registered with the copyright office. The copyright law protects you from someone copying those words, but your ideas are fair game. You obtain protection for your idea in direct proportion to how much of your idea that you write down.

The more you write, the more protection you have. One or two sentences may express your idea, but if someone steals it, you will never be able to identify your one or two sentences in a feature-length motion picture. As a matter of protecting your idea in the marketplace, the more you write down, the better, because copyright law only protects the written word, not ideas—no matter how original. "Ideas are as free as the air."

The Good News

More than a mere glimmer of hope shines on you if your idea gets ripped off. Consider the true (and now very famous) case of Julian Blaustein.

Julian Blaustein was an experienced producer of thirty years with major credits such as *Broken Arrow* (1950), the landmark sci-fi film *The Day the Earth Stood Still* (1951), and *Bell, Book and Candle* (1958). He had supervised more than twenty films a year at 20th Century Fox. In the mid-'60s, he had a great idea: Let's have Richard Burton and Elizabeth Taylor do a film based on Shakespeare's *Taming of the Shrew*. Some people who observed that couple in public would not think that the idea was particularly original. Nevertheless, Blaustein contacted then-relatively-unknown stage director Franco Zeffirelli, who was interested in directing the film. When Blaustein approached the actors' agent about the availability of the world's most famous duo, the agent insisted on hearing the idea. Blaustein disclosed his idea, which included substantial detail of what to cut and what to retain and how to expand Shakespeare's classic.

The agent liked what he heard and pitched the idea to the Burtons, who liked the idea so much that they made a film—with Zeffirelli directing—that incorporated many of Blaustein's ideas. But they made it without Blaustein.

Not nice. Blaustein sued. Blaustein won.

The court said that Blaustein should have a chance to prove that he had an implied oral contract to produce the picture with a reasonable compensation and appropriate credit. Note that Blaustein was an experienced producer. He had only somewhat developed his film idea, but he would not have revealed any of the above details to the parties without the expectation of producing the picture. If you are not a legitimate producer with something of a track record, be aware of that factor as you evaluate your situation. Think of the world of producers as a spectrum between the likes of Blaustein on one hand and a wannabe producer who, during a meeting, makes the simple, naked suggestion that the Burtons should film *Taming of the Shrew*.

The Blaustein victory was based in part on a successful legal battle fought by Victor Desny. Desny was a professional writer with a great idea. The year was 1949, more than two decades after a boy named Floyd Collins was trapped in a cave, a story that the newspapers of the time covered with a vengeance. The Collins story had always fascinated Desny. He wrote a treatment on the incident and included a wholly fictional event as part of his story. He thought that the story was perfect for the famous director Billy Wilder, who was working at Paramount at the time, and asked for a meeting to pitch his idea. Wilder's secretary said that the story was too long for Wilder to read, so Desny condensed his sixty-five-page draft down to three pages and called back two days later. The protective secretary made him read it over the phone while she took it down in shorthand (secretaries could do that in 1949). He mentioned in that conversation that he wanted to sell the story to Wilder and write the script.

Wilder liked the story. He liked it so much that he hired someone else to write the script. Paramount made the movie, *Ace in the Hole* starring Kirk Douglas. The film included the totally fictionalized portion created by Desny.

Not nice. Desny sued. Desny won . . . as well he should have.

The court ruled that Desny had an implied oral contract. An oral contract is any non-written contract. An implied contract is an agreement that arises without any party specifically stating the terms. One of the parties indicates by their conduct rather than by their words that there is an agreement. In contrast to an implied contract, an express contract is one in which the parties have agreed to the terms in specific words, either orally or in writing.

The court said, "Generally speaking, ideas are as free as the air." However, the court found that Desny would not have offered the idea to Wilder except for the prospect that Desny would write it. The court said that a professional writer only pitches ideas for the purpose of employment. Note that Desny had credits but also acted professionally because he kept good records. He had his sixty-five-page, dated story. He had his three-page, dated outline. He recorded his calls to Wilder's office in his writer's diary. The court also said that "the law of implied contracts assumes particular importance in literary idea and property controversies."

What a mouthful! What a case! The courts recognize that writers are not truffle pigs, sniffing out good stories and bringing them to the attention of others only to have the stories snatched from them by those who would use them and grow rich. Courts have little trouble with that concept. The issues today are whether the parties sufficiently establish their relationship to require the idea recipient to pay, whether the idea is the kind of idea that has to be paid for, and whether the material is really used in a way that requires payment.

On the first point, the courts require that both parties be professionals, active in the entertainment business. If your plumber shouts from beneath the sink whilst fixing your drain pipe, "Hey you oughta make a movie about lesbian paraplegics invading Detroit" and you like the idea, you would not be expected to hire him or her to write the script for the film. Therefore, you do not owe him or her any money. The courts have not yet extended idea protection to folks outside the business. Folks outside the business don't like that and often write claim letters. There is no indication right now that the courts have any interest in throwing the net any wider to include more people in the class of protected submitters. In fact, even if you are an active producer, there has to be something more than the mere submission. There has to be some action or event, such as a meeting or other interaction, that creates a contract.

The court in the Desney case made specific mention of the fact that Desny was a professional writer and stated explicitly that he was trying to sell his idea to Wilder. Wilder's secretary said words to the effect that if the idea were used, "naturally we will pay you for it."

On the second point, the idea must be specific enough to convince a jury that it was *your* idea that was ripped off. The more general the idea, the harder it is to demonstrate that it was your idea. Also, the idea must have been first conveyed by you and not have come from someone else. If the person receiving the idea already had received it from someone else, they would not owe you, but rather would owe someone else. Originality, of course, is an aspect of this issue, but different states have different requirements on this point. Courts in most states require that the idea be novel. California courts have said that novelty is not an issue, but note that Desny did create one original scene in an otherwise factual story.

Finally, not every idea's use triggers a payment. Even if your idea becomes a line or scene that is used by someone else, it would not be enough to trigger payment. The use of the idea has to be such that it would deny the person who submitted the idea the ability to make money from their own, separate use of the idea. If you unsuccessfully try to develop a project based on a submitted idea, the person who submitted the idea could still write a script and sell it, so it is a "no harm, no foul" situation. Remember, Desny is not a copyright case. It is a contract case. The courts have not yet given money for a use of an idea that did not produce money to the defendant and deny money to the plaintiff. The ultimate use must also be substantially similar to the submitted idea. In the Desny case, the movie followed the three-page treatment faithfully. In the Blaustein case, every element of Blaustein's idea was used. If this is not the case, then an idea is not stolen, it is an inspiration. Inspiration is good. Theft is bad. Only the taking of someone else's idea is punished. If someone inspires you to create something terrific, good for you and good for them—even if they don't see it that way.

Today, these so-called Desny cases are not uncommon, but they are still tough to win. Here are the exact instructions that the judge gave to the jury when Warren Beatty, Columbia Pictures, and Robert Towne were sued by a certain Ms. Mann under the Desny theory for their film *Shampoo*:

Mann has the burden of establishing, by a preponderance of the evidence, all of the facts necessary to prove each of the following issues:

1. That plaintiff submitted her ideas to the defendants and that the defendants received them.

2. That before plaintiff submitted her ideas to the defendants, she clearly conditioned her disclosure upon defendants' agreement to pay for those ideas of plaintiff's that the defendants used, if any.

3. That defendants knew, or should have known, the condition upon which the disclosure was being made before the disclosure was made.

4. That the defendants voluntarily accepted the submission on plaintiff's terms and thereby implicitly agreed to pay plaintiff for any of her ideas that they might use.

In order to find for the plaintiff, you must find that she has established, by a preponderance of the evidence, each and every one of the foregoing described issues; otherwise, you must find for the defendants.

Non-Disclosure Agreements

Many independent producers are presented with non-disclosure agreements before writers will pitch their ideas. A non-disclosure agreement says that producers will not disclose to others the idea being pitched to them unless they buy the idea. There really is no reason for a producer to sign such an agreement. In Desny's case, Desny could not even get a face-to-face meeting with Wilder. Wilder surely would not have signed an agreement saying that he would not disclose any of the material in order to hear the pitch. He would not want the bother of reading the agreement or the hint of liability that it suggests. Such a thing would have ended the Desny v Wilder story before it began.

As you may note, I am not a big fan of these documents. In my view, such agreements are off-putting at best. At worst, they stop the meeting. The relationship is stillborn: killed by the writer's fear that you will try to steal this particular idea. The writer's paranoid desire to contractually protect against theft (justified as it may be) results in no pitch, no deal, no movie. A writer who never shops an idea ends up in the same place as the writer who shops an idea and has it stolen: nowhere.

PROTECT YOURSELF

Some writers verbalize the agreement that the court in the Desny case implied. They say, "If you don't want to use this idea, please don't pass it on. I understand that if you like it, I get to write it." As an honest producer, you should already possess this point of view.

After a pitch, some writers send a thank-you letter, not unlike the one your mother taught you to write. It might read: "I enjoyed meeting you last Wednesday and discussing my idea for a folk-dance film set in New York in the not-too-distant future. I'm so glad that you liked the characters Monsoon and Dry Season and the way they interacted with their racially mixed Martian parents. Your sympathy with the dog who caught lyme disease from biting the masochistic postal worker was truly encouraging. I hope you want to go forward with this project."

If you receive such a letter, keep it. It is part of a paper trail. If you already were working with any of these ideas that the author discussed, write back, "Yes, but don't forget that we have a script in development with that same great lyme-disease twist, so we won't be able to work on this project together." Or whatever applies. Create your own paper trail at the critical junctures of any idea exchanges.

It is much better for writers to do the work of writing and polishing than to rely on paper agreements for protection. In fact, writers who are too lazy to write down ideas and keep diaries and do the other things necessary to protect themselves probably deserve what they get.

To protect ideas, create a "paper trail" by doing the following:

1. Write down your ideas, the more detailed the better.
   Save all your drafts.

2. Register whatever you write with the Writers Guild of America (WGA). This registration has no legal effect, but it helps establish the history of the creation of your script.

3. Keep a detailed diary of all your meetings, even telephone meetings.

4. Follow up your meetings with written thank-you notes. This confirms your meeting in a pleasant way, while it creates a paper trail.

Always make sure that the cover of your treatment or script contains a WGA registration number and the maximum amount of information about you: your name, your address, your agent, your lawyer. If a major agency represents you, their distinctive covers tell it all. The fire-engine red cover of CAA or the classic silver cover of ICM directs everyone's attention to a phone number that is already in many of our automatic dialing systems.

Whether you take your idea to treatment or script stage, by writing it down and maintaining a paper trail, you are more protected than if it is purely an idea in your head. Most people do not register the copyright of their works at this stage. It is simply too early. Still, you may feel a need to keep a record. That is a correct feeling. Keep a detailed record in a bound book of every draft, every meeting, every significant event in the life of your project.

When Copyright Protection Starts

Interestingly, copyright protection attaches to a work instantly as you are writing the words on the page. The United States used to have a highly formal system in which there was no protection unless you had the correct notice on your work and the work had been registered properly in Washington, D.C. The rest of the world was generally less formal. Their attitude was that if you wrote it, it was yours. You did not have to put notices everywhere and register your claim.

Recently, the United States signed various treaties to move toward world unity in copyright laws. The United States had many reasons for doing this, including protecting trade markets and fighting copyright piracy. The result has been that the legal structure for U.S. copyright has joined the less formalistic world view. This is very important to our economy since this is one of the healthiest aspects of our international trade. American films and music travel around the world, and we want them to travel with maximum protection. The American system now conforms with the rest of the world. American copyright law now protects your work as you are creating it. Formal registration of the script and of the completed film with the Copyright Office are covered in separate chapters. For now, know that the law protects a script as it is being written down and that there is a simple way to register your copyright with the Copyright Office. Go ahead and use the © notice on the script cover.

Writers Guild Registration

Once you have written out your idea, call it a treatment and register it with the Writers Guild of America. The cost is very low ($30 at this writing). A treatment tells the story of the script in abbreviated form. It can be a few paragraphs, a few pages, or more than twenty pages. For purposes of protection of your ideas, the more detailed it is, the better. WGA registration is available to everybody, whether or not you are a member of the Writers Guild. As part of the registration process, the WGA gives the treatment or script a number, puts it in a sealed envelope, and stores it in a vault. You give them two copies, which they keep sealed in their vault for five years. You may extend the registration for another five years. No one can withdraw your script without a court order except you. Today, the entire process can be handled online.

Self-Mailing

People might have told you to mail your treatment or script in an envelope addressed to yourself as a substitute for copyright registration or registration with the WGA. You write. You mail. You receive back your postmarked envelope. You do not open it. You save. Does this work? It has always been a mystery why anybody would want to bother with all of this. Yes, this procedure might very well work if such an envelope were dramatically opened at a trial. It would show with some precision what was written on a certain day. However, if there were a lot of money riding on the outcome, you'd better believe that forensic scientists would testify that the envelope was opened and resealed, had been tampered with, was somehow unreliable, or in some other way was not valid. You know how lawyers are. For the low-cost simplicity and absolute reliability of registering your treatment with the Copyright Office or the Writers Guild, why bother with self-mailing?

The folks in Holland have figured this out, however. In Holland, you can take your script to the customs bureau. They will date-stamp each page for you with an official government stamp. You can then mail that script to yourself (after you copy it so that you know exactly what is in the envelope and can show it to your lawyer if you need to). That mailed script will offer a double proof of the date of authorship: the envelope's mailing information and the stamps on each script page. The stamps on each page appeal to me as a form of proof.

The Ultimate Idea Protection:
Hide Your Candle Under a Bush

That's right. Share your great ideas with no one. Don't let anybody read it. Don't let anybody look at it. It won't be stolen. It won't be ripped off.

Amazingly, some writers and producers are so paranoid that they prevent anybody from seeing their material rather than run the risk of someone stealing it. Most successful writers and producers are less concerned about idea theft. They take the view that ideas are a dime a dozen; what is valuable is how you execute them.

Sure, creative works are stolen all the time. Not nearly as frequently as amateurs believe to be true, but it does happen. The mechanisms discussed in this chapter protect your rights should such a thing happen. Hopefully, you will enjoy your life without having to face off against a word thief.

1.01 NON-DISCLOSURE/NON-CIRCUMVENTION AGREEMENT

THIS AGREEMENT is made as of _____, 20__, between _____ located at _____ and _____ located at _____.

_____, or its representative and/or assigns (hereinafter referred to simply as I or me), has agreed and intends to from time to time disclose to _____ (hereinafter referred to simply as you), certain client contacts, technical, conceptual, financial and other proprietary information which I (individually and collectively) consider to be confidential information relating to proposed motion picture and television program opportunities and/or materials, contacts and concepts relating directly or indirectly thereto (hereinafter referred to as "INFORMATION"), for the sole purpose of allowing you to evaluate such INFORMATION. You and I have agreed to execute and deliver this Non-Circumvention and Non-Disclosure Agreement.

I have indicated that I would like to safeguard such INFORMATION. Accordingly, you agree to maintain such INFORMATION in confidence according to the terms set forth hereinafter:

1. As used in this agreement INFORMATION shall mean all data, documents, proposals, outlines, technical, conceptual, financial and client contacts, names, addresses, telephone/fax/telex numbers, economic and loan or investor information, commercialization and research strategies, vendors, trade secrets and know-how disclosed by me to you, directly or indirectly, either in writing or orally, relating to the proposed projects entitled _____, except such information and know-how which (a) can be shown by you to have been in your possession prior to the disclosure to you by me; (b) at the time of disclosure hereunder is, or hereafter becomes, through no fault of you, part of the public domain by publication or otherwise.

2. This Agreement is a perpetuating agreement for five (5) years from the date above, and is to be applied to any and all transactions entertained by you during the period of this Agreement. This Agreement is also effective upon your heirs, assignees and designees.

3. You, individually, and any associates, hereby agree that you and their corporation, divisions, subsidiaries, employees, agents, or consultants will neither intentionally disclose the INFORMATION to any third party, company and/or individual; nor intentionally use the INFORMATION in competition with my business, for any purpose other than that contemplated under this agreement. In the event you use the INFORMATION, intentionally or otherwise and are informed of such use in writing, you agree to fully compensate me for such use to date of notice and will cease to use INFORMATION unless mutually agreed upon in writing to do otherwise.

15

4. In consideration of the foregoing, you hereby covenant and agree, individually, for yourself and any respective affiliates, partners, officers, directors, corporations, divisions, subsidiaries, employees, agents and/or consultants, to not communicate with (in writing or verbally), make any contact with, deal with or otherwise enter into any agreement and/or understanding with any corporation, partnership, person or other entity introduced by me (and/or my officers, directors, shareholders, partners and/or agents thereof) relating to or arising out of the INFORMATION or in the areas of funding and financing, without my prior written consent. You hereby further agree to keep completely confidential the names of any corporations, organizations, individual or group of individuals, buyers or sellers, introduced by me, in connection with the INFORMATION, as well as all non-public documentation, materials or information supplied to you relating to such INFORMATION.

5. You agree not to make any copies of the INFORMATION, whole or in part, for the purpose other than the purposes contemplated in this Agreement and will, upon my request, return all written materials furnished hereunder and any notes or memoranda of conversations relating thereto, including any copies thereof.

6. Neither this Agreement nor disclosure of the INFORMATION by me shall be deemed by implication or otherwise to vest in you any rights in any concepts, trademarks, patents or other properties of mine and/or my assigns relating directly or indirectly to the INFORMATION and/or any related projects.

7. The parties hereto recognize and agree the remedies at law for breach of the provisions of this Agreement will be inadequate and that I and/or assigns, shall, in addition to any other rights which it might have, be entitled to injunctive relief in the event that such a breach of the Agreement occurs. You further acknowledge and agree that the INFORMATION is unique to me and that your breach of the terms of this agreement will result in material damages to me. Any claim arising out of a breach of this agreement shall be settled by order of the law of the State of California by binding arbitration in accordance with the rules of the American Arbitration Association in Los Angeles, California. The prevailing party in such proceeding may recover attorney fees and costs incurred in connection with such proceeding.

THIS AGREEMENT sets forth the entire agreement between the parties, and supersedes all other oral or written provisions. This agreement may be modified or terminated only in a writing signed by all parties hereto.

AGREED TO AND ACCEPTED:

_____   _____

CHAPTER 2

ACQUIRING THE RIGHTS TO SOMEONE ELSE'S PROPERTY

Producers are often inspired to make a film after they have read a book or seen a play or been exposed to some other kind of property, including an old movie. They say to themselves, "Wow, that would make a great movie." Many times that thought is followed with the thought: ". . . and I'm the right person to make it." To do so, you will have to obtain the right to make the movie from the person or company that created the film or play or book or other item of inspiration.

WHAT RIGHTS TO ACQUIRE

Each property mentioned above is known as an underlying property. An **underlying property** is the source material used as the basis for a script that is not wholly original with the author. When you buy the rights to make a film based on an underlying property, those rights are called the underlying rights. **Underlying rights** are the foundational rights that you must control in order to have the right to make and distribute a film based on an underlying property. **Underlying property** refers to the book or play or story or life rights or previous film upon which a later film is based.

17

All of the rights you need to make and exploit a film are called film rights or motion picture rights. **Film rights** and **motion picture rights** are interchangeable industry terms—a sort of shorthand—for a collection of different rights. Those rights include the right to make a film for initial exhibition on television or in theaters, the right to make sequels and remakes of that film, and the right to distribute the film on videocassettes and other media, even if it is not invented yet. Some people prefer the term audio-visual rights. **Audio-visual rights** are the same as film or motion picture rights, but, as a descriptive phrase, seem to better describe the possible development and use of future technologies. You also want to acquire related rights such as the right to use the title of the underlying work and the right to use the name and likeness of the author of the underlying work for publicity purposes. For instance, if you don't own the film rights to the play *My Big Fat Greek Wedding*, you cannot make a film from a script based on that play. It is also true that even if you have the film rights, when your ownership of the underlying rights runs out, you no longer have the right to exploit the picture you made.

Universal Studios learned that lesson when the U.S. Supreme Court took away its right to distribute Alfred Hitchcock's *Rear Window*. The film was made in 1945 from a script based on a short story by Cornell Woolrich published in 1940 in a magazine. This was when the term of copyright was much shorter, but the copyright could be renewed. When Woolrich assigned the film rights to his original story to Universal, he also agreed to assign the renewal at the appropriate time. But Woolrich died before the renewal time arrived. Due to unique provisions in copyright, the law did not bind his heirs to the original agreement regarding renewal, so when the successor to the rights (Sheldon Abend) offered to resell Universal the underlying rights that they felt they had already paid for, Universal refused. They felt that they had previously paid Woolrich for such rights, and they didn't like the additional price Abend was asking, so they went ahead with their plans to re-release *Rear Window*.

Abend sued. Abend won.

The court ruled that Universal could not do anything with their film during the story's renewal term until they purchased the underlying rights from Mr. Abend.

The point of the *Rear Window* story is that you must own the film rights to an underlying work to have the right to do anything with a film based on that work. The nasty renewal right and all its fascinating problems are becoming less prominent in the copyright landscape. If the underlying work you are interested in was created before 1978, you should consult an experienced copyright attorney to help guide you through the copyright-renewal thicket. Copyright law was revised in 1978, including making the term of copyrights last for the life of the creator of the work, plus seventy years, unless the work is "made for hire." If the work is made for hire (or anonymous or pseudonymous), the copyright lasts 95 years from publication or 120 years from creation, whichever expires first (see Chapter 5 for a definition of work for hire). For works created after 1978, there are still reversion issues and transfer issues, but there aren't renewal problems.

Assume that you have found a property on which you want to base a script for a film. Rarely can you (or do you want to) pay the entire purchase price of those rights before you even have a script or the commitment of a financier. This is why producers like yourself option the property. An **option** is the exclusive right to purchase something in the future, on fixed terms and conditions.

Options are common in many businesses, including the film business. Instead of laying out a large sum of cash up front, the filmmaker offers a small cash amount to the owner of the property. This guarantees that you (the filmmaker/option holder) can purchase the film rights, in the future, under certain specified conditions. You can think of it as buying time.

No matter what kind of property you are optioning, the important thing is to *always, always get it in writing.*

Even experienced attorneys who option property often and communicate clearly need to "get it in writing." Things change, and when they do, you will find that memories change. Take the sad, but true, story of Frank Konigsberg, a highly experienced producer of award-winning movies for television.

In 1987, after a lunch meeting with Anne Rice, the author (and inveterate letter writer), Konigsberg and Rice entered into an oral agreement by which he optioned the rights to her upcoming book *The Mummy*. They agreed that she would create a bible. A **bible** is an industry term used primarily in television for a detailed story description, more detailed than the typical treatment but less detailed than a full script. They agreed that Konigsberg could use this bible to interest television networks in a movie made for television. His plan was to set up the television project while Rice wrote the novel. His option was to commence on the date a television network promised to develop the bible into a script and was to run for two years thereafter. Drafts of a contract were exchanged, but never signed. Rice delivered the bible, Konigsberg paid her $50,000, but still no written contract was signed. Konigsberg assumed that the exchange of money sealed their agreement. Wrong.

Although the novel became a best-seller, Konigsberg was not able to convince a network to proceed with a movie. He tried to extend his still-unsigned option, but Rice refused.

Konigsberg sued to establish co-ownership of the bible and a license to the film rights. Rice denied that Konigsberg had an option agreement and asserted that even if he did, his efforts to extend the rights were not timely.

The court tossed Konigsberg's suit out of court. "No agreement signed by the author," the court intoned. "I know what she said, but what did she sign?" This was the question that hung in the air as the gavel cracked against the small, round, wooden block to mark the end of the matter.

Nevertheless, the wrath of Frank Konigsberg is not so easily squelched, even by a court decision. Worse, such victories often produce some gloating by prevailing plaintiffs. So it was that Anne Rice, feeling too smug to let Konigsberg's defeat go undocumented, wrote Konigsberg a letter. In addition to the expected paragraphs that added salt to his wounds, it contained the following admission of an agreement: "As far as I'm concerned," she proclaimed, "these contracts, though never signed, were honored to the letter . . . You got exactly what you paid for—a bible script and the television rights to the novel, *The Mummy,* for more than two years." Rice claimed that the only thing Konigsberg failed to do was "pick up your option, or extend it."

Not only did her letter fail to shame Frank, it seemed to provide his case with a missing link: an admission of an agreement. So Frank appealed.

In addition to all the other reasons for reversal, he added this letter as new evidence. "A writing?" he railed. "It's a writing you want? I've got a writing. Look at this!" he must have chortled as he added the letter to his legal brief. Surely the court would accept the affirmation of Konigsberg's position by the defendant herself.

The appeal failed. The court's decision states that Konigsberg and Rice were "doing lunch" and "not doing contracts." Why didn't Rice's salty letter to proclaim her vindication after the court's ruling breathe life into the unsigned contracts from the original lunch meeting? "Too late," the court responded. That is not the kind of writing they wanted. You must have a contract signed *reasonably contemporaneously* with the making of the agreement. Rice's letter was too late, too much after-the-fact. Once again, Frank lost. This time Anne Rice did not write a letter.

It is still hard for me to believe that the courts allowed the letter-writing Ms. Rice to stand on a technicality. Often, in this type of case, the court will say to a litigant, "Yes, you are right. The letter of the law is on your side, but your behavior prevents you from using the letter of the law to your advantage. It would be unfair. We do not allow you to assert these technicalities, because to do so would produce an unfair result." Obviously, the courts do not always do this. They didn't do it for Konigsberg and they may not do it for you.

Be sure to put your agreement to writing.

CHARACTER(S)

Within the value of underlying properties, and the films that are produced as a result, lies the identifiable and sometimes valuable *character.* The law defining what constitutes a protectable character and actually protecting it can be quite muddy. It can be muddy because the courts have not always distinguished clearly between two different kinds of characters that are used in movies.

This book and some articles are beginning to point out the distinctions between two distinctly different kinds of characters: One kind of character starts with a drawing and is not so much a character as a copyrighted drawing, figure, or image. The most famous of these characters are highly profitable: Mickey Mouse and many other cartoon characters would be recognizable in any context. You see them at an amusement park, on a magazine page, or in the theater and you know who they are. These characters each have a persona that the owners want to protect, and the owners get very upset with any misappropriation of their property. I call these **visual characters** for lack of a better term. Some legal commentators refer to them as **drawn characters**.

Well-known visual characters are rarely available to independent filmmakers for use in their projects. They are widely licensed for use on merchandise that generates a royalty payment to the copyright holder pursuant to a written agreement that contains quality-control provisions. If you as a producer want to create a new visual character of your own, be sure to have that done pursuant to a work for hire agreement. A good example of a work-for-hire agreement with an explanation of its terms is found at the end of Chapter 5.

A visual character may appear many different times in many different stories without diluting the character in any way. Having a story or a plot is not necessary for the character to be recognizable. Indeed, the character can be printed on a mug or baseball hat and can be recognized. The facial and bodily characteristics are the physical embodiment of that character.

The other kind of character is the story character. **Story characters** are first created in works of literature. Typical examples are two characters created in books a century apart: Frankenstein and James Bond. Dialogue, plot, and interaction with other characters define these characters. Various actors have played these two roles over the years. In spite of the different physical attributes of the actors, the characters are the same. Physical appearance is rarely at the heart of a story character.

Often, a series of books based on a character, such as Sherlock Holmes, exists before you become interested in the character. In that case, you should obtain options on the entire series if possible. If that is not possible, arrange a holdback period and right of first negotiation with regard to those other books or articles in which the character appears.

To obtain rights to a story character from a story, book, or article, you must option and purchase the entire work because this type of character is defined by dialogue, plot, and character interactions. It is not recognizable without these defining elements.

Sometimes, so little of the character's physical description appears in the original text that your work will define the appearance of the character. This phenomenon is discussed in the next chapter with regard to the public-domain literary characters Snow White and Frankenstein. Both Disney and Universal aggressively protect their cinematic versions of these characters.

If your work provides so much of the physical conception of a character that you think you have created a distinctive work, take a photo or drawing of the character and copyright it using Form PA in this book. You can also apply for trademark protection, a procedure that is beyond the scope of this book. (Detailed trademark instructions and forms may be found in my *Do It Yourself Trademark and Copyright, an EZ Legal Guide.*) You will not own the character in general, but you will obtain ownership in the specific physical realization of the character as you created it.

All of this leads us to the fact that characters are separate, independently copyrightable works of creation. If you option the film rights in someone else's property, be sure that you have optioned the film rights in the character in that property. You will be well served to have your agreement state explicitly that you have the right to use the characters in future movies. Central characters often become the focus of a franchise. A **franchise** is a character, concept, or title that is supposed to guarantee a good opening weekend for a film. It is the brass ring that everyone is reaching for. A franchise in the movie business is the most valuable thing you can possibly control. James Bond is the most lucrative franchise in the history of film.

WHOM TO CONTACT

Most producers know instinctively that they are better off talking to the person who created the work than to the agent or other representative of that person. When you talk directly to the creative force, you can share visions, and you can convince the work's creator, who has the ultimate decision-making power, that you are the best person to protect the project.

A good place to turn for information on how to reach a specific person is your local library. Most libraries have a research librarian to help you. Extensive biographical information exists on almost anybody who has done anything. There are *Who's Who* for almost every endeavor. These books routinely lists addresses for the personalities in their pages.

Another source for locating someone is the Internet. You need to have access and some knowledge about how to find your way around. Once you are into the Internet, there is virtually no one of note about whom there is not a great deal of information.

The remainder of this section deals with specific types of properties. You will find guidance on how to contact the right person for a wide variety of properties on which you might want to base a film. No matter what type of property you are after, the more direct your contact is with the actual rights holder, the better off you are.

Fictional Books and Stories

You are reading a book. In your mind's eye you are seeing the movie; it pops right up in your head without an invitation. You have to buy the film rights. Whom do you call?

You can always call the publisher. They are easy to find. That is what the cash-rich studios do. However, in thirty years of practice, I have never heard of a case in which the publisher said, "No, we don't own or control the film rights." Whenever you call a publisher to ask who has film rights, you will receive one of three answers: "Yes, you called the right place, we do own those rights" or "the agent for those rights is X" or "I'll get right back to you." When the publisher calls you back, they tell you that indeed they control the rights, so you should negotiate with them. What happened was that if they didn't already own or control the rights, they contacted the author and gained control of, or at least the right to represent, the film property's rights. This puts another person, and possibly another commission, between you and the original owner.

Most book authors control the film rights to their books. Even if they allowed the publisher or agent to negotiate those rights, they still retain ownership, and generally retain approval rights over any film deal, so you still want to talk directly to the author. The issue is finding them.

The best place to start your search for an author of a book is in the book itself. There is almost always a biography of the author, which often includes the author's city or town of residence. Try the telephone directory for that town. Fortunately, many authors have decided to live in small towns where a mere telephone call or two finds them easily. Acknowledgments often give many clues that can help you find the author. If all else fails, write to the author in care of the publisher. Such letters are generally forwarded unopened to the author.

Fictional magazine stories remain an important source for film material. Fictional magazine stories can be easier to adapt than a full-length book because they do not contain a lot of extra information and plot lines that could not possibly fit into a feature film.

Finding the author of a magazine article is a simple matter of dropping a line to the magazine. The magazine will almost always forward the letter to the author. Most magazines include at least a two- or three-sentence biographical note that will help you find the author directly.

Normally, a magazine story requires both a grant of rights from the author of the story and a release from the publication. The author of an article signs a grant of rights to a magazine much like the agreement signed by the author of a book. The magazine's publisher rarely owns the film rights to articles that they publish, but insurance companies want to be sure. A simple letter from the publisher, saying that it is okay for you to go forward, is sufficient.

Although there is no union for people who write books and magazine articles, there are some organizations to which most authors of books belong:

The Newspaper Guild: (212) 575-1580
www.nyguild.org

The purpose of the Newspaper Guild is to advance the economic interests and to improve the working conditions of its members and to raise the standards of journalism and ethics of the industry.

American Society of Journalists and Authors: (212) 997-0947
www.asja.org

"The nation's leading organization of freelance writers." AJA offers benefits and services focusing on professional development and the opportunity for members to explore professional issues and concerns with their peers.

National Writer's Union: (212) 254-0279
www.nwu.org

The purpose of the National Writer's Union is to organize writers to improve professional working conditions through collective bargaining action and to provide professional services to members.

PEN (Poets, Essayists, and Novelists): (212) 334-1660
www.pen.org

A fellowship of writers working for more than seventy-five years to advance literature, to promote a culture of reading, and to defend free expression.

Author's League of America: (212) 564-8350
www.authorsguild.org
staff@authorsguild.org

The Authors Guild is the oldest and largest group of professional, published authors in the nation. Membership in The Guild supports advocacy initiatives on copyright, free expression, and tax law matters that affect writers.

Author's Guild: (212) 563-5904

www.authorsguild.org

staff@authorsguild.org

The Author's Guild, the nation's largest society of published authors, is a leading advocate for fair compensation, free speech, and copyright protection.

One of these approaches almost always puts you in touch with the author. Once you find them, you can put the question to them directly. At some point, the author usually refers you to someone negotiating on their behalf, but you benefit by having direct initial contact. You can convince the author that you are sincere, hardworking, talented, and the best thing that ever happened to the book's film prospects.

Comic Books

When buying the film rights to a comic book, think "graphic novel" to bring clarity to the process. Generally, the copyright to each element that makes up the comic book is held by the comic book's publishing company. There are several reasons for this. One is that the characters have the potential for becoming so valuable that the ownership of the characters is the biggest asset of a successful comic-book company. Comic-book publishers generally require the writers of the stories and the illustrators and all the other designers who work on a successful comic-book series to assign their creations over to the publishing company.

As explained in Chapter 5, comic books cannot be works for hire unless the people who created the comic books were employees of the company. The comic-book publishing company usually has to obtain assignments. Therefore, your contract generally will be with the publishing company and the terms are similar to a book deal, except for the representations and warranties section and the merchandising section. There are special notes covering all these points in the Sample Option and Purchase Agreement at the end of this chapter.

Non-Fiction Books, Magazine Articles, and Newspaper Stories

Books and periodicals often contain articles about true-life events. In such a case, you might decide to leapfrog over the publication and the writer and go directly to the subject of the book or article. This would involve a life-story rights agreement that would be exactly like the agreement discussed in Chapter 4. The safest thing to do is to sew up the rights to both the life story from the person who lived it and the magazine article from the person who wrote it.

When dealing with two tiers of possible ownership (such as the author of an article and the subject of an article), you have to be very careful about how much you agree to pay any single entity. You do not want the total price to be so high as to make the production package unattractive to a studio or financier. Remember, these are underlying rights.

View this situation both offensively and defensively. You want to tie up as many rights as possible if the story is particularly newsworthy, especially if there are other producers seeking these rights. On the other hand, you still must be careful about over-spending. Remember, if a story has truly grabbed the imagination of Hollywood, competing projects are often developed—and sometimes produced—no matter how many people you may pay for life story rights.

Read the next chapter for the story of the unseemly spectacle of all three major networks broadcasting three different movies-of-the-week about young Amy Fisher, who shot the long-suffering wife of Joey Buttafuoco. Two of the movies were based on the purchase of story rights from different individuals, and the other relied on public domain material.

Songs

Acquiring the right to base an entire film on a song is not too common, but it happens. (*Ode to Billy Joe* and *Harper Valley P.T.A.* are two examples.) These rights are rarely held or administered directly by the songwriter. Because of this, it takes extra effort to talk directly with the songwriter. Songwriters either establish their own publishing company or agree to work with an existing one. A **publishing company**, in the music business, is the company that administers the various rights that flow from ownership of the copyright to a song. Synchronization rights and mechanical rights are defined and discussed in Chapter 15. Chapter 15 also tells you how to find the publishing company.

A publishing company administers synchronization rights, mechanical rights, publishing rights (the right to print the music in folio form), and receives the payments for performance rights (the right to sing the song in public or play a record of it over the air or, outside of the U.S., to perform it as part of a film soundtrack). The right to make a film from a song is a separate right and would not normally be given to the publishing company, but it is a good place to start.

Of course, a song can be in the public domain (see Chapter 3), but be careful. Do not assume that a song is in the public domain. Even "Happy Birthday" is protected by copyright and must be licensed.

It is hard to imagine anyone wanting to make a movie from a song, unless the song was extremely well known. Think of the songs that have been made into movies, such as *Yellow Submarine* and *Harper Valley P.T.A.* (television series). Each of these songs was very well established before anybody wanted to make a movie on the strength of their titles or content. The prices for such rights are therefore high and the profit participation substantial. An independent producer would have to be prepared for this financial challenge.

Plays

Again, the most effective way to begin to option film rights in a play is usually to talk directly with the playwright. If you cannot find the playwright after doing similar research as outlined above, try the Dramatists Guild. It is the only national organization for playwrights, and most successful playwrights belong to it. Member services can verify that the playwright is (or is not) a member of the Dramatists Guild. If so, tell them that you are trying to reach the playwright and ask for the correct contact information.

Dramatists Guild, Inc.
234 West 44th Street
New York, NY 10036
(212) 398-9366

If this does not work, remember that most playwrights are affiliated with specific theaters. This is generally a very informal arrangement, but can rise to the level of a compensated position known as "playwright-in-residence" or "artist-in-residence." No matter what the formality of the relationship, the theaters with which a playwright is associated almost always know a way to contact the playwright. You can identify the affiliated theaters by determining where workshops or world premiers of the playwright's works regularly occur. When you contact a theater, you want to talk to the theater's artistic director or assistant to the artistic director.

If all this fails, look at a program for the play you want to option. Usually the source for permission to produce a play (as a play) is printed on both the program and any published version of the play. Contacting that person or entity should lead you to the holder of the film rights to that play.

One last way to contact "someone official" is to contact the company that licenses the play's amateur performing rights. Fortunately, there are only a few companies in the business of licensing these rights, but note that musicals are generally represented by different companies than straight plays. The oldest and largest licensor:

Samuel French, Inc.
In New York: (212) 206-8990
In Los Angeles: (323) 876-0570
www.samuelfrench.com
samuelfrench@earthlink.net

A couple of other companies with a nice catalogue of plays:

Dramatic Publishing Company
Woodstock, Illinois
1 (800) 448-7469
www.dramaticpublishing.com
plays@dramaticpublishing.com

Dramatist Play Service
New York, NY: (212) 683-8960
www.dramatists.com
postmaster@dramatists.com

When you call any of the above, do not ask, "Who owns the film rights to the play *XXXXXX*?" They will normally just say that they don't know and that they do not have anything to do with film rights. Ask, "Do you handle performing rights for *XXXXXX*?" If the answer is "no," keep trying until you find the company that does handle those rights. When you reach the right company, merely ask for a contact number for the author directly. You are usually given the contact number for the playwright's agent.

Old Movies

If what moves you to make a movie is someone else's movie, you want to obtain both the sequel and remake rights to that movie (or television series). A **remake** is a movie in which you recast and reshoot essentially the same script that formed the basis for a previous film. You use the same characters, in the same story, during the same time period, in the same locale (although sometimes a remake updates the time period). A recent example of a remake was Sydney Pollack's remake of the Billy Wilder classic *Sabrina*.

A **sequel** is a story that uses one or more of the same characters in a different story, set in a different time. Notice that sequels cover events written to occur after or before (a prequel) the "original" story. **Prequel** is something of a slang term to describe the sequel that is set earlier in time than the original story.

When you wish to make a television series into a film, you will almost certainly be working with a studio. The huge box-office revenues resulting from these films when they are well done has driven up their budgets (and the cost of acquiring character rights) into the studio range. Such a sequel usually takes the characters out of the television series and places them in a new story in a new location and a new time period.

The hard part is figuring out who owns the original film rights. Many old contracts were not so clear, and most older films have had their rights splintered and sold off in many different directions. Rarely were the sequel or remake rights the focus of attention when older films were bought and sold because they are often sold as part of a library. A **library** is a group of films whose copyright is owned by one entity. Remember when Ted Turner bought the MGM library? Many people thought that he had grossly overpaid for it, but he laughed all the way to the bank.

The Turner organization had specific instructions not to sell off the library or the even remake and sequel rights of films in the library. Turner felt that he could make a lot of money by colorizing the old films, and he wanted to protect their value for exhibition after he colorized them. He also knew that someday he wanted to be in production, and owning remake and sequel rights would form a rich vein to mine for new pictures. All of those early dreams are being played out today.

In looking for sequel or remake rights to a film, you can start by ordering a copyright report. Chapter 4 tells you how to obtain such a report, which can be anything from two pages to twenty pages long. Note that the original copyright owner of the film almost always owns the remake and sequel rights until those rights are transferred. Examine each of the transfers to create a chain of title as described in Chapter 9. Remember that the sequel and remake rights can be held back or sold separately, so do not make any assumptions. There is one situation in which the copyright holder of the original film will not necessarily own sequel and remake rights to that film. This exception exists if the old film was based on some underlying property (such as a book or a play) and the filmmaker only obtained rights to make a single film.

OPTION AND PURCHASE

Immediately after this section is a form you can use for the option and eventual purchase of the film rights to any underlying property.

Although copyright laws usually don't allow you to copy things out of books for your own use, this book is full of contract forms for your use. Just make any changes to the contract form that suit your needs and then type it up.

To make it easier, you will find recommendations for special provisions for each the underlying properties outlined in this chapter, along with a discussion of the business factors. It is straightforward and shorter than many option and purchase agreements used in Hollywood. One reason is that the "option agreement" and the "purchase agreement" are combined into one document. This combined approach seems more natural for most people. A short-form assignment is attached as an exhibit to use as needed. This is a very important document. Be sure to have that assignment signed right along with the main agreement, even though you will not record it with the Copyright Office until you complete the purchase of film rights. The purchase of the property usually happens just before the commencement of principal photography. Things are moving fast at that point in time and you can't afford any delay. You certainly can't afford to deal with a rights holder who wants to hold you up for their own nefarious reasons. Get the copyright holder's signature early.

**2.01   OPTION AND PURCHASE AGREEMENT
UNDERLYING RIGHTS**

THIS AGREEMENT, effective as of _____, 20__, is made by and between _____ [name of producer] located at _____ (the "Producer") and _____ [name of owner] located at _____ (the "Owner"), concerning the rights to a _____ [e.g., book, play, unpublished story] entitled "_____" and the materials upon which it is based. The following terms and conditions shall apply:

> *Date: By using an effective date right at the beginning of the contract, you eliminate disputes over when a contract was signed and therefore when an option lapses. Few contracts are signed by all parties on the same day, so avoid using the date of signature.*
>
> *Producer: You, as the filmmaker, are the "Producer."*
>
> *Owner: The author of the book is the "Owner," as in an owner of the rights you want to acquire. If there is more than one owner/author, be sure to list all of them here and have all of them sign as parties to the deal.*

1.   DEFINITION OF "WORK": For purposes of this Agreement, "Work" means the _____ [nonfiction/original work/unpublished manuscript] entitled "_____" written by _____ and any and all other literary materials, titles, themes, formats, formula, incidents, action, story, dialogue, ideas, plots, phrases, slogans, catchwords, art, designs, compositions, sketches, drawings, characters, characterizations, names and trademarks now contained therein, as well as such elements as may at any time hereafter be added or incorporated therein, and all versions thereof in any form.

> *Work: Pick the best description of the property you are optioning. If there was a previous title, include that also by saying, "and previously entitled _____." If the Work has been registered with the Copyright Office, you might give that registration number by way of further identification. In the list of included items, be sure to include characters and any other unique elements.*

2.   GRANT OF OPTION: In consideration of the mutual promises contained herein, and the payment to Owner of $_____ (the "Option Price"), Owner hereby grants to Producer the exclusive, irrevocable right and option (the "Option") for _____ months (the "Option Period") to acquire the exclusive motion picture, television, videocassette, and all subsidiary, allied and ancillary rights in and to the Work pursuant to the terms set forth below.

Option Price: You want this to be as low as possible. Sometimes you can even negotiate a free period. Do not be surprised if you run into someone (like me) who says: "No Free Option!" That is my mantra when representing the owner of a property, although I obtain "free" options all the time for my independent producer clients. My argument: It's not "free!" My client will be working, writing (maybe), (if not) hiring someone to write, shopping the project, and generally spending time, effort, and money on the project.

Hint: Since you do <u>not</u> have the deep pockets of a studio, your first job is to convince the author of your passion for the work. Listen to the author's dreams and hopes. You will be the protector of those dreams and hopes. As self-serving as it may sound, it truly is <u>not</u> about the money at the option stage. Except in big studio deals for hot properties, the initial payment is simply not large enough to be the most important aspect of the deal. The likelihood of the film getting made is the important thing. However, the emotional hook— the sizzle that closes your negotiation—can be a simple promise from you: "If you entrust your property to me, I will be as faithful to your work as possible. I will keep you advised every step of the way, and I will do my best to protect you." Be careful of over-promising in this area (or any other area, for that matter).

Option Period: A year or eighteen months is standard for this first period.

3. EXTENSION OF OPTION:

(a) Producer shall have the right to extend the Option Period for one (1) period of twelve (12) months for $_____ non-applicable to the Purchase Price. For the right to the extension of the first Option Period there must be one of the following:

> (i) letter of commitment to direct from an established director;
>
> (ii) the project is set up at a company, major studio or mini-major studio able to fund the project;
>
> (iii) substantial negotiations in progress for complete financing of the film;
>
> (iv) letter of commitment to act in the film from one star; or
>
> (v) a full-length feature-film script has been completed.

(b) Producer shall have the right to extend the Option Period for one (1) additional twelve (12) month period for $_____ non-applicable to the Purchase Price. In order to have a right to a second extension, Producer must secure at least two (2) of the above five (5) items.

Option Extension: *It is standard that you have the right to extend the option. This is important because it takes a very long time to get a film made. Even three years total, as provided here, is a short time. Inexperienced producers often think that they will get their movie made more quickly than anybody else. Based on what? Be realistic. Writers are reluctant to have their material off the market for a long period of time. Frequently, the amounts paid for the second and third years are substantially higher than the amount paid for the initial period . . . and they are non-applicable to the Purchase Price.*

Non-Applicable: *Whether subsequent option payments apply or do not apply to the final purchase price is often a point of negotiation. The initial payment is usually applicable (i.e., deductible). More often than not, additional option payments are not deducted from the purchase price and are therefore labeled non-applicable. The money must be paid before the time elapses under the current option. This payment acts to keep the option open for the extended period of time. If you let your option expire, you no longer have any right to buy the work or to extend the option. The original owner is then free to option the work to another party.*

Progress Requirements: *One way to soften the length of time and/or to get more time is to have your right to renew the option be a result of progress made on the film. That is the approach used above. But do not make those barriers too high. The last sentences of Subparagraph (a) and Subparagraph (b) might work for you—though you don't have to include them in your first draft. If no such demand is made, you can strike this language. (Be sure to tailor the language to your needs.) No studio ever makes this kind of deal. Studios simply pay option prices. Therefore, if you use this approach, you must provide alternatives if the project is set up at a studio. After that, the option may be renewed with a cash payment only.*

4.   EXERCISE OF OPTION: Producer may exercise this Option at any time during the Option Period, as it may be extended, by giving written notice of such exercise to Owner and delivery to Owner of the minimum Purchase Price as set forth below. In the event Producer does not exercise said Option during the period as it may be extended, this Agreement shall be of no further force or effect whatsoever and all rights granted hereunder remain property of Owner. Upon exercise of the option, Producer shall have the right to file the Assignment, Exhibit A, with the Copyright Office.

Hint: *This paragraph is what gives you the ability to purchase the rights you have optioned. It is essential.*

5. PENDING EXERCISE OF OPTION: Producer shall have the right to engage in all customary development and pre-production activities during the option period as it may be extended.

> *Hint: The fact that you optioned the film rights infers this to be true. Stating the fact clearly is better. Often people add "including but not limited to" and then go on for a page or two. That's overkill.*

6. GRANT OF RIGHTS: Effective upon Producer's exercise of the Option, Owner does hereby exclusively sell, grant, and assign to Producer, all rights in and to the Work not reserved by Owner, throughout the universe, in perpetuity, in any and all media, whether now existing or hereafter invented, including, but not limited to, the following: all motion picture rights, all rights to make motion picture versions or adaptations of the Work, to make remakes and sequels to and new versions or adaptations of the Work or any part thereof, to make series and serials of the Work or any part thereof; the right, for advertising and publicity purposes only, to prepare, broadcast, exhibit, and publish in any form or media, any synopses, excerpts, novelizations, serializations, dramatizations, summaries and stories of the Work, or any part thereof; and all rights of every kind and character whatsoever in and to the Work and all the characters and elements contained therein, except those specifically reserved herein.

> *Hint: This is exactly what you are purchasing. This is why you are making the payments. This paragraph can also run on for pages, but the above is all-inclusive. It puts the burden on the Owner to be specific about reserved rights.*
>
> *Hint: If you obtain sequel rights at the same time you buy the film rights—as you always should—you can take any story character out of the film and use that character in other films. The author of the book usually retains the right to write a sequel to the book being optioned. Comic books always retain that right. When this occurs, be sure to obtain the right of first refusal and last negotiation with regard to such an author-written sequel. Note that the language here says that you also purchased the film rights to the characters. A very sharp owner will not allow you to own the characters without a hefty additional payment.*
>
> *Caution: Some Owners want to approve the final script. The studio <u>will not</u> allow the author of the book to have approval over the screenplay. In fact, a studio will not allow <u>you</u> to have the final approval over the screenplay. Do not make this type of promise to a writer. At most, you can allow the Owner to read the final shooting script and to have a short period of consultation.*

7. PURCHASE PRICE: As consideration for all rights and property herein granted, and all warranties, and covenants herein made by Owner, Producer agrees to pay Owner the following sums not later than the commencement of principal photography of a production:

(a) $_____ if the final budget for the motion picture based on the Work does not exceed two million dollars ($2,000,000) less any moneys paid as option exercise money and less the option payment for the initial period;

(b) If the final budget exceeds $2,000,000, One Percent (1%) of the final budget for the motion picture based on the Work (exclusive of insurance, interest, completion bond and finance charges) less any amounts paid for option exercise; however, in no event shall the amount of such payment exceed Fifty Thousand Dollars ($50,000).

> ***Purchase Price:*** *Price can be a flat fee or a percentage of the film's budget, or a combination. Most film budgets allow 1% of the budget for purchase of the book, with a floor and ceiling. The* **floor** *is the minimum price you pay, regardless of the budget. The* **ceiling** *is the maximum price you pay, regardless of the budget.*

8. ADDITIONAL COMPENSATION:

(a) **Contingent Compensation:** Producer also agrees to pay Owner ___ percent (__%) of one hundred percent (100%) of the net profits from any production based on the Work for which Owner receives any other payment under this Agreement. "Net Profits" shall be defined, accounted for and paid in the same manner for Owner as for Producer, whether Producer's contingent compensation is called Net Profits, Adjusted Gross Profits or otherwise.

> ***Note:*** *Net Profits have gotten a bad name. Try using Contingent Compensation. The language in this agreement avoids all accusations of Hollywood accounting, at least by you, because Owner gets a piece of what you get. If you are going to pay for the film yourself or through your family and friends or a company you own or control, be sure to spell out your definition of Contingent Compensation. Be as specific as possible to avoid future conflicts. 1% to 1.5% is common. 2.5% is about as high as is ever paid. Note that the label "contingent compensation" folds in profit participation at various levels.*

(b) **Bonus Compensation:** Producer shall pay Owner $_____ in addition to any other money due Owner under this agreement upon the happening of the following: _____.

Performance Bonus: Often there are bonuses if a film grosses over a certain domestic box office as reported in Weekly Variety or Hollywood Reporter (e.g., $10,000 if the film grosses $100 million in domestic box office.) Usually such performance bonuses are advances against contingent compensation. Do not grant bonuses for things like awards or Oscar nominations. These events do not always translate into money for you.

Books: Best-Seller Bonuses are common. You want to be sure to put a cap on such bonuses and specify the list that qualifies. "$10,000 per week for each week on the New York Times Best-seller List up to 10 weeks" would be a common provision.

Plays: Often, there are Broadway production or Pulitzer Prize-winning or Tony Award-winning bonuses. These provisions persist in spite of the clear diminution of Broadway's importance to the national theater scene. This is due in part to the fact that there is no shorthand substitute by which to measure success. The Mark Taper Forum in Los Angeles birthed back-to-back Pulitzer Prize-winning plays, but still does not rate the mark of success that a Broadway production rates. More film rights are optioned from productions in Los Angeles than from Broadway, but this is overlooked and underrated. Broadway stoically remains the hallmark of a play's success and the trigger for bonus payments.

Magazine Story or Song or Comic Book: There are rarely bonuses involved with songs or magazine stories or comic books. The merchandising aspects of anything related to a comic book are very important, and may be difficult to secure for a film. They are usually reserved by or at least shared with the publisher.

9. MERCHANDISING: Owner shall be entitled to receive a royalty equal to ten percent (10%) of Net Merchandising Receipts attributable to the use of any character in the Work in Merchandise of any kind, it being the intent of the parties to create the broadest possible definition to Merchandise. Such amounts shall be reducible by the aggregate amount paid on account of all royalties to others for use of names, likenesses or images or Producer's logo or other intellectual property that receives a royalty on any given piece of Merchandise to not less than seven and one-half percent (7$^1/_2$%) of Net Merchandising Receipts. Net Merchandising Receipts are all receipts of any kind or nature received by Producer less only third-party sales commissions not to exceed 25%.

> **Comment:** *10% is a generous offer. Many producers would start with 2.5% for the underlying property and 2.5% for the writer for a total budget of 5%, leaving plenty of room to move to a 10% budget.*

10. CREDITS:

(a) In the event a motion picture based substantially on the Work is produced hereunder, Owner shall receive credit in the following form:

Based on the book by _____

or if the film has a different title from the Work, then:

Based on the novel "_____" by _____

> **Hint:** *This is a standard source-material credit. A **source-material credit** is the credit that acknowledges the original, pre-existing material upon which the first-draft script was based. The title of the underlying work is not listed unless it is different from the title of the film. This is not a credit for writing services.*

(b) Such credit shall be accorded on a single card in the main titles on all positive prints of the picture and in all paid advertising in which the director has received credit, except for advertising of eight (8) column inches or less; group and list advertisements; teasers; publicity; special advertising; billboards; television trailers; film clips ("excluded ads"). Nothing contained in this Paragraph shall be construed to prevent the use of so-called "teaser," trailer or other special advertising, publicity or congratulatory advertising. All other matters regarding prominence, placement, size, style and color of said credits shall be in Producer's sole discretion.

> **Hint:** *This is a very precise description of your obligations as far as credit. It is acceptable to the studios and to any legitimate distributor. Often you will be asked to expand this credit provision by adding "screenwriter" or "producer" after "director" in the third line.*

(c) No casual or inadvertent failure to comply with credit requirements hereunder shall be deemed a breach of this Agreement.

> **Hint:** *This is very important to you, since there can always be a slip-up. Often the Owner insists (and you should agree) that you take reasonable steps to correct any mistake when it is brought to your attention.*

11. RESERVED RIGHTS: All publication rights, including audio-book rights, are reserved to Owner for Owner's use and disposition, including but not limited to the right to publish and distribute printed versions of the Work and author-written sequels thereof (owned or controlled by Owner) in book form, whether hardcover or softcover, and in magazines or other periodicals, comics or coloring books, whether in installments or otherwise, subject to Producer's limited rights to promote and advertise, including the right to use a synopsis of up to 10,000 words for promotional purposes.

> ***Reserved Rights:*** *Owners of underlying rights invariably want to reserve certain rights. The standard reserved rights for books are the rights of publication and author-written sequels that are set forth in the sample agreement. You want to get all the rights you can, but these rights are often allowed to remain with the owners of the property. Frequently, there are no reserved rights for a spec script. If you are optioning a spec script, try issuing your first contract without this paragraph. If you do that, strike the words "not reserved by Owner" from the first sentence of Paragraph 6 and eliminate the next two paragraphs as well. Note that if the writer of the spec script is a member of WGA, there are definite provisions that control certain non-film rights in the spec script.*
>
> ***Books:*** *Authors want sole publishing rights and the right to rerelease the book using film art on the cover to coincide with the release of the film. It is up to them to raise this issue. It is ultimately the studio's decision, but this is a safe item to give away.*
>
> ***Magazine Story:*** *Publication rights are the only rights normally reserved by the owners of magazine articles.*
>
> ***Song:*** *There probably aren't enough of these deals done to say that anything is ironclad, but I would think that everything except the right to make a film would be reserved by the songwriter.*
>
> ***Plays:*** *Everything having to do with the play as a play will be reserved by any author with an ounce of self-esteem. That includes publication of the play, performance of the play, and the creation of any other plays that are derivatives of the play. Some producers want to require a holdback period for the performance of the play. A **holdback period** is a period during which certain rights that are possessed are not used. Personally, I don't think it is necessary, but I know that many producers ask (and many playwrights give) a holdback period of six to twelve months from release of the film during which the playwright will not authorize the performance of the play.*
>
> ***Old Movies:*** *The right to continue releasing and otherwise exploiting the previous film is always retained by the owner.*

12. RIGHT OF FIRST NEGOTIATION: If Owner desires to dispose of or exercise a particular right reserved to Owner herein ("Reserved Right"), then Owner shall notify Producer in writing and immediately negotiate with Producer regarding such Reserved Right. If, after the expiration of thirty (30) days following the receipt of such notice, no agreement has been reached, then Owner may negotiate with third parties regarding such Reserved Right subject to the next paragraph.

> *Comment: The above and below paragraphs spell out your rights when the Owner exploits Reserved Rights. It is pretty self-explanatory. This is a strong protection from anyone making a fortune on the hard work you went through to get a film made. You can shorten some of these time periods, but do not quickly give up these rights if the Owner has Reserved Rights. You don't need these two paragraphs at all if there are no Reserved Rights. Publishing rights are the first ones to let go of, if asked to do so, unless you are in the publishing business.*

13. RIGHT OF LAST REFUSAL: If Producer and Owner fail to reach an agreement pursuant to Producer's right of first negotiation, and:

(a) Owner makes and/or receives any bona fide offer to license and/or purchase the particular Reserved Right or any interest therein in a context other than an auction ("Third Party Offer"), Owner shall notify Producer, if Owner proposes to accept such Third Party Offer, of the name of the offeror, the proposed purchase price, and other such terms of Third Party Offer. During the period of ten (10) days after Producer's receipt of such notice, Producer shall have the exclusive option to license and/or purchase said Reserved Right upon the same financial terms and conditions of said Third Party Offer. If Producer elects to exercise the right to purchase such Reserved Right, Producer shall notify Owner within said ten (10) day period, failing which Owner shall be free to accept such Third Party Offer. If any such proposed license and/or sale is not consummated with a third party on terms no less favorable than those offered to Producer within thirty (30) days following the expiration of the aforesaid ten (10) day period, Producer's Right of Last Refusal shall revive and shall apply to each and every further offer or offers at any time received by Owner relating to the particular Reserved Right or any interest therein; provided, further, that Producer's option shall continue in full force and effect, upon all of the terms and conditions of this Clause, so long as Owner retains any rights, title or interests in or to the particular Reserved Right, or

(b) Owner seeks to obtain bona fide offers to license and/or purchase the particular Reserved Right or any interest therein by means of auction ("Auction"), Owner shall notify Producer of the time, date, location and rules of such Auction within (30) days thereof. Owner shall be entitled to license and/or sell the Reserved Right to the highest bidder at such Auction, provided that the terms and conditions of the license and/or sale to any party other than Producer shall be at least as favorable to Owner as those terms and conditions last offered by Producer to Owner under Clause 3 above. If any such license and/or sale is not consummated with any party in the course of said Auction, Producer's Right of Last Refusal shall revive and shall apply to each and every further Auction relating to the particular Reserved Right or any interest therein; provided, further, that Producer's option shall continue in full force and effect upon all of the terms and conditions of this Clause, so long as Owner retains any rights, title or interests in or to the particular Reserved Right.

●   ●   ●   ●   ●

Go to Chapter 8, Provisions Common to Most Agreements, to finish up this contract. You should use all the paragraphs contained there except Expenses, unless the Owner brings that up.

CHAPTER 3

PUBLIC DOMAIN

An old saying goes, "A little knowledge can be a dangerous thing." Many people seem to know just enough about public domain to be dangerous. **Public domain** literally means "owned by the public." No individual or corporation owns the copyright in the material, so they don't need to be asked to use it. As a member of the public, you are as free to use the material as anybody else. This chapter explains the concept and provides some contemporary examples to help you understand public domain and its best use in making your film.

WHAT IS PUBLIC DOMAIN?

The law says that there are four ways a property can become public domain:

1. Facts and events are already in the public domain. No one can "own" the date of an election, or the fact that the grass is green, or the fact that 2 + 2 = 4. BUT if you write about any of these facts in an original way, your original writing is protected by copyright.

2. Very old works for which the copyright has expired are in the public domain. How old? Take the current year and subtract 75. If the work was created in the United States before January 1 of that year, it is definitely in the public domain. Between January 1 of the year you just figured (this year minus 75) and January 1, 1951, the work might (or might not) have fallen into the public domain for failure to renew the copyright.

3. Works created before 1978 may have fallen into the public domain because they did not meet the formalities of proper copyright notice under the old U.S. Copyright Law or because application for term renewal was not timely filed. Before 1978, the copyright term had a life divided into two parts. The first part was 28 years long, but the second part (the renewal period) could be either 28 or 47 years for a total of 56 or 75 years. Today, copyright lasts until the death of the author plus 70 years, except if it is a work for hire. If it is a work for hire, then the copyright lasts the shorter of 75 years from first publication or 100 years from creation. For works protected by foreign copyright, the length of the copyright can be an exotic search of a crosspatch of laws. You no longer must meet these formalities of notice and renewal for works created after March 1989 in order to be eligible for copyright protection in the U.S.

4. Publications and other works created by employees of the United States government and its agencies, as part of their job, are in the public domain. The documents may be unavailable for your use because they are classified or because of privacy considerations, but they are still in the public domain.

Remember that "familiar" does not mean public domain. "Happy Birthday" is a very familiar song, and it has been around a long time, but it is a protected property. In fact, restaurants whose employees sing it to customers have to pay an annual fee to ASCAP for the performance royalties. You have to pay fees to use it in your film for the reasons explained in Chapter 15. "Rudolph the Red-Nosed Reindeer" is very familiar and has been around a long time, but the song and the Rudolph character are protected property. Should you try to use this classic character, born in a song, without permission, you will quickly be contacted by Rudolph's lawyer.

"Old" does not necessarily mean public domain either. To determine a cut-off area, subtract 75 years from the current year. If something was written on or before December 31 of that year and registered for copyright in that year, and nothing more happened to the work other than the registration of the copyright, the work is now in the public domain. However, a later translation of that work could still be well-protected by copyright. Copyright might protect a revised edition of a book or the remake of a film. Therefore, before you conclude that a work is in the public domain, you should purchase a copyright report. A **copyright report** is a detailed history of the work and related registered items. Unless the answer is obvious, you should review the copyright report with a lawyer to decide whether copyright protects the work or not. While you are free to search the records of the Copyright Office yourself, the task would be daunting. It would also omit reports published in the trade newspapers about the piece you are searching, which are included in private reports. The Copyright Office does not issue any such reports. It just records and organizes that material which is submitted. Copyright reports can be obtained from the following companies:

Thomson and Thomson
1750 "K" Street N.W., Suite 200
Washington, DC 10006
(800) 356-8630
www.thomson-thomson.com
dc_orders@t-t.com

Law Offices of Dennis Angel
1075 Central Park Avenue, Suite 306
Scarsdale, NY 10583
(914) 472-0820; (212) 239-4225
www.lawyers.com/dennisangellaw
dangelsq@aol.com

Even if a photo or a piece of film is in the public domain, be careful. Chapter 4 discusses the rights of the people who appear in public domain photos and film clips. Other elements in a film clip, such as music, might also have protection. See a lawyer before you spend a lot of money on a project that relies on what you believe are public domain elements.

FACTS AND EVENTS

If you have an urge to buy life story rights, it is generally because of someone involved in an interesting and publicized story. The facts of the story are in the press, and, as stated above, facts are public domain. So, why do people devote so much time and energy to buying these rights if everybody is free to use the facts because they are not protected by copyright?

Even when something is in the public domain, it is often a good idea to acquire an underlying property. You can sign a contract directly with the person whose story you wish to tell, or you can purchase the film rights to a book or magazine story about that person. The reasons are several fold. First, E&O Insurance (see Chapter 13) is generally easier to obtain if you purchase such underlying rights. The insurance companies feel that if the story was published, and therefore available to the public and no lawsuit followed, it is less likely that the film will draw a lawsuit.

The second advantage of buying underlying rights is that the writer of such a story may very well have some juicy, hard-to-find piece of information that was not used in the article and that they may share with you if you purchase the film rights to the story. In fact, the person who lived the story always has such information. Simply put, you make a better movie with the participation of these people. Finally, it often helps to have a spokesperson for publicity purposes who is familiar with, or directly involved with, the subject, but is not a direct participant in making the film. Purchasing film rights from a person usually makes them available for such promotional purposes.

Also note: People possess rights of privacy and publicity that you cannot invade, and a right not to be put in a false light (as set forth in detail in Chapter 4). When you purchase someone's life story rights, they waive the right to file a lawsuit based on a violation of those rights.

The Amy Fisher Story

One of the most bizarre examples of the interplay between public domain facts and life story rights is the Amy Fisher story. You may recall that Amy Fisher was a seventeen-year-old girl who claimed to have had an affair with Joey Buttafuoco. Three different television networks made her story into three different movies. Here is the chronology:

May 19, 1992	Amy goes over to Joey's split-level house on Long Island with a gun. Joey's wife, Mary Jo Buttafuoco, answers the door and takes a bullet to the head.
May 20, 1992	The story is fast becoming the hottest tabloid tale of the moment.
June, 1992	NBC purchases the life story rights of Amy Fisher. Tri-Star purchases the life story rights of Mr. and Mrs. Buttafuoco. ABC purchases nothing: They rely on public domain material.
Dec. 1, 1992	Amy Fisher enters a plea bargain and is sent to jail for five to fifteen years.
Dec. 28, 1992	NBC airs *Amy Fisher: My Story*, starring Noelle Parker. This is the tale told through the eyes of Amy herself.
Jan. 3, 1993	ABC airs *Beyond Control: The Amy Fisher Story*, starring Drew Barrymore. They base it exclusively on public domain facts as they were reported in the transcripts of the trial and in the press.

Jan. 3, 1993   CBS airs *Casualties of Love: The Long Island Lolita Story*, starring Alissa Milano. This is the Buttafuoco side of things.

As you might guess from the above, NBC portrayed Joey as an adulterous lover and portrayed Amy more kindly. CBS portrayed Joey as an innocent victim of Amy's obsession. ABC, relying on public domain material found in news accounts, didn't draw conclusions about who was right or wrong or good or evil. One thing is for sure: Amy shot Mary Jo and for that she sat in jail.

Astonishingly, each made-for-television movie was a genuine rating success. Even the network executives involved were "stunned" (their word). One NBC executive said, "It's sad . . . it's crazy."

Sensational Criminal Stories

This feeding frenzy raises two other issues about films based on sensational criminal activities. One is the "Son of Sam" statute passed in many states, including New York. The other issue is that your money may be better spent on stars for your film, rather than acquiring rights that are available to you through the judicious use of matters in the public domain.

The Son of Sam statute began in the State of New York in response to some hefty payments made to a notorious convicted murderer for his—you guessed it—life story rights. The public outcry demanded a legislative response. The idea was to prevent felons from selling their stories. However, the legislative response was not uniform among the states, partly because it is difficult to devise a scheme that survives constitutional scrutiny. The schemes generally apply only to persons who have been convicted. If you feel the urge to pay a felon for life story rights, see a lawyer. At least you won't run afoul of the law. Personally, I have never and will never pay money to a felon for his or her story.

ABC's telling of the Amy Fisher tale garnered the highest rating of the three networks without buying any life story rights. They saved their money and spent it on a star, Drew Barrymore. One of the hottest movies made for television was HBO's *The Positively*

True Adventures of the Alleged Texas Cheerleader-Murdering Mom,
starring Holly Hunter. That film was based on public domain
matter, including a tape-recorded conversation with "Mom" that
was originally taped for the police investigating Mom. The conversation was spoken verbatim by the actors in the film.

Events during the O.J. Simpson murder trial inspired the California
Legislature to pass a related law. This one prohibits witnesses to a
crime from selling their stories to the media before the end of the trial.
That law has not been tested, but look for some court decisions, and
look for the spread of this kind of statute throughout the country.

If you are creating a script based on facts that are in the public
domain, be sure that you keep copies of all the research materials
that support your script. Be sure that you have two sources for
each factual assertion, (e.g., 8/8/89 interview with Joe Blow, court
transcript of Jane Smith p. 7671). You cannot fictionalize any
aspect of a person's life just because you have the right to portray
the public domain facts about that person. (For information about
people and their rights, read Chapter 4.)

If you are going to create this type of script, you should require
the writer to prepare an annotated script. An **annotated script** has
references to the various sources the writer relied on when writing
the script. You annotate a script by placing handwritten numbers
directly on the factual assertions in the script. These numbers
correspond to numbers arbitrarily assigned to the various sources
used by the writer as the basis for the script. Members of the
Writers Guild have the protection of some relatively new rules
about annotated scripts. If you require a WGA member to submit
an annotated script, you must inform the writer at the beginning of
the assignment because it is a lot of extra work to save all the
research in an orderly manner and then to go through and annotate
a script. At the end of this chapter, there is an Annotation Guide for
Scripts Based on Facts. You can attach it to the contract of any
writer you hire to write the script for a film based on factual events.

Here is a good piece of news for those of you who are
researching scripts based on facts. The author of the "true crime"
books *Where Death Delights* sued the producers of the television

series *Quincy* for infringement of the copyright of some fictional stories that the author wrote. Even though the stories were totally fictional, the author represented them to the reading public as true. Therefore the reading public could treat them as true, putting the stories in the public domain.

In court, as a plaintiff, the author said that any reader should have known that the stories were fiction because of their absurdity. The court held the author to his original representation of his stories as "true crime" stories. The moral is that you do not violate copyright law when you retell a story or a fact that you find in a book or article if the author of the book or article said that it was true. An author cannot promote a book as true and then claim that it is a work of fiction in order to pursue a lawsuit for copyright infringement when someone uses the story. This is true even when a typical reader would not necessarily view the contents of the book as plausible. One case even involved stories supposedly told to the author by aliens from outer space. When the stories were copied, the courts found the representation on the jacket and in publicity about the book's truthfulness to be controlling; therefore there was no copyright infringement. This is also true for "fictionalized" elements of biographies. The author of a biography of the actress Frances Farmer found that out when he sued the producers of the movie *Frances*. "Too bad" said the court. "You presented the book as true, so even the pseudo-facts are in the public domain." Of course, you should see a lawyer if you are planning a film based on material you did not purchase.

FACTS—AN EXCEPTION

One area that is particularly relevant to television producers is "hot news," although it has no relevance to someone involved in the longer, more leisurely process of creating a documentary film, feature film, or other project with a less-pressured process. A **hot news exception** protects facts for a short period of time.

If a news-gathering agency spends resources and energy to gather fast-breaking news, the facts that it collects are protected from organizations who would like to piggy-back on that effort, without spending the bucks to gather the news themselves. To cite a specific case, the International News Service was prohibited from taking factual information from Associated Press news articles and then reselling this information to its own subscribing newspapers. All of this falls in the area of unfair competition.

The National Basketball League tried to use the AP case to stop Motorola from sending out its sports scores to pager subscribers. The court said, "Oh, no, no, no." The NBA doesn't spend energy collecting this data. The scores and stats that result from NBA games are facts and therefore free for anybody to use. It was Motorola's team of fact-gatherers that did the work of collecting the data and sending it out to subscribers.

OLD PROPERTIES

If a tale like the Grimm brothers' *Snow White* is in the public domain, what rights must be acquired, and from whom, if you want to create your own *Snow White*? You could ask the same question for Mary Shelley's *Frankenstein* and many other books.

The Grimms' fairy tale *Snow White and the Seven Dwarfs* is in the public domain. Disney's copyright is in their film based on that book. The Disney copyright applies only to the items that Disney created independent of the underlying work. For instance, the Grimm brothers describe Snow White to the tiniest detail in the book, so she must have a certain appearance to be faithful to the book. It turns out that Disney's *Snow White* looks very much like the Grimm brothers described her. Disney added very little new to the *Snow White* character. The Grimms only describe the seven dwarfs in the book as seven "friends," and they are otherwise quite amorphous. These "friends" were not necessarily human or living and did not have names, sex, or a description of any kind. Disney owns the copyright on those dwarfs, their names, appearances, and personalities. In the book, the mirror itself is the talking beauty consultant. In Disney's film, it is the mirror frame that talks back to whomever listens. This is why Disney sued Lou Scheimer and Filmways when he created an animated film using some of those elements, but they did not sue Spike Jones for his humorous version of *Snow White* that used none of Disney's elements.

If you are creating something based on an old work in the public domain (such as Mary Shelley's *Frankenstein*), be sure you go back to that work to create your derivative work. Universal is very protective of the cinematic *Frankenstein* they created many years ago. Several elements in Universal's creation are quite different from Shelley's original physical description. Shelley wrote about skin stretched tight over the bone structure, thin black lips, and extended arms. Universal's distinctive bolt through the neck, the flat head, the jacket that does not fit, the visible stitching of the skin, and other elements—when taken together—create a distinctive, protected character. Universal is very aggressive in protecting its copyright, but you are free to create your own monster based on Shelley's work. Shelley's *Frankenstein* is in the public domain all over the world because it was created in the nineteenth century. Kenneth Branagh held close to the original book in his film *Mary Shelley's Frankenstein*, which protected him from any claims by Universal.

TECHNICAL FLAWS

When a picture or the screenplay that it incorporates falls into the public domain, anybody is free to make a derivative work from either one. This is true of any public domain work. Courts have held that each of the following methods of creating new works that are derivative of existing public domain films can produce a copyrightable property. However, the new elements are protected by copyright. The public domain film is still in the public domain, but as you can see, the following techniques created a new, protected, highly exploitable film:

1. A colorized version of a black and white film. Ted Turner gained protection for his colorized versions of a number of classics, including *Blackboard Jungle*.

2. A new version of a public domain motion picture can be newly registered and protected by copyright when you pan and scan the public domain version. **Pan and scan** refers to the process by which motion pictures are adapted from the wide-screen theater format to a narrower format fitting on the old-style television screens. Pan and scan shows only a portion of the original film frame. The heirs of John Wayne won a summary judgment on this issue (without a trial) when they sued UAV for infringing the copyright of their derivative version of their dad's 1963 film, *McLintock!* Note that anybody can pan and scan a film, and, for better or worse, the pan-and-scan copy is protected. Note also that if you try to register a pan-and-scan film, be sure to identify the new film as a pan-and-scan version, because a mere change in format is not copyrightable. If the copyright office cannot tell from your application whether your new version is copyrightable, correspondence will ensue that can chew up a lot of time.

3. One can always redo the soundtrack with new music or obtain exclusive rights to the music in the film instead of the usual non-exclusive rights that are traditional for film music. In the case of *McLintock!*, the heirs were successful in obtaining copyright protection after they digitized the soundtrack of the 1963 movie, remixed it, stereoized (the court's word, not mine) the previously monaural sound, and upgraded its quality. The court said that all of this added up to a "creative mixing and balancing of sounds."

GOVERNMENT PROPERTIES

Any document created by a government employee while working for the government is in the public domain because the employer is the government, which means that the public owns the document.

But not every government document was created by a government employee. It is not common for the government, at any level, to contract out for services. Before you incorporate a government document or property into your work, be sure that you're dealing with a government document that was prepared by a government employee during the course and scope of his or her employment. Once you have made such a determination, you may use the document without worry, unless it is classified or otherwise protected.

The array of government documents that are available to you is truly bewildering. Documentary filmmakers have long enjoyed the use of clips from films created for the government by government employees.

RECAPTURE

Taking steps that have the practical effect of recapturing works from the public domain is a new and interesting area. Everyone knows of the enormous potential value in the monopoly granted by the law of copyright. Millions of dollars hang in the lawful ownership of the copyright to the most inane creations. As mentioned above, prior to 1978, some creations fell into the public domain in the U.S. through an inadvertent noncompliance with the old technical requirements. The new Copyright Act provides for the recapture of certain foreign creations that failed to meet these technical requirements. The feeling in Congress was that some foreign owners were unfairly penalized because they were unaware of the technicalities of U.S. law. Shrewd lawyers often work to come up with schemes that give their clients similar control over the use of their film, even if they do not give the clients the copyright itself.

The company controlling the name and likeness of the Three Stooges tried to exercise copyright-like control over their old public domain films by asserting that people who wanted to use clips from those films had to pay for use of the name and likeness of the Three Stooges. In fact, the company convinced most of the studios to pay up. They had a pretty good deal going. But New Line went ahead and used a clip from a Three Stooges movie, playing it on a television in the background of a scene in the feature film *The Long Kiss Goodnight*. The jig was up. The court said that as long as the clip from the public domain film was used purely as a clip, then the owners of the Three Stooges could not block the use of their name and likeness.

Images of the Three Stooges on T-shirts, mugs, and other items would produce a different result, but the clips could be used—as clips—without payment of any sort. That's why some of the actors on *Cheers* sued the folks who bought the rights from the producers of *Cheers* to build bars in airports that looked like the *Cheers* set. These bars' use of big dolls that looked like the actors, however, implied an endorsement of the airport bar by the actors. And similar non-copyright considerations allowed the illustrator of the public domain *Peter Rabbit* books to sue when those famous illustrations were redrawn, photographically reproduced, and used in a manner different from how they appeared in the original work. The court found that the illustrator's trademark in the character illustrations had been infringed, even though the books themselves are in the public domain.

Documentary filmmakers frequently pay archives for the privilege of using clips from public domain films. The reason they pay a fee is for the archive's time and trouble. It costs the archive money to store the films and to service a request for a clip from the film. It also costs money to catalog the various shots in the films so that you can find them easily. So you can expect to continue paying for clips from archives, even if the film from which the clip comes is in the public domain.

With domestic films, there are ways to "recapture" something very similar to the copyright, even if the film itself is in public domain. Consider *It's a Wonderful Life*. That classic film, starring Jimmy Stewart and my longtime client Donna Reed, was seen nonstop during the Christmas season because it was in the public domain. However, the music was not in the public domain. Films contain music that has a separate copyright and a separate ownership. *It's a Wonderful Life* contains a considerable amount of preexisting music, licensed for use in the film. Though the film itself fell into the public domain, the music was still protected. A team of very clever copyright specialists contacted the copyright holders of some of the music in the film and made exclusive licensing deals with them. That act provided the working equivalent of a copyright recapture for *It's a Wonderful Life* through the music contained in the film. Chapter 15 explains how that recapture happened.

BEWARE OF SHORTCUTS

Beware of lists that claim to set forth works that are in the public domain. Beware of people who claim that the copyright for a master recording or the photo they want to sell you is in the public domain if they do not provide carefully documented proof. Take the information they provide to an experienced copyright lawyer. You may want to buy your own copyright report. The question of whether a given work is in the public domain can occasionally be cut and dry, but it is more often than not a sophisticated and entangled question for which you should receive the best possible advice.

There are many twists and turns. For instance, being in the public domain in one country does not mean that a work is in the public domain in all countries. The laws of various countries are becoming more homogenized, and the countries without any copyright law are virtually nonexistent today. Nevertheless, there is still a large variation around the world. For instance, *Peter Pan* is in the public domain in the United States due to its age. However, the Parliament of Great Britain has given it special status so that it has permanent copyright protection. Therefore, Steven Spielberg had to make peace with the Great Ormond Street Children's Hospital in London, which owns the copyright to *Peter Pan*, before he could distribute the film *Hook* (which is clearly a derivative of *Peter Pan*) in Great Britain.

3.01   ANNOTATION GUIDE FOR SCRIPTS BASED ON FACTS

Annotated scripts should contain for each script element, whether an event, setting or section of dialogue within a scene, notes in the margin which provide the following information:

1.   Whether the element presents or portrays:

   a)   Fact, in which case the note should indicate whether the person or entity is real; with respect to a person, whether (s)he is alive and; with respect to all of the foregoing, whether a signed release has been obtained

   b)   Fiction, but a product of inference from fact, in which case the information described in 1.(a) should be provided; or

   c)   Fiction, not based on fact

2.   Source material for the element:

   a)   Book

   b)   Newspaper or magazine article

   c)   Recorded interview

   d)   Trial or deposition transcript

   e)   Any other source

NOTE: Source material identification should give the name of the source, page reference (if any) and date (e.g., *The New Yorker* article, page 27, August 1, 1988). To the extent possible, identify multiple sources for each element. Retain copies of all materials, preferably cross-indexed by reference to script page and scene numbers. Coding may be useful to avoid repeated, lengthy references.

Descriptive annotation notes are helpful (e.g., setting is hotel suite because John Doe usually had business meetings in his hotel suite when visiting L.A., *New York Times*, Section 1, page 8, April 1, 1981).

CHAPTER 4

PERSONAL RIGHTS

People have rights, too! In the third decade after George Orwell's *1984*—which was supposed to have been the watershed for dehumanization—legal protections for individual rights and the number of rights that are protected seem to be on the rise. Just because you have the right to use a photo does not necessarily mean you have the right to use the likeness of the person depicted in the photograph. That is a separate permission that you must acquire separately. The right to use a film or video clip does not necessarily give you permission to use the likeness of the person(s) appearing in the clip. You may also have to get the permission of the people who are recognizable in the clip to use the clip itself.

RIGHTS OF PEOPLE

Personal rights are the rights held by individuals. Generally, they were created by the courts based on the writings of legal scholars. Most states have legislated them into existence. These rights are based on the notion that every person has the right to control the way they are presented in public, unless they have placed themselves in the public eye or are participants in matters of public interest. Even then, individuals have the right to insist on accuracy and the right to prevent the commercial exploitation of their names or likenesses.

Fictional films usually do not run afoul of the rules about the rights of publicity and privacy, unless they identify a real person in their films. That is why script-clearance procedures are so important. Through those procedures, you learn if you are inadvertently identifying a living person, and, if you are, you can change the name of the character before you start shooting. See Chapter 14 to learn more about script clearance.

Producers of fact-based films—such as documentaries, biopics (biographical motion pictures based on the life of a famous person, living or dead), or historical films—need to be very aware of the rights of individuals.

Right of Privacy

The **Right of Privacy** is an individual's right to be left alone. This is the personal right that a filmmaker is most likely to invade innocently. Intent is not considered by courts in this case. It doesn't matter who you were aiming at, it only matters who you hit. If you violate someone's right of privacy, your innocent state of mind is of no help in avoiding liability. It may reduce what you owe, but you will still owe something.

The Right of Privacy can take several forms. For your purposes, it covers several traditional items: You cannot "out" someone in any way. You cannot reveal the private facts of someone's life. You cannot intrude into someone's private space in the course of your filmmaking. These activities invade someone's right of privacy.

Everyone has a bubble of privacy around them. That privacy bubble can be burst in various ways. One is the disclosure of private facts. Not lies. Not distortions. Facts. These private facts, however, must be of a kind that, when disclosed without permission, would be highly offensive to a hypothetical ordinary and reasonable person—you know, the kind that exists nowhere except in the minds of judges and the high-priced lawyers who try to persuade them. There is no interest in "protecting any shrinking soul who is abnormally sensitive about such publicity."

So I went in search of the cases that could show us fact situations that did and did not qualify as "highly offensive" (not just slightly offensive) to the masters of our litigation fates. I think I have a feel for what some judges are thinking, but I offer no guarantees—and there is no clear and simple way to describe the definitional watershed. Probably the simplest way to express the demarcation of "offensive" is to say that you should be highly sensitive to religion, sex, and politics, that is, views on matters of social importance. Why? Because that is where normal people are sensitive and that is where lawsuits are spawned and that is where filmmakers most commonly lose.

Since the right of privacy protection slams hard into the First Amendment right of free speech, free press, and the public's right to know, there is a well known exception: If the matter is of public interest, you can reveal it. There is something intuitive about all of this. If a congressman is diddling an intern, that is of public interest and can be mentioned, even though an office affair between consenting adults in a nongovernmental workplace would probably not be fair game. In practice, the courts have stripped elected officials of virtually all of their privacy rights based on the public's right to know.

Crimes are always reportable. However, the California Supreme Court has explicitly held an exception to that for stories about former criminals who have long been rehabilitated and are living a life of quiet obscurity. The U.S. Supreme Court said something very similar: "The ordinary citizen surely has a similar privacy interest in the aspects of his or her criminal history that may have been wholly forgotten."

An Illinois federal court reached a contrary result in a case in which all of the facts that were revealed were in the public court records.

Producers of documentaries and magazine shows on television are most likely to run afoul of someone's right of privacy, but the producer of a fictional film could do the same thing in a two-step process. First, someone is convinced (and their friends and family are convinced) that a certain character in a film is really them and, second, that the movie reveals private facts about them. The most common problems come up in movies that are admittedly based on films that were based on true-life stories.

The best way to avoid accidentally tripping over the right of privacy is to obtain a **Script Clearance Report**. The companies that prepare such reports check out names and locations against real people and places in the area of your film's setting. If you cannot afford such a report, then go through your script yourself and see if a normal viewer could reasonably identify a real person based on the information they observe in your film. If you are shooting in a fictional store in Queens, pick up the phone book and see if an establishment exists by the same name anywhere around the New York area. Better yet, seek out generic names for use in your film. Don't give your characters full names when using a first name only would do. Details, such as both a first and last name, are rarely essential to cinematic storytelling, and if handled improperly, they can get you into trouble.

This is an area where you must exercise extreme care. Frederick Wiseman, the well-known, award-winning documentary director, ran into a brick wall at the beginning of his career. The court enjoined his masterpiece film *Titicut Follies* from being commercially exhibited for thirty years. When a court **enjoins** something, it issues an order for people not to do a certain thing—in this case, Wiseman was stopped from commercially exhibiting *Titicut Follies*. Few people saw it after its initial public screenings because of flawed releases. Well, that was the official reason. There is a whole book on the litigation alone.

The film depicted the inner workings of a Massachusetts hospital for the criminally insane. The head of the hospital signed on behalf of the hospital and on behalf of most of the patients depicted. The hospital administration liked the film when they screened it privately, but when they showed it publicly, an understandable outcry followed. The emotionally brutal treatment depicted in the film was very different from what the public expected.

The state arranged for legal guardians for some of the patients, enabling them to sue on the grounds that the hospital did not have authority to waive the patients' rights of privacy. The result of the lawsuit was technically correct. The film languished, virtually unseen, on the shelf until the last patient went to the grave with the right to privacy well intact. Since those rights die with a person, the film can now be seen more widely. Wiseman now gets all of his releases on audio tape, usually at the end of the interview.

Right of Publicity

Professor J. Thomas McCarthy, a leading authority in the use of name and likeness, succinctly defines an individual's **Right of Publicity** as the inherent right of everyone to control the commercial use of his/her identity. In his book, he says, "The right of privacy protects the soul. The right of publicity protects the pocket book." The right of publicity has to do with using someone's face or name to sell your product without permission to use that particular face or name. Be sure that you have permissions for all the things you use in your advertising. In the body of your film, you have every right to accurately portray a public figure, but in advertising your film, be very sure that you have written permission to use every name and likeness that apppears in the advertisements.

The rule is: "You have to pay up before you put someone's mug on a coffee mug and try to sell it to the public." The same thing goes for your movie poster. That is the bottom line. Professor McCarthy's treatise (mentioned above) is over a thousand pages with cases and history and theory and explanation. All you need to know is that different rules apply to the advertisements for your film than apply to the content of your film. No matter what, you need permission before you use someone's name or likeness in your movie poster or other advertising.

Misuse of a star's name and likeness has produced much litigation in what are called pre-sales. **Pre-sales** refers to selling the right to distribute a film in a certain territory before the film is complete—usually before filming has even started. That is one of the main activities at the film market that takes place during the Cannes Film

Festival held in France during May of each year and the American Film Market (now shortened to AFM) held in February in Santa Monica, California, and MIFED held in the fall in Milan, Italy. If you pursue your dream of being an independent producer, you will be spending a lot of time at these markets, because this is where a lot of production financing is arranged and is completed when films are sold.

As you wander around these markets, you will see many posters for films that have not been shot. The producers are trying to raise the money for these productions through pre-sales. The posters, however, can only list a name if you have written permission from the actual actor—not from his or her agent or lawyer.

If you do not have written permission to include someone's name in the publicity for your picture, you are on safe ground to include a factual statement about the involvement of a certain person in the production of your picture. You can say: "So and so directed the film." The more you include in addition to a simple factual statement, the more it looks like you are using the person's name to help sell your film, which, of course, you are. As your press release talks more and more about a person, it moves along a spectrum of safety from the very safe simple statement to the unsafe area of invasion of the right of publicity.

In negotiating the permission to use an actor's likeness on a poster, you will generally run into a request for approval over the likeness by the person you are negotiating with. Try to limit the approval right by requiring the actor to approve at least 50% of the likenesses within a fairly short period of time. Only the biggest stars are entitled to 100% approval over their likeness, and only the biggest stars have more than three or four days to give that approval. Also, approval should be deemed given after the third batch of photos is sent. The actor should not be allowed to unreasonably extend his or her legitimate request for an approval right to trump your need to advertise your picture. There is no extra charge for the right to advertise someone in your picture—the cost is wrapped into the overall cost of the services to be rendered.

The negotiation on the use of a name in advertising comes in the credit paragraph of a contract struck with just about everybody who will work on your picture. The toughest name-use negotiations are always with the above-the-line personnel. **Above-the-line** personnel are the key creative elements of a picture and the key financiers. These generally include all producers, lead actors, the director, and the writer. The issues most commonly encountered in name use in advertising are placement, prominence, and appearance in the main titles of the motion picture and in all paid advertising for the picture, except congratulatory ads and award campaigns. It is a little easier going with the below-the-line personnel. **Below-the-line** personnel include everybody who isn't above-the-line personnel: the crew, non-star actors, suppliers, and licensors. There the credit provision is usually the assurance of appearance in the end roll credit on all positive prints of the picture. These people's names usually do not appear in paid ads. The actual line that separates above-the-line from below-the-line personnel is a line across the page of the budget that separates the budget into two parts. The bottom part for other cast, crew, locations, equipment, and suppliers is fairly stable and predictable. The cost of the major talent and the script in the top part is subject to heavy negotiation and escalation, depending on whom you are able to attract to your project.

Usually an entirely separate paragraph dealing with publicity will appear in your contracts with the writer and the director and lead cast members. It sets out when the person must be mentioned in publicity and sets forth some restrictions on the artist issuing their own publicity. These restrictions are particularly important in the early stages of the project. The producer must maintain some degree of control so that word does not go out into the world before the producer is assured that all the elements are lined up. Sometimes a sensitive negotiation can be sidetracked by premature publicity about a picture—especially premature publicity that identifies attached creative elements before their attachment has been firmly cemented with a contract.

Note that the right of publicity is in the nature of a property right. Every citizen has it whether they are a celebrity or not. Obviously, it is a right that is more relevant and comes up more often in the life of the rich and famous than in the lives of the rest of us, but the right of publicity is a right that we all have. We all have the right to control the commercial exploitation of our name and likeness.

Many states have passed laws to protect one's right of publicity. However, it is the courts, not the legislatures, that have created most of the law in this area. You, of course, must be guided by the most protective state in the union.

Because the right of publicity is a property right, it lives past an individual's death and may be passed on to one's heirs. In contrast, the invasion of the right of privacy and false light and defamation are personal rights, so the injury is personal and dies with the person. You can't defame a dead man, but you can violate a dead man's right of publicity. In fact, all the state laws dealing with the right of publicity make it clear that the right can be left in a will and that the right lasts for a long time after death. Most of the statutes provide for terms that are 50 to 70 years in length after death.

SOUNDALIKES AND LOOKALIKES

Sometimes you cannot sign up the performer you want, so you are tempted to hire someone who sounds like or looks like the person you wanted to hire in the first place. They are called **soundalikes** and **lookalikes**. Not a good idea. Unless you are scrupulously accurate and forthcoming about the fact that you are using a soundalike or a lookalike, you are in trouble. Given the high cost of litigation, a good rule to follow is, "When in doubt, don't."

Don't think that you can skirt around these problems by invading someone's right to publicity with less than a picture and name splashed all over the place. Sometimes, the use of a distinctive voice, such as the one owned by Bette Midler or Tom Waites, is sufficient to identify the performer, even if an imitator supplies the voice. This is especially true in the context of advertising. Waites recovered $200,000 from Frito-Lay when it used someone who sounded so much like him that everyone thought it was him, even though he had always been very outspoken about not endorsing products. Soundalikes and lookalikes are of no help to you if you are using them to trick the public into thinking that you have the endorsement or the backing of a celebrity when you don't really have their backing.

Those whom the courts have punished for using soundalikes or lookalikes have really crossed the line. Take the Bette Midler case. The advertising agency for the Ford Motor Company really wanted Bette Midler to sing their song for a commercial. Midler did not want to do it. So they hired one of her former backup singers and paid her to sing as much like Bette Midler as she could. Having shared the stage with Midler for many years, she came very close. The advertising agency was happy. Ford was ecstatic. The public was confused. We all thought that Bette Midler was singing the Ford song. That little bit of intentional deception cost Ford and its ad agency a bundle. And rightly so. Honesty, accuracy, and disclosure are the guideposts to staying out of trouble, especially when dealing with rights of people.

I have warned you not to ask unless you are sure that you need the permission that you are seeking. Nowhere is this advice more important than in the area of using soundalikes and lookalikes. The reason is that an early inquiry is a tangible piece of evidence that, at the inception of the project, you wanted the star. It is easy for a jury to believe that when you did not get the star, you hired a cheap substitute.

When your purpose is to save money and you cannot get the star you want, go in a different direction altogether—do not try to fool folks. It's not nice, and it can be much more expensive than hiring the star in the first place. It is certainly more expensive than going in an entirely different direction. Don't you really think that they could have sold just as many Fords with another campaign or another talent in the campaign they did run?

Even political figures, who have virtually no privacy rights, have publicity rights. You cannot imply a commercial endorsement of your product or film by a political figure without the permission of the political figure. Speech and comment about political figures are among the most protected areas of free speech as long as there is no endorsement of a product implied.

DEFAMATION: LIBEL AND SLANDER

Defamation is the publication of anything false which is injurious to the reputation of another or which tends to bring them disrepute. A defamation designed to be read is **libel**. An oral defamation is **slander**.

Growing up, we all learned that it is not nice to tell lies. When the lies are about other people, they can cost you big bucks.

As a filmmaker, libel and slander issues do not come up often unless you are making a documentary or a biopic, or some other type of film that is offered up as a truthful version of the facts. Television movies often wander into this territory.

If you are offering your film as truthful, you want to have double sourcing on everything. **Double sourcing** simply means that you have two separate and independent sources for each factual assertion in your script. This is especially important for anything that might offend anyone, but especially the subject of the remark or representation. The second source should be truly independent of the first source. For instance, two different newspaper articles written from the same press conference or press release is not really a double source. The same fact verified by a second person not at the press conference would be a double source.

False Light

It used to be that the law only punished lies that damaged a person. Clint Eastwood fought one of his many battles with one of the grocery-store tabloids. *The Star* reported that he was romantically linked with someone other than the woman he had been involved with for many years. It was untrue. Everyone in Clint's life knew that it was untrue. On the face of it, this created a "no harm, no foul" situation. Clint felt deeply wronged by this false report.

He sued.

He won.

The courts created a new tort called false light. **False light** means that the statements were not true and caused some harm or embarrassment to Eastwood. In this situation, he was falsely reported to be dating someone else. Because he was a public figure, the court said that he had to show that there was gross negligence in their reporting of the situation. The rest of us only have to prove ordinary negligence.

Even if you are making a documentary and you accurately depict a person in context, you can still put them in false light in the editing room. Consider Michael Moore, whose *Roger & Me* offered many a good laugh. Unfortunately, some of those laughs were at the expense of certain persons who thought that the humor came from putting them in a false light. Remember the scene shot at the Great Gatsby Garden Party? One guest came off as an arch-conservative, insensitive to the evicted. In actuality, he was the liberal chairman of the Democratic Central Committee and had helped Michael in the past.

He sued.

The jury agreed with him. The jury found that Michael Moore had put the plaintiff in a false light. Michael didn't feel the need to obtain a formal release to use the man in the documentary because the man knew Michael, knew about the documentary, and consented to be in it. Everything would have been fine, but the way the film was edited put this man in a false light. Michael needs all the protective language he can get to protect against false light claims.

Defenses to Defamation and False Light

There are a number of common defenses to a suit for defamation. None of them is as good as never getting sued in the first place. Be careful when you make statements about individuals who are living and identifiable.

Truth: This is the classic defense. Everybody seems to know that truth is a defense. Even if a statement is not completely true, you should win with a public figure if you have checked the facts out and you have a reasonable basis for believing they are true. Unfortunately for you, reasonable people may differ on what amounts to a reasonable basis for believing anything. Check the facts carefully. Double source any dubious or inflammatory claims.

Opinion: Everybody has a right to their opinion. If you are stating an opinion, make it very clear that it is an opinion. "Jack is a thief" is libelous. "I don't trust Jack" is an opinion. This can be tricky. The courts don't let you off the hook with merely a prefunctory statement such as "It is my opinion that . . ." and then go on with a string of libelous statements. It must be clear to the reasonable listener that the statement is an opinion, not a fact.

Humor: Humor is a defense because, if everyone hears a comment as a joke, you have not damaged the reputation of whatever or whomever is the butt of your joke. However, there is a big difference between something that draws laughs or chuckles from most listeners and something that insults someone and, upon realizing that your words insult the person, you say, "It was only a joke" or "I was only kidding."

In some ways, humor as a defense is a variation on the opinion defense. In both cases, you are not stating a fact and you do not want your statement taken as factual.

THE VERBAL RELEASE

Here is the good news for documentarians. You can obtain valid and binding verbal releases on film. The key is to make sure that the subjects give a full and informed release. While the camera is rolling, tell the subject of your interview that you are making a documentary film. Tell them what it is going to be about. Then explain that with documentaries, you never know how they are going to be distributed, but television, videocasettes, and libraries are the most obvious and likely methods of distribution. Let the person know that you will try to enter the film in film festivals, and if you are successful, there is a chance for a theatrical release. (Don't forget to tell your subject that you may sell clips from your documentary for use on news programs or in other documentaries.) This explanation takes time, but if the interview continues—as it usually will—you have recorded a valid release by the person's continued participation after your careful explanation.

Lily Tomlin learned this the hard way. She allowed documentary filmmakers to prepare a documentary about her Broadway show, *The Search for Signs of Intelligent Life in the Universe*. Tomlin allowed the crew back stage during rehearsals building to opening night. Tomlin did not ask that they leave or turn off their cameras when tensions were high and some participants revealed more of themselves than they intended.

Tomlin hated the result. She tried to stop distribution of the film on the grounds that she never signed a release and neither did any of the people around her. The court watched a good portion of film in which Ms. Tomlin and everyone involved in the show acknowledged that they were being filmed for a documentary. No objections were made when they thought a flattering portrait was being prepared, and no objections were made even at less flattering times. The court said that if they wanted to retain approval rights, they should have spoken up at some time during the process. The court felt common sense dictated that was too late to complain after the film was finished and ready to be sent out into the world.

THE WRITTEN RELEASE

It is best to have a written agreement. With a written agreement, you can specify the scope of the rights being granted. You can obtain specific waivers.

What follows is a so-called Life Story Rights Agreement that you can use when you want to obtain the right to produce a movie based on someone's life story. This document is not an acquisition of an underlying right in the sense of the Chapter 2 acquisitions. Rather, it is a person's waiver of certain personal rights and an agreement by them to cooperate and consult in the making of the film of which they are a subject.

The Agreement is formatted like a normal acquisition of underlying rights because that is the tradition in Hollywood, and because most lay persons have the notion that they own something called life story rights.

For a simple release in letter form see the end of Chapter 19.

4.01   **LIFE STORY RIGHTS AGREEMENT**

THIS AGREEMENT is made, effective as of _____, 20__, between _____, located at _____, ("Producer") and _____, located at _____, ("Owner"), concerning Producer's acquisition of all motion picture, television and allied rights worldwide, in and to Owner's name, likenesses, life story and background materials as follows:

> **Comment:** *Refer to Chapter 7 if you have any questions as to how to fill out this introductory paragraph.*

1.   DEFINITION OF LIFE STORY: For purposes of this Agreement, "Life Story" shall mean the irrevocable, exclusive, perpetual and universal rights to use Owner's name, likeness, sobriquet, voice, and biography; depict, portray, impersonate or simulate Owner in any way whatsoever, and make use of all the incidents of Owner's life preceding, surrounding, following and otherwise in any way relating to incidents about the Owner's life that the Producer deems in its sole discretion necessary or appropriate to produce one or more motion pictures, whether wholly or partially factual or fictional; and use any and all information and materials in Owner's possession or under Owner's control, which Owner shall, at Producer's request, disclose and provide to Producer freely, completely and candidly, in such forms as, without limitation, copies of any newspapers or magazine clippings, photographs, transcripts, journals, notes, recordings, home movies, videotapes or other physical materials relating to Owner's life story and all Owner's thoughts, observations, recollections, reactions and experiences surrounding, arising out of, concerning all those events, circumstances and activities relating to Owner's life story (all the aforementioned rights hereinafter collectively referred to as "Life Story").

> **Comment:** *This paragraph defines the "Life Story" that you purchase. A living person seldom wants you to have the rights to make a picture of that portion of their lives that they have not yet lived. On the other hand, you seldom need any rights to the future. Whatever attracted you to this person's life has already happened. Therefore, feel free to narrow the above by describing that part of a person's life which you want to option. Insert the description you need in place of the second appearance of the words "the Owner's life." Use plain English and you are on safe ground. Note that personal photos, notes and journals are also pulled into this agreement. Also note that if the Owner wrote books or articles, it is important to obtain those also. Add a description of such books just before the final parenthetical statement and the books will be included in the definition of Life*

Story. If you don't include such books, you may have bought the cooperation of the person and certain waivers, but someone else can buy the film rights to the book. The money you spend in this area must put you ahead of the person who relies on facts in the public domain or there is no reason to spend the money. You will want this paragraph to be as inclusive as possible. Note also in the ninth line "or more." Very few people will want to give you the rights to make more than one movie. If they do, they will definitely want more generous payments than the ones provided in paragraph 9b. At a minimum, they will want (and deserve) payments that are equal to the payments for the first motion picture. If you take out "or more," be sure to take it out of paragraph 5 a) 2 also.

2. **GRANT OF OPTION:** In consideration of the payment of _____ ($___) to Owner, and of the mutual promises contained herein, receipt and sufficiency of which is hereby acknowledged, Owner hereby grants to Producer for twelve (12) months from and after the effective date of this Agreement (the "Option Period") the exclusive, irrevocable right and option (the "Option") to acquire the exclusive motion picture, television, videocassette and all subsidiary, allied and ancillary rights in and to the Life Story, as defined above.

Hint: This is the first money you spend on the long journey of developing a screenplay and then making a movie. Even established companies try to get ninety days free. This gives you a chance to set the project up with a company that can fund development activities.

3. **EXTENSION/EXERCISE OF OPTION:** Producer shall have the right to extend the Option Period for a one (1) year period by sending notice to Owner prior to the expiration of the previous period, along with an additional payment of _____ ($___). Producer may exercise this Option at any time during the Option Period, as it may be extended, by giving written notice of such exercise to Owner. The sums paid under this Agreement, with respect to the initial and one (1) year extended Option Period, shall be credited against the first sums payable as compensation under the terms of the Compensation clause below. If Producer fails to exercise this Option, then the sums paid to Owner hereunder shall be and remain the sole property of Owner.

Hint: Many projects based on life-story rights are for television. The range of prices for television projects is narrow. Most projects pay $35,000 to $100,000 for life-story rights whether there is one person or several persons to receive this money. Cable outlets generally pay less than broadcast networks.

> *Comment: Try to get three years if you can. It always takes longer than you think to get a movie made. Note that the first payment is generally not applicable, meaning that there is no deduction on account of the first payment, so if you are asked for this concession, you should feel comfortable in granting it.*

4. PENDING EXERCISE OF OPTION: Producer shall have the right to prepare screenplays, budgets, teleplays, treatments or other material, and engage in other customary development and pre-production activities. It is understood that if the Option is not exercised, Producer shall have no further right in and to the Life Story, but Producer shall own all rights of every kind in and to material Producer prepared.

5. RIGHTS GRANTED:

(a) Upon exercise of the Option by Producer, Producer shall acquire and Owner shall be deemed to have assigned, conveyed, sold and transferred to Producer all motion picture, television, home-video, allied, subsidiary and ancillary rights in and to the Life Story for use by Producer, and Producer's successors and assigns, throughout the world and in perpetuity, including, without limitation, the following rights:

1) the right to develop one or more scripts based on the Life Story;

2) the right to make one or more motion pictures based on the Life Story, any part thereof or any sequences or characters therein (including, without limitation, theatrical productions, television series, and made-for-television movies and made-for-home-video productions);

3) the right to distribute, exhibit and otherwise exploit any such motion pictures in any and all media and by any means now known or hereafter devised, including, without limitation, all forms of theatrical and non-theatrical distribution and exhibition (including, without limitation, free broadcast, pay, cable, subscription and pay-per-view);

4) the right to manufacture, distribute and otherwise exploit all forms of videocassettes, videodiscs and similar devices of any such motion pictures and to combine such motion pictures with other programs on such videocassettes, videodiscs and similar devices;

5) the right to make changes to the Life Story, to create fictional episodes, characters and/or dialogue for dramatic purposes,

and to use any portion or portions of the Life Story for any purpose of this Agreement;

6) the right to edit and alter any motion pictures based on the Life Story and to make foreign versions thereof;

7) the right to publicize, advertise or otherwise promote any such motion pictures and in connection therewith to prepare and use synopses (not to exceed 7,500 words each) of the Life Story;

8) the soundtrack recording, music publishing, legitimate stage, live television, radio broadcasting and merchandising rights to the Life Story, to any such motion pictures based thereon and to any of the characters contained therein;

9) the right to make remakes and sequels to any such motion pictures;

10) the right to copyright any such motion pictures, sound recordings, musical compositions and all other copyrightable works based on or derived from the Life Story and to secure copyright and trademark protection to all works based on or derived from the Life Story; and

11) the right to sublicense or authorize others to exercise any of the foregoing rights, subject to Producer's obligations hereunder provided.

> **Comment:** *Well, finally, one of those long, interminable grant-of-rights paragraphs. I thought that you ought to see one, and if you are ever going to use it, you might as well use it with someone who lives outside of Hollywood and who might need a little longer rendition of what rights are being granted. Also, you need some waivers from the holder of the bundle of rights known as life-story rights. Those waivers can be very scary when you stop and think about it. Sometimes they appear less ominous when buried among all the detail that this long version of the grant-of-rights paragraph provides.*

(b) Notwithstanding anything contained in this clause to the contrary, it is Producer's intention to portray Owner's and Owner's Life Story as factually as possible with the understanding that Producer has the right to deviate from the facts of the Life Story in order to enhance the dramatic value. Owner shall be entitled to review and be consulted on the final shooting scripts of the motion pictures produced hereunder, it being understood that further changes to such final shooting scripts may be made by Producer. No approval rights are granted whatsoever in connection with any scripts created or motion pictures produced hereunder, which rights shall be held solely and exclusively by Producer and shall include, without limitation, control over all dramatic elements of said scripts and motion pictures.

> **Comment:** *This is an important piece of reassurance for the owner. Your obligations are minimal. Be sure you actually consult with the owner if you promise to do so. Many producers don't offer the reassurances in paragraph (b) until asked to do so.*

6.   RESERVED RIGHTS: The Owner specifically reserves literary publishing rights to the Life Story (other than literary publishing rights of up to 7,500 words for use by Producer in advertising any motion picture based on the Life Story). However, if Producer produces a movie hereunder and if Owner writes a book, Producer owns all motion picture rights in book without further payments.

> **Hint:** *This is a fairly standard reserved right. You need your 7,500 words for the synopsis you send out with your publicity packet. Most producers start by asking for 10,000 words for the synopsis. The last sentence is good to ask for, but you don't always get it.*

7.   WAIVER: Owner hereby waives and relinquishes any rights or remedies at law, in equity or otherwise, and further releases Producer and Producer's employees, agents, successors, licensees and assigns from, and covenants not to sue Producer, or any of them, with respect to any claim, cause of action, liability or damages of any nature whatsoever arising out of or in connection with the exercise of any of the rights herein granted to Producer. Such liabilities include, without limitation, defamation, libel, slander, false light, false advertising, intentional or negligent infliction of mental distress or invasion or appropriation of any right of privacy or publicity in any jurisdiction. These waivers are hereby made by Owner, both on Owner's behalf and on behalf of Owner's next of kin.

> **Comment:** *This is at the heart of a Life Story Rights Agreement. You are obtaining the waiver of all the suits based on the personal rights held by the person whose life story you are purchasing. These rights can be violated intentionally or accidentally. There is peril in making major modifications to this paragraph.*

8.   CONSULTING SERVICES: Owner shall be available to Producer as consultant in connection with the first motion picture produced hereunder at mutually convenient places, dates and times, to provide Producer with information and materials regarding the Life Story and to assist Producer in obtaining releases from any persons designated by Producer. Such consultation will involve, among other things, cooperation with Producer and any writers employed by Producer or Producer's assigns in connection with the writing of the teleplay or other forms of adaptation of the Life Story. Owner shall be entitled to compensation for the above employment in the amount of ten thousand dollars ($10,000), payable upon commencement of principal photography of said motion picture.

> **Comment:** *This paragraph is important in a life-story rights agreement. The only reasons to pay a person for their life-story rights are to receive their cooperation in obtaining the rich details of their story and to obtain waivers if you wander away from the literal truth to achieve dramatic impact. If you do not receive this consultation, you might as well save your money and just rely on public-domain materials. This paragraph is usually reassuring to the Owner.*

9. **COMPENSATION:** As full consideration for all rights, licenses, privileges, waivers and property herein granted, and for all warranties, representations and covenants herein made by Owner, Producer agrees to pay Owner as follows:

(a) Guaranteed Compensation: An amount of fifty thousand dollars ($50,000), payable upon the earlier of exercise of the Option or commencement of principal photography of the first motion picture produced hereunder.

(b) Remakes and Sequels: In the event Producer, or a successor-in-interest, produces any sequel and/or remake feature motion picture based on the first motion picture produced hereunder, Owner will be paid an amount equal to fifty percent (50%) of the amounts payable to Owner pursuant to the paragraph above in connection with each such sequel and/or remake.

> **Comment:** *The 50% is taken from the rather standard compensation for a screenwriter when a sequel is made from a script. However, for the owner of life story rights, you should be willing to go to 100% if asked to do so.*

10. **CREDITS:** The Owner shall be entitled to receive the following screen credit in the main titles of any and all motion pictures produced hereunder: "Based on the life of _____".
Owner shall be entitled to an end-roll screen credit in connection

with consulting services performed hereunder, the form and placement of which shall be at Producer's discretion. Inadvertent failure
by Producer to comply with these credit provisions shall not be
deemed a breach of this Agreement.

> **Hint:** *You may not be able to give this credit if your film
> disparages a living person who has not signed a release. A credit
> that identifies the main character serves also to identify other
> people portrayed in the film even if you change the names of
> those characters.*
>
> **Comment:** *If the Owner is not happy with the details about the
> words "at Producer's discretion," change these words to "subject
> to good-faith negotiation within customary motion picture in-
> dustry parameters."*

• • • • •

*Go to Chapter 8, Provisions Common to Most Agree-
ments, to finish up this contract. You should use all the
paragraphs contained there. In the Representation and
Warranty paragraph, eliminate (a) and reletter the
other subparagraphs. You may have to tone down (c)
and (d) for certain life stories.*

PART II

GETTING A
COMPLETED SCRIPT

There are only four ways to obtain a script:

Write it alone
Hire someone else to write it
Write it with someone else
Buy a completed script

Of course, you could steal it, but if that is your plan, why would you be reading this book? If you are writing alone, you can skip this entire part, although you may have occasion to return to the last chapter in this part when you are constructing other contracts. If you are writing with someone else as a writing team, start with Chapters 6 and 8. If you hire someone, start with Chapters 5 and 8. If you are acquiring a completed script, go to Chapters 7 and 8.

CHAPTER 5

Hiring a Scriptwriter— WORK FOR HIRE

Suppose you have a great idea. Maybe you have optioned the book of your dreams. However, you either do not have the time or do not have the inclination to write the script. Maybe your talents are as a producer and you know your limits as a writer. So you decide to hire someone else to do it. This chapter details the process of finding and working with the writer. It also details your best protection through the special copyright term "work for hire."

CHOOSING A WRITER

This is not as easy as it may seem. Hiring a screenwriter can be a tricky task. Too many producers hire whomever they meet or happen to know without really addressing the writing issues in a tough manner. To spend a great deal of time working on a script with a screenwriter who is not right for a project can be an enormously frustrating experience for all concerned. Take care with the selection process. The best screenwriter in the world does not hit a home run every time, and less experienced screenwriters are less predictable, partly because they have a smaller body of work for you to read before you decide whether to let them write your script.

Here are three tips to hiring a writer:

1. Interview more than one writer.

2. Read lots of the writer's scripts.

3. Check out the writer's work habits. (Talk to people who have worked with the writer.)

Be sure that the scripts upon which you make your choice have as much in common with your project as possible. Make sure that the screenwriter wrote the scripts you read without a partner, unless you plan to work with the partner also. When you read a script written by a writing team, finding out who brought what to the table is virtually impossible, especially if your only source for that information is the one team member whom you plan to hire.

WHAT IS WORK FOR HIRE?

Once you decide whom to hire to write your script, you want to structure the deal as a work for hire. A **work for hire** is defined in U.S. Copyright Law as either:

A. a work prepared by an employee within the scope of employment; or

B. a work specially ordered or commissioned for use as one of a very limited number of specified works.

Category A is easy to determine, but does not usually apply to an independent filmmaker. It is, however, the category under which a great deal of television is written and produced. Examples of employees whose job it is to create the works identified as Category A include term writers at a studio, animators at Disney, and the actors hired during principal photography. The creative works (and copyright therein) prepared by these employees are, by definition, the immediate property of the employer under the work for hire doctrine.

Category B, however, is of great help to independent filmmakers. It is an anomaly of copyright law. Many people in the film business do not understand that this is a very special tool of our industry. It creates a mechanism so that certain items can be created as a work for hire, even though the person doing the creating is not a full-time employee.

To appreciate just how unusual this aspect of copyright law is, take a quick look at the specific items to which it applies. Here is the exact list of items as it appears in U.S. Copyright Law:

1. a contribution to a collective work
2. as a part *of a motion picture or other audiovisual work,*
3. as a translation
4. as a supplementary work
5. as a compilation
6. as an instructional text
7. as a test
8. as answer materials for a test
9. as an atlas

Notice how they buried films among all that apple-pie stuff like newspapers, tests, and atlases? Looking at that collection of works, it is amazing that films are among them. In fact, the legislative history of this provision of the law shows that the movie tycoons pushed it through Congress. All of the other items helped to justify the request for the work for hire concept to apply to motion pictures.

If the work does not fall within one of the above categories, you cannot commission it as a "work for hire." For instance, a novel or a play cannot be commissioned as a work for hire. Even if a work does fall within one of the above categories, the parties must expressly agree in a written instrument signed by the person who would otherwise be the author that the work will be considered a work "made for hire." This agreement must be made before or about the same time as the work is created.

Be sure that you understand the implications of this extraordinary provision. Without this provision, the words of a writer are the copyrighted property of the writer as they are being typed. The writer can then assign or license the work to another, but the writer is always the "author" for purposes of copyright law. If the work was created as a work for hire, the words belong to the employer as they are created. The employer is the author for all purposes. There is no point in time when the words belong to the person who typed them on paper.

A work for hire is comparable to the assignment of an original work if the transaction goes well. If there is a dispute, the author who has assigned the materials to a producer would have certain remedies through which they could conceivably get the property back. This is not possible, however, if the work was a work made for hire. Since the writer never owns the property in a valid work for hire situation, there is no way that the person creating the words and typing the words on paper can get the ownership by bringing an action to cancel the transfer or to break the license.

It is also important to note that the duration of a copyright that initially resides with an individual is the author's life plus 70 years. For a work for hire, the duration of a copyright is 95 years from publication or 120 years from creation, whichever expires first. An assignment from an individual to a corporation does not lengthen the life of the copyright. The law establishes the life of the copyright at the moment of creation according to whether the person writing is doing so as a work for hire or not.

INDEPENDENT CONTRACTOR

Note that an underlying question in all of this is whether the actual creator of the work is an employee or an independent contractor. The definition of **independent contractor** is detailed below. If the actual creator is an employee and the work was created within the scope of that employment, then the work was a "work for hire." If the creator was an independent contractor under written agreement, then the work can only be a work for hire if it is one of the nine kinds of work listed above.

When the issue is contested, the courts use various factors to decide whether a person is an employee or an independent contractor. The contract between the parties is not an important factor in deciding whether a person is an employee or an independent contractor. The court recognizes that the producer and writer will often create contract language to shift income-tax burdens, to reduce unemployment insurance payments, or to gain other short-term financial benefits. The only reason that the court looks at the contract is to see if it sheds any light on the various factors that the court does consider important, such as the details of time, place, and manner for preparing the work.

When determining employment status, the most important factor is who controls the time, the place, and the manner in which a task is to be performed. If it is the individual writer, that person would be considered an independent contractor. This time, place, and manner test can cover a lot of legal ground. Other factors the courts consider: Who owns the equipment? Does the person hired have an independent business? Does the person have employees to help achieve the goals? What remedies do you have if you are unsatisfied with the end result? As a producer, the important thing to know is that writers are almost always independent contractors. Film actors are employees and can never be independent contractors.

When you plan to commission a work to be created as a work made for hire, follow the Golden Rule of Filmmaking:

ALWAYS, ALWAYS GET IT IN WRITING.

You read earlier how important it is to have options in writing. It is even more important when it comes to agreements to create a work for hire. The requirement to have something in writing is part of this unique anomaly of copyright law. The courts have been very strict in interpreting that requirement. They say, when it comes to a work for hire, you must:

1. have a written agreement (in legalese, often known as "a writing"),
2. signed by the person against whom it is to be applied,
3. at substantially the same time as the writer commenced the work.

What the court seems to say is that under the Copyright Law, the written agreement does not merely prove the contents of your agreement, it changes the character of the thing being created. In that sense, it is part of the creation and so must be in a tangible form, just like the work itself must be reduced to a tangible form in order to receive copyright protection. As an intellectual abstraction, the court's reasoning cannot be faulted. But the erasure of all the normal defenses of estoppel or waiver or the inability to prove an agreement by performance (or reliance) seems an extremely harsh result in some circumstances. Your job is to know that you're working in a profession controlled by a very special area of the law—you are dealing in intellectual property. Only rarely do courts allow an oral transfer of copyright licenses to be confirmed in writing after the fact.

WRITERS GUILD OF AMERICA (WGA)

As producer, you must sign the Minimum Basic Agreement (MBA) of the WGA if you plan to hire a writer who is a member of that union. There is absolutely no reason to sign the MBA if you do not plan to hire a union writer. By signing this agreement for any given project, it does not mean that all of your other projects need to be brought under the MBA requirements. Merely create a separate corporation to sign the MBA. You then have two companies or producing entities, and you are considered double vested. **Double vested** means that you control two (or more) production or development entities, one of which is a signatory of the MBA and the other of which is not. Almost all independent producers become double vested at some point in their lifetime. Even the major studios have figured out ways to be double vested.

Once the MBA is signed, that company must create and produce all its properties under the terms of the union agreement. However, you as an individual can be involved with, own, or control other companies that remain non-signatories. Caveat: Once you bring a project within the MBA, you cannot then assign it back and forth for the purpose of having a non-guild writer work on it for a while and then switch it back later. This is a cardinal rule of conducting yourself as a double-vested producer. Once you have made a WGA project out of any given script, it stays a WGA project.

Although one occasionally meets a writer who is able to earn a living as a screenwriter without being a member of the WGA, it is safe to say that most television and studio film writers are members of the WGA. It is equally true that many independent films are written by non-union members. However, writers often request that there be a provision in the contract that if they qualify and join the WGA, any future writing services from them to you will only be rendered after you have signed the MBA. Even as an independent producer, you should have no real problem with such a request and it does help the screenwriter.

THE WORK FOR HIRE AGREEMENT

When you're ready to hire a writer, the contract at the end of this chapter should serve your needs to ensure that you are complying with the work for hire provisions of American copyright law.

As stated before, you are authorized to copy this agreement. A work for hire contract need not be overly long, although studio contracts for such work can be twenty to forty pages. What follows is a simple, straightforward agreement, which comes with a Certificate of Authorship. As in the case of the Assignment provided as part of the Option and Purchase Agreement at the end of Chapter 7, this one-page document can be registered with the Copyright

Office without disclosing the financial details of the relationship. Note that the Certificate of Authorship, therefore, is much more than a mere statement of who wrote a certain script. It also confirms the work for hire arrangement and provides the "fail-safe" assignment discussed in the text. You may see Certificates of Authorship that include a lot of extra things. Legally, they add almost nothing to the basic contract.

5.01   WRITER AGREEMENT - WORK FOR HIRE

THIS AGREEMENT is made and entered into, effective _____,
_____ , by and between _____,
located at _____, (hereinafter
"Producer") and _____, located at
_____, (hereinafter "Writer") with re-
spect to Writer's writing services in connection with the proposed
motion picture project currently entitled "_____"
(the "Picture") on the following terms and conditions:

Date: *By using an effective date right at the beginning of the
contract, you eliminate disputes over when a contract was signed
and therefore when a contract begins and ends.*

Producer: *You, as the filmmaker, are the Producer, so fill in
your name and address or the name and address of your
production company before that word.*

Writer: *Fill in the name and address of the writer and the
name of the Picture. From here on, capitalize those words that
refer to yourself, the Writer, and the Picture.*

---

1. ENGAGEMENT:

(a) **First-Draft Screenplay:** Producer hereby engages Writer,
and Writer hereby accepts such engagement, to write and deliver
to Producer as a work for hire a first-draft screenplay ("First Draft")
based upon material supplied to Writer by Producer (the "Assigned Material"). Writer shall commence writing services upon
execution hereof and shall deliver the First Draft to Producer
within ten (10) weeks thereafter.

Schedule: *This paragraph and the ones that follow present a
carefully thought-out model that tracks the writing schedules set
forth in the WGA agreement. You can modify the schedule
according to your discussions with the writer you hire, but keep
a schedule in your contract. Many of the problems that come up
between a writer and a producer are a function of different
expectations and attitudes about time. You have a much better
chance at a good, working relationship with the writer you hire
when you start out with a written schedule.*

Comment: *If you have read this chapter, there is nothing to be
added here about the importance of work for hire.*

> *Hint:* Many contracts concerning writing services refer to the minimum payments or other minimum rights set forth in the MBA, even though the producer is a non-signatory. This a common way to shorthand such things as wages, credits and creative rights when the writer is not qualified to enter the guild. For instance, in the above paragraph, you could replace the last sentence with "Writer shall perform services according to the minimum schedule of payments contained in the MBA of the WGA." If the contract is to be pursuant to the WGA, state that clearly and require the Writer to become or remain a member in good standing.

(b) **Option For Rewrite and Polish:** Producer shall have an irrevocable and exclusive option ("Option"), for a period of three (3) weeks after delivery of said First Draft, to engage Writer as a work for hire to write and deliver to Producer a rewrite of the First Draft ("Rewrite") and a polish ("Polish") thereof. Producer may exercise said Option by written notice to Writer at any time during the Option period. Writer shall commence Writer's services with respect to the Rewrite upon exercise of said Option, and shall deliver the Rewrite to Producer, incorporating such changes to the First Draft which Producer may require, no later than four (4) weeks after commencement of services.

Producer shall have a period of three (3) weeks from the date of Producer's actual receipt of the Rewrite (the "Reading Period") to study the Rewrite and to confer with Writer regarding any changes to the Rewrite which Producer may require, and Writer shall remain available during the Reading Period to so confer with Producer. Writer shall commence Writer's services with respect to the Polish on or before the expiration of the Reading Period, and Writer shall deliver the Polish to Producer, incorporating such changes to the Rewrite which Producer may require, no later than two (2) weeks after commencement of services.

> *Hint:* By stating this as an option, you have the right, but not the responsibility, to obtain additional services from this writer.

(c) **Postponement of Services:** Producer may require Writer to postpone writing either the Rewrite or Polish for a maximum period of six (6) months, provided that Producer pay Writer the applicable fixed compensation for such services as if the services had been timely performed. Writer shall render such postponed services thereafter when required by Producer, subject only to Writer's professional availability.

> *Comment:* This is a fair balancing of interest of the producer to pace progress during development and the writer's interest not to be hassled by a producer who can't decide what to do.

(d) **Time of the Essence:** Time of delivery is of the essence to Producer.

2. EXCLUSIVITY: At all times during the writing periods hereunder, Writer's services shall be furnished by Writer to Producer on an exclusive basis. At all other times, Writer's services shall be furnished on a non-exclusive "first-call" basis.

> *Hint: This paragraph does not add much in most situations, since writers work at home, but it does give you certain rights in case of a flagrant violation. Writers have to avoid contractual conflicts, but as a practical matter most writers don't work exclusively on a single script. They are always noodling about multiple projects.*

3. COMPENSATION: Upon condition that Writer shall fully perform all material services required to be performed by Writer and that Writer is not in default, Producer agrees to pay to Writer, as full consideration for all services to be performed by Writer hereunder, and for all rights herein granted, and all representations and warranties made, the following sums in the following manner:

(a) **Fixed Compensation:** As follows:

(1) <u>First Draft</u>. $_____, payable one half (1/2) upon execution of this Agreement and one half (1/2) upon delivery to Producer of the completed First Draft.

(2) <u>Rewrite</u>. In the event Producer exercises Producer's Option hereunder, Producer shall pay to Writer $_____, payable one half (1/2) upon commencement of Writer's services and one half (1/2) upon Writer's delivery to Producer of the completed Rewrite.

(3) <u>Polish</u>. In the event Producer exercises Producer's Option hereunder, Producer shall pay to Writer $_____ in connection with the Polish, payable upon commencement of Writer's services in connection therewith.

(b) **Additional Compensation:** If the Picture is produced, writer shall receive two and one-half percent (2.5%) of the final locked budget of the picture (less overhead, insurance, bond and interest charges) with a ceiling of $_____ and a floor of $_____, less any amount previously paid to writer, payable on or before the first day of principal photography.

*How much?: For experienced writers, there are quotes that are used as a basis for payment. A **quote** is merely the price that a writer received for a past assignment. Such quotes tend to establish a floor for the price that the writer accepts in the future. If one of those past scripts was produced and did very well at the box office, that fact usually increases the price. If the film made from the script was a bomb, that fact can soften the price from the past quote. Be sure to verify that the quote given to you was legitimate.*

Hint: If you don't have much money up front, be prepared to pay more when principal photography begins. However, there are limits. Every film has its own economics. No matter how much money there is to spend on a production, there is a limit to the amount of the film's budget that goes go to the script. That is why this paragraph is structured as a percentage of budget. The real test of a script is whether it is made into a movie. You can never afford to pay up front for the full value of the script if the picture isn't actually made. Even studios do not throw around the big bucks unless they are sure that the film is going to be made. Instead, there is a standard paragraph calling for additional payments to the writer in the event that the film is made. If you are on a real shoestring, even these will be deferred until money comes in as in the next paragraph.

(c) **Contingent Compensation:** An amount equal to five percent (5%) of one hundred percent (100%) of the Net Profits, if any, from the Picture, if Writer receives sole "screenplay by" credit in connection with the Picture, or an amount equal to two and one-half percent (2.5%) of the Net Profits, if any, from the Picture, if Writer receives shared "screenplay by" credit in connection with the Picture. "Net Profits" shall be subject to good-faith negotiation within customary industry parameters.

Note: The word "profit" in the film industry has become a joke due to some ingenious studio accounting practices. "Contingent compensation" avoids much of the negative reaction triggered by the word "profit."

Hint: More for reasons of history than logic, the contingent participation that goes to writers has settled in at 5% for sole writing credit, reducible to 2.5% for shared writing credit. That is the standard in the industry in spite of the fact that the contingent compensation is not mentioned in the MBA of the WGA. So, if a writer asks for such participation, it is hard to argue against it. In a situation where a screenwriter is also your partner, you might go above that, but you would be doing so as a function of the role that the screenwriter plays as a partner, not for the screenwriter's role as a screenwriter. The key is the definition of net profits. The language above leaves everything to be negotiated in the future. The most generous language you can possibly agree to is a definition that links the writer's definition to the producer's. For example: "Net Profits shall be defined, calculated and paid on the same basis as Producer's contingent compensation, whether such compensation is designated Net Profits, Profits, or by some other name." This is a generous provision because all of the various categories of profit participation are treated as one.

4. CREDIT:

(a) **Billing:** In the event the Picture is produced hereunder, and Writer has performed all services required of Writer hereunder, Writer shall be entitled to "screenplay by" credit in connection with the Picture as determined pursuant to Exhibit A. All other matters regarding prominence, placement, form, size, style and color of Writer's credits shall be in Producer's sole discretion. Any paid ad credit to which Writer is entitled hereunder shall be subject to Producer's and any distributor's usual and customary exclusions; nothing herein shall be construed to prevent so-called award or congratulatory or other similar advertising with respect to the material or Picture which omits the name of the Writer.

__Hint:__ Note the deferment to Exhibit A. Read it carefully to understand the process being proposed. Do not commit irrevocably to the writer's credit unless you are planning to finance the movie yourself, or you have the financial commitment well in hand. The WGA requires producers who sign their agreement to follow the guidelines they have adopted. Even if you are not a signatory, it is best to use their guidelines. The WGA provides a well thought-out, detailed guideline to determining credits, which ought to hold down disputes. It is difficult for a writer to argue against the use of the WGA credit guidelines. Exhibit A was prepared by the oldest and largest law firm based in Los Angeles and avoids the pitfalls of merely referencing the WGA agreement, which carries with it certain procedural requirements not available to you unless you sign the WGA agreement.

(b) **Inadvertent Non-Compliance:** No casual or inadvertent failure to comply with the provisions of this Paragraph shall be deemed to be a breach of this Agreement by Producer unless writer gives Producer notice of a failure to comply hereto and Producer fails to exert good-faith efforts to correct prospectively such within a reasonable time thereafter.

__Comment:__ This is a standard, important provision.

5. RESULTS AND PROCEEDS OF SERVICES:

(a) **Ownership:** Producer shall solely and exclusively own all rights, title and interest in and to the Assigned Material, the Work, each Form of Work and all of the results and proceeds of Writer's services hereunder. Writer agrees that all material written, composed, prepared, submitted or interpolated by Writer hereunder constitutes and will constitute a work specially ordered or commissioned by Producer for use as part of a motion picture or other audio-visual work, and accordingly, the parties expressly agree that said material is and shall be considered a "work made for hire" for Producer; Producer is and shall be considered the author of said material for all purposes and the owner of all of the rights comprised of the copyright.

> *Hint: This paragraph is at the heart of a writer's agreement. It says that everything that the writer writes is yours as the producer. As a Work for Hire, you (or your production company) will be listed as the Author for copyright purposes.*

(b) **Certificate of Authorship:** Writer will execute and deliver to Producer in connection with all such material the Certificate of Authorship attached hereto as Exhibit B.

> *Hint: See comments on that form.*

6. WRITER'S INCAPACITY:

6. WRITER'S INCAPACITY: If, by reason of mental or physical disability, Writer shall be incapacitated from performing or complying with any of the terms or conditions of this Agreement ("Writer's Incapacity") for a consecutive period in excess of five (5) days or an aggregate period in excess of seven (7) days during the performance of Writer's services, then:

(a) **Suspension:** Producer shall have the right to suspend the rendition of services by Writer and the running of time hereunder so long as Writer's Incapacity shall continue, but in no event shall any suspension hereunder exceed a duration of sixty (60) days.

(b) **Termination:** Producer shall have the right to terminate this Agreement and all of Producer's obligations and liabilities hereunder upon written notice thereof to Writer; except, however, said termination shall not terminate Producer's obligations and liabilities hereunder with respect to any Form of Work theretofore delivered by Writer to Producer in conformance with the terms and conditions hereof (including, without limitation, any obligations and liabilities that may have accrued relating to the payment of Additional Compensation and the according of credit hereunder).

(c) **Right of Examination:** If any claim of mental or physical disability of Writer is made by Writer or in Writer's behalf, Producer shall have the right to have Writer examined by such physicians as Producer may designate. Writer may have Writer's own physician present at any such examination.

> **Comment:** *The above paragraph and the next four paragraphs all deal with your rights when you believe the writer is in default. Some independent producers think this all looks too ominous and leave these provisions out. Because the money involved is so much less than that involved in studio deals, it is usually okay just to "cut your losses" and go to another writer. You have the right to terminate even if it is not spelled out in the contract.*

7. WRITER'S DEFAULT: If Writer fails or refuses to write, complete and deliver to Producer any material herein provided for within the respective periods herein specified, or if Writer otherwise fails or refuses to perform or comply with any of the material terms or conditions hereof other than by reason of Writer's Incapacity ("Writer's Default"), then:

(a) **Suspension:** Producer shall have the right to suspend the rendition of services by Writer and the running of time hereunder so long as Writer's Default shall continue, but in no event shall any suspension hereunder exceed a duration of thirty (30) days.

(b) **Termination:** Producer shall have the right to terminate this Agreement and all of Producer's obligations and liabilities hereunder upon written notice thereof to Writer; except, however, said termination shall not terminate Producer's obligations and liabilities hereunder with respect to any Form of Work theretofore delivered by Writer to Producer in conformance with the terms and conditions hereof (including, without limitation, any obligations and liabilities that may have accrued relating to the payment of Additional Compensation and the according of credit hereunder).

(c) **Anticipatory Default:** Any refusal or statement by Writer, personally or through Writer's agent, that Writer will refuse to keep or perform Writer's obligations and/or agreements hereunder shall constitute a failure to keep and perform such obligations and/or agreements from the date of such refusal or indication of refusal and shall be a Writer's Default hereunder.

8. TERMINATION RIGHTS: Termination of this Agreement, whether by lapse of time, mutual consent, operation of law, exercise of a right of termination or otherwise, shall:

(a) **Compensation:** Terminate Producer's obligation to pay Writer any further compensation; except, however, said termination shall not terminate Producer's obligation to compensate Writer as provided hereunder with respect to any Form of Work thereto-fore delivered by Writer to Producer in conformance with the terms and conditions hereof (including, without limitation, any obligation that may have accrued relating to the payment of Additional Compensation hereunder).

(b) **Refund or Delivery:** If termination occurs prior to Writer's delivery to Producer of the material on which Writer is then currently working, then Writer (or in the event of Writer's death, Writer's estate) shall, as Producer requests, either immediately refund to Producer the compensation which may have been paid to Writer as of that time for such material, or immediately deliver to Producer all of the material then completed or in progress.

9. SUSPENSION RIGHTS: No compensation shall accrue or become payable to Writer during the period of any suspension. If Producer shall have paid compensation to Writer during any period of Writer's Incapacity or Writer's Default, then Producer shall have the right (exercisable at any time) to require Writer to render services hereunder without compensation for a period equal to the period for which Producer shall have paid compensation to Writer during such Writer's Incapacity of Writer's Default; unless Writer immediately refunds to Producer said compensation paid to Writer, upon receipt of notice from Producer to commence such services hereunder.

10. WRITER'S RIGHT TO CURE: If any Writer's Default is inadvert-ent and reasonably curable, Writer shall have a period of three (3) calendar days from the date of notice of default to cure (one time only) such Writer's default; provided that if such Writer's Default occurs during the principal photography of the Picture, Producer's notice to Writer of default to cure need not be in writing and the foregoing three (3) day cure period shall be reduced to twenty-four (24) hours. Any such cure by Writer shall not preclude Producer from exercising any rights or remedies Producer may have hereun-der or at law or in equity by reason of Writer's Default.

• • • • •

Go to Chapter 8, Provisions Common to Most Agree-ments, to finish up this contract. Each one of the provi-sions set out there ought to be included in this contract for all the reasons listed next to those provisions, except the Ownership paragraph that duplicates one of the paragraphs above. In fact, the signature block is lo-cated among those provisions—no signatures, no agree-ment. (All of those paragraphs refer to "Owner." Change "Owner" to "Writer" to make the language match.)

EXHIBIT A
CREDIT DETERMINATION

A.   Screen credit for the screenplay authorship of a feature-length photoplay will be worded "Screenplay By" or "Screenplay _____."

B.   Except in unusual cases, screen credit for the screenplay will not be shared by more than two (2) writers and in no case will the names of more than three (3) be used, provided, however, that two (2) established writing teams, recognized and employed as such and of not more than two (2) members each, may share screen credit for the screenplay. The intention and spirit of the award of credits being to emphasize the prestige and importance of the screenplay achievement, the one (1), two (2), or at most three (3) writers or two (2) teams chiefly responsible for the completed work will be the only screenwriters to receive screenplay credit.

C.   The only exception to the foregoing shall be a photoplay on which one (1) writer (or a team) writes both the original story and screenplay. In this case, the credit may be worded "Written By."

D.   The term "screenplay" means the final script (as represented on the screen) with individual scenes, full dialogue and camera setups, together with such prior treatment, basic adaptation, continuity, scenario, dialogue, added dialogue or gagging as shall be used in and represent substantial contributions to the final script.

E.   The term "photoplay" means a feature-length photoplay.

F.   No production executive shall be entitled to share in the screenplay-authorship screen credit unless he does the screenplay writing entirely without the collaboration of any other writer.

G.   When more than one (1) writer has substantially contributed to the screenplay authorship of a photoplay, then all such writers will have the right to agree unanimously among themselves as to which one (1) or two (2) or, in exceptional cases, three (3) of them, or two (2) teams of the nature above mentioned, shall receive credit on the screen for the authorship of the screenplay. If at any time during the course of production all such writers so agree, then the Producer will not be obligated to issue the notices specified in Paragraphs K through R of this schedule.

H.   The Producer shall have the right to determine in which of the following places the screenplay credit shall appear on the screen:
      1. On the main title card of the photoplay,

2. On a title card on which credits are given only for the screenplay,

3. On a title card on which credits are given for the original story,

4. On a title card on which credits are given for the sources of the material upon which the screenplay was based.

I. A writer whose contribution is judged by the Producer to represent a substantial portion of the completed screenplay shall, for the purpose of this Agreement, be considered a substantial contributor. As a substantial contributor, he shall be entitled to participate in the procedure for determination of screen credits.

J. The screen credits and also the work of writers making substantial contributions but not receiving screen credit may be publicized by the Producer.

K. Before the screen credits for screen authorship are finally determined, the Producer will send a written notice to each writer who is a substantial contributor to the screenplay. This notice will state the Producer's choice of credits on a tentative basis, together with the names of the other substantial contributors and their addresses last known to the Producer.

L. The Producer will make reasonable efforts in good faith to communicate with such writers. No notice will be sent to writers outside the United States or writers who have not filed a forwarding address with the Producer. In the case of remakes, the Producer shall not be under any obligation to send any notice to any writer contributing to the screenplay of the original production unless such writer received screen credit in connection with the original production.

M. The Producer will keep the final determination of screen credits open until a time specified in the notice by the Producer, but such time will not be earlier than six o'clock, p.m. of the fifth business day following dispatch of the notice above specified. If, by the time specified, a written notice of objection to the tentative credits or request to read the script has not been delivered to the Producer from any of the writers concerned, the tentative credits will become final.

N. However, if a protest or request to read the script is received by the Producer from any writer concerned within the time specified in Subdivision M hereof, the Producer will withhold final determination of credits until a time to be specified by the Producer, which time will not be earlier than forty-eight (48) hours after the expiration time specified for the first-notice mentioned in the foregoing paragraphs.

O. Upon receipt of a protest or request to read the script, the Producer will make a copy of the script available for reading at its place of business. The Producer will also notify by fax the writer or writers tentatively designated by the Producer to receive credit, informing them of the new time set for final determination.

P. If, within the time limit set for final determination of credits, exclusive of any writer or writers waiving claim to screen credit, all of the writers entitled to notice have unanimously designated to the Producer in writing the name of the one (1) or two (2) or, in exceptional cases, three (3) writers or two teams to whom screen-play credit shall be given, the Producer will accept such designa-tion. If such designation is not communicated to the Producer within the time above mentioned, the Producer may make the tentative credits final or change them as the Producer sees fit within the requirements as to wording and limitation of names.

Q. The writer shall have no rights or claims of any nature against the Producer growing out of or concerning any determination of credits in the manner herein provided, and all such rights or claims are hereby specifically waived.

R. Any notice specified in the foregoing paragraphs shall be sent by the Producer by faxing, mailing, or delivering the same to the last known address of the writer or may be delivered to the writer personally.

S. In the event that after the screen credits are determined as hereinabove provided, material changes are made in the script or photoplay which, in the sole and absolute discretion of the Producer, justify a revision of the screen credits, then the proce-dure for determining such revised credits will be the same as that provided for the original determination of credits.

T. The writer shall not claim credit for any participation in the screenplay authorship of any photoplay for which the credits are to be determined by the procedure herein provided for prior to the time when such credits have in fact actually been determined, and no writer shall claim credits contrary to such determination.

U. No casual or inadvertent failure to comply with any of the provisions of this Exhibit shall be deemed to be a breach of the contract of employment of the writer, or entitle him to damages or injunctive relief.

EXHIBIT B
CERTIFICATE OF AUTHORSHIP

I, _____, hereby certify that for good and valuable consideration, receipt of which is hereby acknowledged, I have been commissioned to perform writing services in connection with a motion picture presently entitled "_____" pursuant to an agreement (the "Agreement") between me and ("Producer"), dated as of _____, 200__, and that any and all stories, screenplays and other material created, composed, submitted, added or interpolated by me (the "Work") in connection therewith are "work made for hire" for Producer. I further certify that Producer is the "author" of the Work for all purposes, including, without limitation, the copyright laws of the United States, and the owner of the Work and all of the results and proceeds of my services arising out of or in connection with the Agreement, including, without limitation, the theme, plot, characters, ideas and story contained in, and all copyrights (and all extensions and renewals of copyrights) in and to the Work, and all rights therein and thereto, including the right known as "droit moral," and the right to make such changes therein and such uses thereof as Producer may from time to time determine. I hereby waive the benefit of any provision of law known as "droit moral" or any similar or analogous law or decision in any country of the world.

IN WITNESS WHEREOF, I have executed this Certificate of Authorship as of this _____, 200__.

_____
(Writer)

Hint: Many people add provisions that turn this simple Certificate of Authorship into a contract of its own. The agreement to which it is attached controls all the terms and conditions of the work. Therefore, it is not necessary to clutter this simple certificate with other terms and conditions. Also, it is never a good idea to repeat subject matter because you could end up with internal inconsistencies in your contract.

CHAPTER 6

WRITING WITH
A PARTNER

For a variety of rational and irrational reasons, you may want to write with a partner rather than hire someone to do all the writing. Usually, the notion is rooted in common dreams at a minimum and more often in a strong friendship. You should know that you are entering territory that all too often ends in heartache, anger, and litigation. This chapter deals with the pitfalls and preventions.

A SPECIAL KIND OF PARTNERSHIP

This writing relationship almost always begins with a great deal of passion and commitment and enthusiasm. It rarely begins with an agreement that covers what happens after the hot, Oscar®-quality script is completed, because both parties know that it will sell instantly for a bucket of money. But what if it doesn't?

When hard choices are faced, the parties usually struggle individually and collectively to figure out what to do with the script. I have seen many examples of this situation turning sour, ripping apart long-standing friendships and leaving both writers feeling used, misunderstood, and unappreciated. Even though you are sure it would never happen to you, it is better to avoid the possibility by reaching an early agreement. If you have a problem making these decisions before you even start writing, imagine how difficult it would be if the choices you face are a series of unhappy choices concerning a completed script that did not sell or if you have just been offered that bucket of money, but your partner thinks the work on the script was not 50/50.

Copyright law controls your relationship with a writing partner, unless you have written collaboration agreement. Most people are quite surprised at the absolute power of a writing partner when there is no written agreement. A writing partner can stop a deal "deader than a doornail," as my grandmother used to say.

"But that does not make any sense," you protest. "My partner would never do that," you say. Actually, it happens every day— and it is a heartbreaker for everyone involved. Save yourself a lot of grief. Sign a collaboration agreement up front for a happier experience with your writing partner, unless you are willing to completely let go of all control of the finished project.

The dispute can be a completely good faith dispute based on an honest difference of opinion between two intelligent people. When a script sells, one writer might want terms that the other writer does not care about. Often, one writer would like to do business with a producer with whom the other writer is not comfortable. Often, one writer wants to walk away from a deal if the money is not enough while the other writer wants to go forward, just to get the picture made.

The example at the end of this chapter is a simple collaboration agreement that spells out each partner's rights. It overrides the sometimes dire circumstances imposed by copyright law.

But we can't rush to the contract without a story or two.

Just as I began revising this book, I was hired as an expert witness in the last of the James Bond litigation concerning Ian Fleming and his collaborator on *Thunderball,* Kevin McClory. Ian Fleming had written a half dozen thrillers about a fictional member of her majesty's secret service, James Bond. Fleming had tried to sell these books to Hollywood to no avail. There was a short period of hope when one of the books was optioned for a television show, but that never went anywhere.

Fleming hooked up with Kevin McClory to write a script. Kevin had some conditions. It would be a new story, not based on any of the books. There would be a new protagonist—a worldwide, world-threatening criminal organization, not some individual satisfied with individual crimes. It would be a new James Bond—witty, urbane, who loved and used plenty of high-tech gadgets, not the stodgy, somewhat sour character of the novels. And there would be women galore, beautiful world-wise women, the likes of which had never before made an appearance in the Fleming novels.

Ian Fleming and Kevin McClory wrote *Thunderball.* They never wrote out a collaboration agreement. They sold *Thunderball.* Still no collaboration agreement.

Fleming thought their deal was for the script only and wrote a novel based on the script called, surprisingly enough, *Thunderball.* Since they had written *Thunderball* together, McClory thought they jointly controlled all rights in the script and that he should receive credit and income from the novel.

McClory sued in England. There was a settlement reached mid-way through the trial that was reduced to two pages. It settled the particular lawsuit, which is why to this day you will see Kevin McClory's name on every copy of the *Thunderball* novel that was printed after the suit was settled. But still no collaboration agreement!

The very next Bond film produced another lawsuit and another settlement. That was 1976 and the two have been at it ever since, at least until the year 2000, long after Fleming was dead and the battle involved those who acceded to Fleming's rights. Finally, it is over. Or have I spoken too soon? After such a long period of rancor between the two sides, it is hard to imagine that there will be a truce that counts. The last couple of lawsuits ended in a whimper. McClory has very few legal options left. The court ruled that after his initial victories, McClory should have kept up the legal challenges. Instead, he chose to carry on the fight mostly in the press.

He (and the studio claiming through him) lost the last lawsuit on the theory of laches. **Laches** is a legal theory that says that even if you have a technical right to bring a lawsuit, if you waited too long to bring your suit, you lose.

McClory's position was that he and Fleming had created a new, cinematic James Bond that shared only a name and occupation with the James Bond of the first six novels, and therefore he was entitled to share in the income stream earned from that character. Bond is the most profitable character in movie history. It is a real puzzlement that McClory chose the court of public opinion instead of a court of law to wage most of his battles. After a couple of early wins, he seems to have lost his stomach for the whole thing, but he was still angry enough to take out full-page ads from time to time.

So, even when the script does sell and the movie is made, there can be something other than a happy ending. Please, for your own sanity and happiness, prepare this simple collaboration agreement.

JOINT WORK

What does the law say when you write a script with someone and you do not have a written agreement or—even more common—you have not really discussed the issue? You just assumed that you two would co-own the resulting script. You assumed that you would get some proportional share, if not 50%. First rule to remember in the area of copyright is that your agreement has to be in writing or it does not count for a thing. That is also true as between joint authors. Without any written agreement to the contrary, each joint author receives the right to an equal undivided interest in the copyright and the right to deal in any of an author's rights, subject only to an accounting to the other author and payment of his or her share.

The trick is to figure out if you are really joint authors under the copyright law. The disputes usually arise when one person thinks the activity was co-writing and the other person thinks the activity was a friend being a producer or a director or a dramaturge. When the suggestion is made that the activity was co-writing, hurt and indignation flare. That leads quickly to anger and shortly thereafter to litigation. The courts have protected authors from claimjumping by overreaching research assistants, editors, and former spouses, lovers, and friends and other people that authors talk to about what they are writing.

Courts used to say that the plaintiff had to have made some separately copyrightable contribution in order to have any ownership right in a script or film. That is untrue in many cases in which there are true collaborators. The two writers sit in a room talking all day, one of them pecking away occasionally on the computer, but they are creating together. The person not at the computer is comfortably making a 50% contribution, even though the other person is the only one typing in the information.

The courts are now saying that the key ingredient is the mutual intent, when the writing or filming was taking place, to create a work of joint authorship. Without that intent, the courts say, there cannot be a work of joint authorship. Since that almost always takes both parties admitting that fact and you would not be in a dispute if you agreed, these cases have become very hard to win.

All of these cases seem to grow out of people not reducing their expectations to writing. Worse yet, there is a strong undercurrent to the cases that the person thinking they were treated badly never articulated what they thought was a fair treatment in the first place.

Malcom X, like all movies, was the result of a lot of contributions by a lot of people. One of them was Jefri Aalmuhammed, who was credited in the end-roll credits as Islamic Technical Consultant. He sued Spike Lee and Warner Bros. and a lot of people, claiming joint authorship in order to obtain credit on the film and to share in the profits. Everyone agreed that he had made enormous contributions to the film, its dialogue, and even some characters. Even a couple of scenes that he wrote found their way into the finished film. But Warner Bros. was the copyright holder. They didn't even share copyright ownership with Spike Lee, so any effort to say that they <u>intended</u> to share the copyright with anyone else was going nowhere.

Let's be clear. If Aalmuhammed had spoken up earlier and tried to reach an agreement whereby he would share the copyright or even screen credit for co-writing the script, he would have—in all likelihood—failed in his efforts. However, that would have been much better than waiting for the film to be complete and then spend a lot of time and money and psychic energy on a lawsuit. He could have been totally aware of the situation and chosen how he wanted to behave, given the fact that he was not going to receive credit or ownership. This book is rife with examples of the virtue of expressing your needs and wants clearly and early.

The court also talked a lot about superintendence in the *Malcom X* case. The court's opinion focused on who had the final say. Joint authors have an equal say. If all the suggestions of one person can be accepted or rejected without any reason by the other person, that other person has **superintendence** over the script or film. It is that superintendence that identifies a sole author as opposed to someone who is coauthoring.

The notion of superintendence also played a central role in the decision in the musical *Rent*. After a seriously flawed workshop production of *Rent*, Ms. Thomson was brought in to help fix it, and fix it she did. However, all of her suggestions and input were subject to the approval of the author. Even though she wrote up to 9% of the final dialogue for the show, not a word went in without Larson's approval. And there were no other indicia of authorship ever discussed such as shared credit, so Ms. Thomson lost her claim to co-ownership of *Rent*, although she retained ownership of the lines in *Rent* that she wrote. Her only alternative was to pull out her 9% of dialogue. Those words would have been fairly useless to her and harmful to *Rent,* so the parties were able to reach a financial settlement after the decision was rendered, but the result was dissatisfying to everyone. It would have been much better to settle all of this up front.

SILENCE IS GOLDEN

While you always want to give credit where credit is due, never ever put someone's name on a script without the intent that the script is indeed coauthored. More than once I have been consulted by someone who placed someone else's name on a few copies of a script "to make them feel good," "to send to their family," or "to get them off my back about the credit thing." What better proof of co-authorship could there possibly be than if you, yourself, put someone else's name on a script? Be clear about the connection between the credit that you ultimately intend to use and the credits that show up on all those interim drafts.

Mike Batt, the British composer and producer, discovered that when he included a track of absolute silence on the debut album entitled *Classical Graffiti* by The Planets, a group of eight sexy young adults looking to follow in the footsteps of such crossover successes as violinist Vanessa Mae and Bond, the handsome string quartet. He called the track "A One Minute Silence" and then, in homage to the late John Cage, the composer of a "silent" musical composition entitled *4'33"*, Mike Batt listed the composers of "A One Minute Silence" as "Batt/Cage."

It's all a joke, right? Wrong. The Mechanical-Copyright Protection Society, the British organization that collects royalties for composers and publishers of music, sent a license form to Batt on behalf of Cage's publishing company. They wanted half of the mechanical royalties for that track of the CD, since a separate payment is made for each track of a CD. Batt's rejoinder (and the ironic observation of more than one otherwise serious music critic in London) was that Batt's silent minute was very different from John Cage's four minutes and thirty-three seconds of silence he had recorded years earlier. Hmmmm. Sometimes, the law of copyright and the money flow that it controls can lead to some Byzantine results. After a brief splash in the press, this particular dispute was settled privately.

HIRING COLLABORATORS

As a producer, you may hire a team of writers or option a script written by two or more writers. In these instances, a collaboration agreement not only protects the writers. It can also protect you.

If the writers get in a squabble after you become involved as a producer, you will be drawn into the controversy, your project will be affected. This is not what you want. Making a movie is hard enough without the writers being at war.

If you are dealing with a team of writers, ask to see their collaboration agreement. More often than not they will not have one. In that case, be very careful that your option and purchase agreement spells out carefully your rights vis-a-vis the writers.

You must be sure that you have the right to move the script along; that if you hire them to write as a team, you can fire them as a team for the breach of either one; that you can hire someone else to write in the future; the order of names for purposes of credit is settled or under your control; and that it is clear how the money is to be paid to them. Don't get involved in their problems. Quietly cover all of these issues in your option and purchase agreement.

The collaboration agreement that follows is structured in response to the fact situation in which you as the producer will be co-writing with another person who will be carrying the laboring oar with regard to the writing. If you are two writers starting out on a script without any purchaser in mind, there will be a few variations that are pointed out in the comment section to the agreement.

COLLABORATION AGREEMENT

This Agreement, effective as of _____, 200__, is between _____ (Writer A), whose address is _____, and _____ (Writer B), whose address is _____, regarding collaboration on a proposed script for a feature-length film with a working title of _____ (herein the "Work").

> **Comment:** *Fill in the names in the agreement in the same order as you want them to appear in the credit. The credit paragraph is on the next page, but you will want to start off the agreement in the same way. Fill in the most permanent address available for each writer, which is often not his or her current residence.*

> **Hint:** *This agreement will be more user-friendly if you use the writers' last name rather than Writer A and Writer B.*

1. Each Writer will provide the other with access to all material prepared to date on the Work. The Writers agree to be available to each other at convenient times to supply additional information and for consultations, conferences and story meetings.

2. Writer A will write the script of the Work. In writing the Work, Writer A agrees to adhere to material supplied to Writer A by Writer B or by others to whom Writer B introduces Writer A and not introduce any extraneous incidents or anecdotes without first obtaining Writer B's personal approval. Notwithstanding anything to the contrary contained herein, Writer B shall have personal approval over the contents of the script. Writer A shall deliver the first draft screenplay on or before _____, _____.

> **Comment:** *Both the paragraph above and the paragraph below assume that you are clearly the producer on this project and you have entered into this collaboration agreement because you have a great idea, but no money; these paragraphs also assume that you will be helping and performing some writing service, especially with regard to the idea and developing the story, but that "Writer A" will be doing most of the work at the computer. If you are two friends starting out to write a script together, you can describe your working relationship in the above paragraph and modify the next paragraph to cover the situation if one of you wants to quit or, worse, starts slacking off on the work.*

3. Should Writer A be unable to deliver a complete and satisfactory script because of Writer B's failure to cooperate with Writer A, Writer A shall have the right to terminate this Agreement, but Writer A may retain any moneys already paid to him or his

designee for his work and Writer B retains all rights in and to the material created. Should Writer A deliver a script that is unacceptable for any reason directly relating to the quality of Writer A's work, Writer B may terminate this Agreement and Writer A shall have the obligation to return any moneys paid to Writer A under this Agreement. If this Agreement is terminated for any of the aforementioned reasons, it is specifically understood that Writer B shall have the unencumbered right to enter into an agreement with regard to the Work with another writer.

4. If either party shall be unavailable for the purposes of collaborating on such revision or screenplay, then the party who is available shall be permitted to do such revision or screenplay and shall be entitled to the full amount of compensation in connection therewith, provided, however, that in such a case wherein there shall be a revision in the original selling price, the party not available for the revision or screenplay shall receive from the other party $_____ or _____% of the total selling price.

> **Comment:** *Often, when a script is sold, the purchase agreement contains a provision that the writer is obligated to write one or more revisions to the script. If you are writing with someone else, it is a good idea to have that number separated out in the purchase agreement so that you do not have to get into an argument with your co-writer if you end up doing all the work on the rewrite or vice versa.*

5. Upon completion of the Work, it shall be registered with the Writers Guild of America, West, Inc. (the "WGA") as the joint work of the parties. If the work shall be in the form such as to qualify it for copyright protection under the Copyright Act, it shall be registered for such copyright protection with the United States Copyright Office in the names of each of the parties, and each party hereby designates the other party or parties as such party's true and lawful attorney-in-fact to so register such Work on behalf of the other party or parties, which right is coupled with an interest.

> **Comment:** *The last sentence of the above paragraph contains a new phrase that you might not be familiar with, "a right coupled with an interest." **A right coupled with an interest** refers to a legal concept concerning making someone your agent, representative or attorney in law or attorney-in-fact. When you appoint someone as your representative and that person has an interest in the subject, you cannot cut off that representation so easily. It is not impossible, but it certainly is not as easy as when you would normally just be able to write a letter and withdraw the power to represent you.*

6. The credit on the Work where credit appears, and in any and all forms and in any and all media in which the Work is used or licensed, will be the same size, color and boldness and shall read as follows:

Written by [A] _____ and [B] _____

7. Writer A and Writer B represent and warrant that each is free to enter into this Agreement, and that insofar as material created by each is concerned, the work is original, it does not contain any libelous or other unlawful matter; and it does not invade any right of privacy nor infringe any statutory or common-law copyright. Each writer agrees to hold the other harmless from and against any and all claims of libel or of copyright infringement or of invasion of privacy or similar rights arising out of material created by each writer in the Work.

8. The parties agree that all income received from the worldwide sale or disposition of any and all rights in and to the Work (including but not limited to print publication rights, dramatic motion picture, television and allied rights) shall be divided between the parties as follows: __% to Writer A and __% to Writer B. Neither party shall enter into any other agreement or dispose of rights in or to the Work unless it is done so under this Agreement. The parties will each be paid directly by any third party.

> **Hint:** *Without an agreement to the contrary, the law imposes an even split, no matter how uneven the contributions are. The last sentence benefits everybody by eliminating future accounting disputes.*

9. Neither party may enter into any agreement for any of the rights in and to the Work without the written consent of the other party. Co-signature of agreements for the disposition of any such rights shall constitute written agreement by both parties.

> **Hint:** *This language reflects the law without an agreement. As a producer, you will probably want to replace this language with the following, which shifts control to you: "Writer B has the right to market, develop and exploit the work so long as Writer A is kept fully informed and all receipts are divided as provided herein."*

10. If the parties cannot agree on how to exploit the work after one or both of them have completed the work or cannot agree on how to complete the work, then writer A will take over the project for two years to complete and market the property and may enter any agreement with a bone fide third party, so long as A keeps B advised of all significant activities, advises B before entering into an agreement transferring rights of any kind in the property and provides in the agreement of transfer for direct payment to B of B's share of the proceeds as provided in this agreement. After the

two–year period elapses, A's rights pursuant to this paragraph will shift to B, subject to all the same conditions for the next two years. The right to complete, market and exploit the script will continue to switch back and forth until the script is sold.

> **Comment:** *This is a scheme that prevents the script from being the victim of a disagreement between two collaborators. The project can still move forward. It is not ideal, but then the situation is not ideal either. This paragraph creates a workable solution where none else might be available. Feel free to craft your own solution to this problem.*

11. If any disposition is made for any rights in or to the Work, this Agreement shall be in force and effect and continue for the life of the copyright therein.

12. The parties agree that Writer B shall be responsible for all expenses incurred in the preparation of the Work until such time as funds are received from any source, at which time expenses shall be reimbursed after payment of commissions and before the agreed to split between Writer A and Writer B.

> **Comment:** *This is the standard agreement when Writer B is a producer. If you two are writers who will be looking for a producer once the script is completed, you should each bear your own expenses. If the script requires a research trip somewhere or some other substantial expenditure, the party making the expense should be reimbursed **off the top. Off the top** means that the reimbursement is made before the agreed split of proceeds.*

13. Any controversy between the parties hereto involving the construction or application of any of the terms, covenants or conditions of this Agreement shall, on written request of one party served on the other, be submitted to arbitration before a single arbitrator in Los Angeles, California according to the Rules of the AFMA. The cost of arbitration including attorney fees shall be borne by the losing party or in such portions as the arbitrator decides.

> **Comment:** *The virtues of arbitration are many to the independent producer. Whatever you do, you want to stay out of court. Many people like to have mandatory mediation before going to arbitration. **Mediation** is the process by which the parties to a disagreement agree to talk through the problem with a neutral third party who is trained to bring people into agreement. Mediation is a good idea, but often involves some money, always involves some time delays and is something that many people would like to decide upon when a dispute arises. If it is appropriate, mediation is easy enough to institute.*

Writer A   Writer B

CHAPTER 7

BUYING SOMEONE ELSE'S COMPLETED SCRIPT

Every movie starts as a gleam in someone's eye . . . a hope, a dream. A good script is hard to find and when you find one, it screams out to be made. As a producer, you will come up with many of your own ideas to make into films. At the same time, aspiring writers everywhere are writing their own ideas into their own scripts. If you are planning to option a completed script and have therefore skipped Chapter 2, review it now. There is a lot of helpful information there about options in general and why you need them in writing. To be fully prepared for your negotiation, you should also read both the previous chapter and the following chapter, which cover related deal points.

SPEC SCRIPTS

Many writers will submit their completed spec script to you in the hope that you will produce it. A **spec script** is a script written on speculation—the speculation that you or some other producer will want to option and/or purchase the script and make a movie based on it. No one paid the writer, so the writer owns all rights in the script.

The script will have been brought to your attention by either the writer of the script or a go-between, such as an agent, a manager, or a lawyer. Either way, you should talk directly to the screenwriter about the film you want to make, if you can.

If by any chance the screenwriter's address and phone number are not on the cover of the script, you can call the Writers Guild of America, west at (213) 951-4000 or the Writers Guild of America, east at (212) 757-4360 and ask for member-contact information. This service tells you the name and phone number of the person to contact for any writer who is WGA member. If the writer you wish to contact is not a WGA member, try the phone book. Again, talk directly to the writer if at all possible.

If the script is by co-authors, review the information in Chapter 5 about collaboration agreements. Even on the option and purchase of a simple script by one author, you need to be sure that you are dealing with the correct person. You'll note that within the boilerplate provisions discussed in Chapter 7, there are certain representations and warranties. But you still are better off making a personal inquiry rather than relying on the "boilerplate" guarantees that an anxious author might not even read.

When you talk to the author, ask about all the details of the creation of the work. You need to be sure that the writer is the exclusive owner of what they are attempting to sell you. You must be totally comfortable that you are dealing with everyone who needs to be dealt with. If you were to ask, "Did you get any help on this script?" or "Did anyone help you write it?" the answer is usually "no." So ask the question a little differently to get a more complete answer. Ask, "Who did you work with on this script?" Make notes on this conversation, keep it in your chain-of-title file. Again, you should review the information on collaboration agreements and rights of co-authors.

The actual option and purchase agreement is fairly simple and straightforward. The tough part is finding a really good script that is worth the effort and energy needed to turn it into a film. That takes a lot of reading and a firm knowledge of what you like and why. Before laying out any money or energy or time on the project, you want to be sure that you have in mind the same film that the writer has in mind. Find out if you share a vision of the ultimate film: What is the tone of the film? Who would be a good director and why? What actors do you see in the lead roles? What budget are you going to try for? Where do you want the film to be shot?

BUYING
SOMEONE
ELSE'S
COMPLETED
SCRIPT

117

Once you have purchased a script, you have the legal right to take it in whatever direction you want, but you and your project are better off if everyone starts out headed in the same direction. For one thing, if you like the script so much, you probably want any script changes to be made by the original writer. (Even if no additional writing is indicated, a polish is almost always required when the director and the stars become attached.) Generally, you can negotiate a better deal with the original writer involved because the original writer knows the material and the original writer is more motivated to see the film made than a replacement writer would be.

A sample Option and Purchase Agreement can be found at the end of this chapter. It has all the standard provisions and explanations or useful hints concerning many of them. This agreement can be typed into your system and modified slightly for a variety of uses before you line up your money. It would not hurt to have a lawyer review your changes, but common sense is your biggest ally. As soon as you complete the paperwork on this (or any other) option agreement, mark your calendar with at least two important dates: the date that the option runs out and one month before. This may be the most valuable tip in this book.

Once an option terminates—once its time runs out—there is nothing you can do to revive it without the owner's agreement. The option is dead after the last day of its existence. You cannot revive it without the owner allowing you to do so. It is not like an agreement with a contractor who shows up a day late with paint brush in hand and paints your house. In that case, you owe the painter the agreed-upon amount of money. If you show up a day late with your extension check in your hand, nothing happens. The option is dead. Nothing you do replaces the act of extending your option in a timely fashion. The writer is under no legal or moral obligation to grant you a new option or to revive the old one.

PROTECTING YOURSELF
AGAINST UNSOLICITED SCRIPTS

Writers are submitting their scripts all over town. As a producer, you may receive dozens of spec scripts that are not what you are looking for. If you later produce a film that in any way resembles a spec script that a writer submitted to you, that writer might very well file a claim of infringement. (See Chapter 1 for an example involving Warren Beatty and his film *Shampoo*.)

You can gain some protection against unsolicited scripts (and those who send them to you) by the use of a submission agreement. A **submission agreement** provides that if you read a script, the writer will not bring a claim against you for copyright infringement if you produce a similar movie without the writer's participation. The use of these agreements grew out of the cases discussed earlier in this book. There is a handy example of an agreement at the end of this chapter. Print it out and address it to yourself. You can then have the writer sign it.

Most studios, the independent producers who occupy offices on their lots, and other established people do not want to read scripts that come to them "over the transom." If the script is not from an agent or a known entertainment attorney, they do not want to receive it in their offices, much less read it. Not only are the odds against it being much good, the long shadow of litigation looms over every uninvited project that creeps into one's office.

If you are reading scripts by writers who are not represented, you should have the writers of these scripts sign some type of submission agreement. The writer has very little choice—the signing of these documents is generally nonnegotiable. There are simply too many new scripts registered with the Writers Guild each year. It usually doesn't make sense to read scripts from writers you don't know or who do not even have an agent. You do not care if the writer chooses not to sign the agreement and therefore not to submit the script to you. By refusing to sign, the writer has just saved you the trouble of reading one more (probably bad) script.

The submission agreement is an egregious document. In fact, some of these agreements go so far that they are not enforceable. The writer is between a rock and hard place on this one. On its face, it says that you can do anything you want with the submitted material, but obviously, an overt act of plagiarism would not be protected. Infringement cases are hard to win, but you do not want to be sued. Submission agreements give you some protection.

7.01   **OPTION AND PURCHASE AGREEMENT**
SPEC SCRIPT

THIS AGREEMENT, effective as of _____, 200__, is made by and between _____ located at _____ (the "Producer") and _____ [name of owner] located at _____ (the "Writer"), concerning the rights to a motion picture script entitled "_____" and the materials upon which it is based. The following terms and conditions shall apply:

> *Date:* By using an effective date right at the beginning of the contract, you eliminate disputes over when a contract was signed and therefore when an option lapses. Few contracts are signed by all parties on the same day, so avoid date of signature.
>
> *Producer:* You, as the filmmaker, are the "Producer."
>
> *Writer:* The author of the script is the "Writer," and the owner of the rights you want to acquire. If there is more than one author, be sure to list all of them here and have all of them sign as parties to the deal. See Chapter 6 for more information to protect yourself when two or more writers have collaborated to write a script.

1.   **DEFINITION OF "WORK":** For purposes of this Agreement, "Work" means the motion picture script entitled "_____" written by _____ and any and all other literary materials, titles, themes, formats, formula, incidents, action, story, dialogue, ideas, plots, phrases, slogans, catchwords, art, designs, compositions, sketches, drawings, characters, characterizations, names and trademarks now contained therein, as well as such elements as may at any time hereafter be added or incorporated therein, and all versions thereof in any form.

> *Work:* Pick the best description of the property you are optioning. If there was a previous title, include that also by saying, "and previously entitled _____." If the Work has been registered with the Copyright Office, you might give that registration number by way of further identification.

2.   **GRANT OF OPTION:** In consideration of the mutual promises contained herein, and the payment to Writer of $_____ (the "Option Price"), Writer hereby grants to Producer the exclusive, irrevocable right and option (the "Option") for _____ months (the "Option Period") to acquire the exclusive motion picture, television, videocassette, and all subsidiary, allied and ancillary rights in and to the Work pursuant to the terms set forth below.

BUYING
SOMEONE
ELSE'S
COMPLETED
SCRIPT

121

Option Price: You want this to be as low as possible. Sometimes you can even negotiate a free period. Do not be surprised if you run into someone (like me) who says: "No Free Option!" That is my mantra when representing the owner of a property, although I obtain "free" options all the time for my independent producer clients. My argument: It's not "free!" My client will be working, writing (maybe), (if not) hiring someone to write, shopping the project and generally spending time, effort and money on the project.

Hint: Since you do <u>not</u> have the deep pockets of a studio, your first job is to convince the author of your passion for the script. Listen to the author's dreams and hopes. You will be the protector of those dreams and hopes. As self-serving as it may sound, it truly is <u>not</u> about the money at the option stage. Except in big studio deals for hot properties, the initial payment is simply not large enough to be the most important aspect of the deal. The likelihood of the film getting made is the important thing. However, the emotional hook—the sizzle that closes your negotiation—can be a simple promise from you: "If you entrust your property to me, I will be as honest to your work as possible. I will keep you advised every step of the way, and I will do my best to protect you."

Option Period: A year or eighteen months is standard for this first period.

3. EXTENSION OF OPTION:

(a) Producer shall have the right to extend the Option Period for one (1) period of twelve (12) months for $_____ non-applicable. For the right to the extension of the first Option Period there must be one of the following:

> (i)   letter of commitment to direct from an established director;
> (ii) the project is set up at a company, major studio or mini-major studio able to fund the project;
> (iii) substantial negotiations in progress for complete financing of the film; or
> (iv) letter of commitment to act in the film from one star.

(b) Producer shall have the right to extend the Option Period for one (1) additional twelve (12) month period for $_____ non-applicable. In order to have a right to a second extension, Producer must secure at least two (2) of the above five (5) items.

Option Extension: It is standard that you have the right to extend the option. This is important because it takes a very long time to get a film made. Even three years total, as provided here, is a short time. Inexperienced producers often think that they will get their movie made more quickly than anybody else. Based on what? Be realistic. Writers are reluctant to have their material off the market for a long period of time. Frequently, the amounts paid for the second and third years are substantially higher than the amount paid for the initial period . . . and they are non-applicable.

Non-Applicable: Whether subsequent option payments apply or do not apply to the final purchase price is often a point of negotiation. The initial payment is usually applicable (i.e., deductible). More often than not, these additional payments are not deducted from the purchase price. The money must be paid before the time elapses under the current option. This payment acts to keep the option open for the extended period of time. If you let your option expire, you no longer have any right to buy the work or to extend the option. The original owner is then free to option the work to another party.

Progress Requirements: One way to soften the length of time and/or to get more time is to have your right to renew the option be a result of progress made on the film. That is the approach used above. But do not make those barriers too high. The last sentences of Subparagraph (a) and Subparagraph (b) might work for you—though you don't have to include them in your first draft. If no such demand is made, you can strike this language. (Be sure to tailor the language to your needs.) No studio ever makes this kind of deal. Studios simply pay option prices. Therefore, if you use this approach, you must provide alternatives if the project is set up at a studio. After that, the option may be renewed with a cash payment only.

4. EXERCISE OF OPTION: Producer may exercise this Option at any time during the Option Period, as it may be extended, by giving written notice of such exercise to Writer and delivery to Writer of the minimum Purchase Price as set forth below. In the event Producer does not exercise said Option during the period as it may be extended, this Agreement shall be of no further force or effect whatsoever. All rights granted hereunder become property of Writer. Upon exercise of the option, Producer shall have the right to file the Assignment, Exhibit A, with the Copyright Office.

Hint: This paragraph is what gives you the ability to purchase the rights you have optioned. It is standard.

5. PENDING EXERCISE OF OPTION: Producer shall have the right to engage in all customary development and pre-production activities during the option period as it may be extended.

BUYING
SOMEONE
ELSE'S
COMPLETED
SCRIPT

123

> *Hint: The fact that you optioned the film rights infers this to be true. One of the things you want is to be able to change the script. That means creating a derivative work, which requires permission of the copyright owner who is the writer. This is where you obtain the writer's permission. Stating the fact clearly is better. Often people add "including but not limited to" and then go on for a page or two. That's overkill.*

> *Comment: Many writers will want a guarantee that they will write the first revision, if any, of the script. Fair enough. If you don't think the writer is up to taking the script to the next level, look at this payment as part of the cost of the script.*

6. GRANT OF RIGHTS: Effective upon Producer's exercise of the Option, Writer does hereby exclusively sell, grant and assign to Producer all rights in and to the Work not reserved by Writer, throughout the universe, in perpetuity, in any and all media, whether now existing or hereafter invented, including, but not limited to, the following: all motion picture rights, all rights to make motion picture versions or adaptations of the Work, to make remakes and sequels to and new versions or adaptations of the Work or any part thereof, to make series and serials of the Work or any part thereof; the right, for advertising and publicity purposes only, to prepare, broadcast, exhibit and publish in any form or media, any synopses, excerpts, novelizations, serializations, dramatizations, summaries and stories of the Work, or any part thereof; and all rights of every kind and character whatsoever in and to the Work and all the characters and elements contained therein.

> *Hint: This is exactly what you are purchasing. This is why you are making the payments. This paragraph can also run on for pages, but the above is all-inclusive. It puts the burden on the Writer to be specific about reserved rights.*

7. PURCHASE PRICE: As consideration for all rights and property herein granted, and all warranties, and covenants herein made by Writer, Producer agrees to pay Writer the following sums not later than the commencement of principal photography of a production:

(a) $_____ if the final budget for the motion picture based on the Work does not exceed two million dollars

($2,000,000) less any moneys paid as option exercise money and less the option payment for the initial period;

(b) If the final budget exceeds $2,000,000, One Percent (1%) of the final budget for the motion picture based on the Work less any amounts paid for option exercise; however, in no event shall the amount of such payment exceed Fifty Thousand Dollars ($50,000).

> ***Purchase Price:*** *Price can be a flat fee or a percentage of the film's budget, or a combination. Most film budgets allow about 2.5% or 3% of the budget for purchase of the script, with a floor and ceiling. The **floor** is the minimum price you pay, regardless of the budget. The **ceiling** is the maximum price you pay, regardless of the budget.*

8. ADDITIONAL COMPENSATION:

(a) **Contingent Compensation:** Producer also agrees to pay Writer ___ percent (__%) of one hundred percent (100%) of the net profits from any production based on the Work for which Writer receives any other payment under this Agreement. "Net Profits" shall be defined, accounted for and paid in the same manner for Writer as for Producer, whether Producer's contingent compensation is called Net Profits, Adjusted Gross Profits or otherwise.

> ***Note:*** *Net Profits have gotten a bad name. Try using Contingent Compensation. The language in this agreement avoids all accusations of Hollywood accounting, at least by you, because Writer gets a piece of what you get. If you are going to pay for the film yourself or through your family and friends or a company you own or control, be sure to spell out your definition of Contingent Compensation. Be as specific as possible to avoid future conflicts. The standard is 5% for sole credit, 2.5% for shared credit.*

(b) **Bonus Compensation:** Producer shall pay Writer $_____ in addition to any other money due Writer under this agreement upon the happening of the following: _____.

> ***Performance Bonus:*** *Use this paragraph only after the Writer requests it! Often there are bonuses if a film grosses over a certain domestic box office as reported in* Weekly Variety *or* Hollywood Reporter *(e.g., $10,000 if the film grosses $100 million in domestic box office.) Usually such performance bonuses are advances against contingent compensation. Do not grant bonuses for things like awards or Oscar nominations. These events do not always translate into money for you.*

9. CREDITS:

BUYING
SOMEONE
ELSE'S
COMPLETED
SCRIPT

125

(a) In the event a motion picture based substantially on the Work is produced hereunder, Writer shall receive credit in the following form:

Written by _____

unless the credit guidelines of Writers Guild of America would produce another result, in which case the credit will be determined according to those guidelines.

(b) Such credit shall be accorded on a single card in the main titles on all positive prints of the picture and in all paid advertising in which the director has received credit, except for advertising of eight (8) column inches or less; group and list advertisements; teasers; publicity; special advertising; billboards; television trailers; film clips ("excluded ads"). Nothing contained in this Paragraph shall be construed to prevent the use of so-called "teaser," trailer,or other special advertising, publicity or congratulatory advertising. All other matters regarding prominence, placement, size, style and color of said credits shall be in Producer's sole discretion.

> *Hint:* This is a very precise description of your obligations as far as credit. It is acceptable to the studios and to any legitimate distributor.

(c) No casual or inadvertent failure to comply with credit requirements hereunder shall be deemed a breach of this Agreement.

> *Hint:* This is very important to you, since there can always be a slip-up. Often the Writer insists (and you should agree) that you take reasonable steps to correct any mistake when it is brought to your attention. If asked, you should agree to add, "provided Producer takes reasonable steps to prospectively cure upon written notice from Writer."

• • • • •

Go to Chapter 8, Provisions Common to Most Agreements, to finish up this contract. You should use all the paragraphs contained there except Expenses, unless the Writer brings that up.

EXHIBIT A
ASSIGNMENT (Short Form)

FOR good and valuable consideration, receipt of which is hereby acknowledged, the undersigned Writer does hereby sell, grant, assign and set over unto _____ (hereinafter referred to as "Producer"), and Producer's heirs, successors, licensees and assigns, forever, the sole and exclusive motion picture rights, television motion picture and other television rights, videocassette rights and certain subsidiary, allied and ancillary rights, including merchandising rights and limited publication rights, for advertising and exploitation purposes only, throughout the universe in perpetuity, in and to that certain script (e.g., original literary/musical) described as follows:

Title: "_____"
By: _____

including all contents thereof, all present and future adaptations and versions thereof, and the theme, title and characters thereof. The undersigned and Producer have entered into a formal option and purchase agreement dated _____, 200__, relating to the transfer and assignment of the foregoing rights in and to said Work, which rights are more fully described in said Option and Purchase Agreement. This Assignment is expressly made subject to all of the terms and conditions of said Agreement.

IN WITNESS WHEREOF, the undersigned has executed this assignment on _____, 200__.

WRITER: _____

> ***Hint:*** *This document is signed along with the main agreement so that you don't have to obtain it later. You do not use it until you actually exercise the option agreement and own the film rights to the Work (book, song, article). When you exercise the option and own the Work, one of the first things you do is to file the assignment with the Copyright Office for all the reasons stated in the Chain of Title chapter (Chapter 9). Use the Cover Sheet provided in Chapter 9 to record the assignment.*
>
> ***Comment: Consideration*** *is legalese shorthand for whatever is of value that you give up for what you get. Money is the "consideration" that most people think of. Your promises can also be consideration. It is okay to reference the fact of consideration without spelling out details, especially in a document like this that will be open to the public.*

SUBMISSION AGREEMENT

[date]

[Producer's name]
[Producer's address]

Dear [Producer's name]

I desire to submit to you for your consideration the following described material (herein called "Submitted Material"), written, composed, owned or controlled by me and intended to be used by you as the basis for one or more theatrical motion pictures:

I recognize the possibility that the Submitted Material may be identical with or similar to material which has or may come to you from other sources. Such similarity in the past has given rise to litigation so that unless you can obtain adequate protection in advance, you will refuse to consider the Submitted Material. The protection for you must be sufficiently broad to protect you, your related corporations, and your and their employees, agents, licensees and assigns and all parties to whom you submit material. Therefore, all references to you includes each and all of the foregoing.

As a material inducement to you to examine and consider the Submitted Material, and in consideration of your so doing, I represent, warrant and agree to the following terms and conditions:

1. I acknowledge that the Submitted Material is submitted by me voluntarily, on an unsolicited basis, and not in confidence, and that no confidential relationship is intended or created between us by reason of the submission of the Submitted Material. Nothing in this agreement, nor the submission of the Submitted Material, shall be deemed to place you in any different position from any other member of the public with respect to the Submitted Material. Accordingly, any part of the Submitted Material which could freely be used by any member of the public may be used by you without liability to me.

2. You agree that you shall not use the Submitted Material unless you shall first negotiate with me and agree upon compensation to be paid to me for such use, but I understand and agree that your use of material containing features or elements similar to or identical with those contained in the Submitted Material shall not obligate you to negotiate with me or entitle me to any compensation if you have an independent legal right to use such other material which is not derived from me (either because such features or elements were not new or novel, or were not originated by me, or

were or may hereafter be independently created and submitted by other persons, including your employees).

3. I represent and warrant that I own or control individually, or together with those other persons signing this letter, the Submitted Material, that the Submitted Material is free of all claims or encumbrances and that I have the exclusive right to offer all rights in the Submitted Material to you.

4. I agree that no obligation of any kind is assumed or may be implied against you by reason of your consideration of the Submitted Material or any discussions or negotiations we may have with respect thereto, except pursuant to an express written agreement hereafter executed by you and me which, by its terms, will be the only contract between us.

5. Any claim, controversy or dispute arising hereunder shall be settled by arbitration before a single arbitrator in accordance with the rules of AFMA. The award of the arbitrator shall be binding upon the parties and judgment thereon may be entered in any court. The prevailing party shall be entitled to all arbitration costs, and reasonable attorney fees.

6. I have retained a copy of Submitted Material. I assume full responsibility for any loss of the Submitted Material, irrespective of whether it is lost, stolen or destroyed in transit, or while in your possession, or otherwise.

7. Except as otherwise provided in this agreement, I hereby release you of and from any and all claims, demands and liabilities of every kind whatsoever, known or unknown, that may arise in relation to the Submitted Material or by reason of any claim now or hereafter made by me that you have used or appropriated the Submitted Material, except for fraud or willful injury on your part.

8. No statements or representations have been made except those expressly stated in this agreement. This agreement may be modified only by subsequent written agreement signed both by you and me.

Very truly yours,

_____

Writer
[Writer's address]
[Writer's phone number]

Encl.: Submitted Material as Described Above.

CHAPTER 8

PROVISIONS COMMON TO MOST AGREEMENTS

Many independent filmmakers think that boilerplate means one of the following: "I don't have to read that." "Skip over this; it's lawyer stuff." "Boring." "I never understand that stuff." "I'll never need to use that stuff." There is an element of truth to each one of these reactions. However, these sections in a contract are the ones that come into play almost every time there is a problem. These paragraphs are the ones you turn to in most disputes.

CONTRACTS AND NEGOTIATION

A short course on contract law is well beyond the scope of this book, but you should understand a few key points (besides the importance of getting everything in writing) if you ever negotiate any of the deals on your film.

A deal closes when the parties agree to the extent that they can move forward with the performance of the deal. Everybody is bound to perform. The tradeoffs have been made. The compromises have been made. The deal is closed.

Unless you have a specific agreement to the contrary, no deal is closed until all the points of the deal are closed. This truth about the way American law works has given rise to various catchphrases you may have heard: "It ain't over till it's over." "It ain't over till the fat lady sings." "I'll trust it when the check clears the bank."

Even if you are aware of this truth, you will still be upset if you think that you have a deal on all points except one, and then find the other party backing off on some of the points of the deal where agreement had been reached.

To have an enforceable contract, you have to have agreement on four elements:

1.   What you are getting.
2.   What you are paying for what you are getting.
3.   How long the contract will last.
4.   Whom the contract is between.

You can work out everything else along the way.

Offers and Counteroffers

If you receive a written offer, you can write "accepted" across it and the deal is done. Be careful when you counteroffer. There is a widely held misconception that you can always accept an offer. When you make a counteroffer to someone who has made an offer to you, the law looks at the transaction in a very particular way. The law says that you rejected the offer that was made to you and put a new offer on the table. The other party may *let* you accept a previous offer, but they are not bound to do so. You do not have a legal right to demand that the other party's old offer stay on the table.

Written vs. Oral

Samuel Goldwyn once boomed, "An oral agreement isn't worth the paper it's written on." When it come to matters of copyright, you must get it in writing. There are no exceptions. It is required by the

Federal Copyright Law. The law requires a few other contracts to be in writing, but for contracts in the other areas of law there are some exceptions. Examples of contracts that "must" be in writing include contracts that sell land and contracts lasting longer than one year. The major exception is when there has been reliance on an oral agreement. For contracts that convey an interest in a copyright, even reliance does not excuse the need for a writing. Otherwise, contracts do not have to be in writing. The problem with an oral agreement is the enforcement of it. If you get into a dispute, you can be sure that the other side will remember the agreement differently from the way you remember it.

Remember, the paper does not fulfill the agreement—people do. No contract can protect you against bad people who are determined to do bad things to you.

The Structure of a Contract

No matter what the subject of a contract is or how much money is involved, a contract ought to be well organized and easy to read. In fact, you should never sign (or present) a contract that you don't understand. Here are some rules of thumb for you to remember when you are putting together your own contracts:

The first paragraph should name the parties, provide their addresses, and identify them in parentheses. Once identified, you always refer to the party by the short identifier instead of the long name. Most of the agreements in this book are between the Producer and the Owner. Be sure that the identifiers are consistent throughout the contract. The first paragraph also gives an effective date for the commencement of the contract.

Note that the words Producer and Owner are capitalized in the paragraph above and in the paragraphs that are at the end of this chapter. That is because they are defined terms. A **defined term** is a term (or word) that is defined somewhere in the contract and has a special meaning throughout the contract. For instance, Owner refers to the specific person identified as such in the first paragraph of the contract. Always capitalize the word throughout the contract to show that you are not referring to any old owner, but rather to a specific person. Never use the word in the contract in its generalized meaning. If you absolutely must use the word in a nonspecific way (i.e., not referring to the Owner defined in paragraph one), be sure to use it in lower case. When you use the word as it has been defined in the contract, it should be capitalized.

Number your paragraphs in the order in which they appear.

Put captions on your paragraphs. **Captions** are the titles of the paragraphs. They can help you quickly find specific subject areas in the contract.

Be sure to limit each paragraph to one subject.

Don't discuss any subject in more than one place.

Try not to refer to other paragraphs in the contract by number. As you work on a contract, paragraph numbers can change without all the references to the paragraphs changing, which can create confusion later.

Describe the basic deal early in the contract in clear, easy-to-understand language. Follow the basic deal with the less important things. Then move on to termination provisions and close with the provisions common to most contracts that are at the end of this chapter.

Always, always, always be sure that the signatures on the bottom of the contract match the parties at the top. There is a huge difference between an agreement with a corporation and an agreement with an individual. If a person is signing for a corporation, be sure they set out their position with the corporation. If a person is signing as an individual and you are going to be paying that person more than $600, it is a good idea to have that person include their social security number.

A few of the agreements in this book are complete in and of themselves. Most of them only have the introductory paragraphs containing the basic deal terms. In order to form a usable contract, they need to also contain the provisions that are provided at the end of this chapter. When they need these provisions, that is noted below the basic deal terms of each contract.

International

If you are to make money from your film, it must be sold around the world. This activity is normally handled by a foreign-sales agent, but you might like to know something about how it works to sell rights to distribute your film all over the world. Put your contract in English. English has become the language of international commerce in general. In the film business, even people from non-English speaking countries will generally put their film contracts in English.

BOILERPLATE

Take a few minutes to read through the language and the legal explanations in this chapter, and then you can use them in your agreements without thinking through them for each individual contract. You should have a smattering of knowledge about these important provisions, and now is a good time to acquire that knowledge. Too many producers wait to learn about these paragraphs until there is a crisis or dispute that boilerplate controls!

Having some background in these matters also makes the negotiation go more easily. It discredits you and your position if you have never read the language or do not understand it yourself. You are the filmmaker. You are supposed to be taking care of all these details. The writer, the director, the actors, and the crew all look to you for leadership on the business side of things. Be informed and you will make better deals and those with whom you work will have more confidence in you and you will sleep better at night.

Some of the clauses are included merely because they are so common. Some, such as the arbitration clause, can be extremely important to you. Others define what happens in certain circumstances and are therefore helpful in keeping you out of controversy.

It is always good to have these things spelled out so that there are no future misunderstandings. Why should you get into an argument? A good contract does more than protect you from scoundrels. A good contract helps both parties avoid future confrontations. Be sure to add the appropriate "boilerplate" provisions to the agreements you take from other parts this book. These provisions are so important that you are directed to this chapter by several other chapters.

Do not include any special heading (such as "boilerplate provisions") for these paragraphs. Just number them in sequence, starting with the next number available to you in the contract you are creating.

> *Comment:* Number these paragraphs sequentially from the last paragraph in the contract in which they are being attached. If they are being applied to a writer-for-hire agreement, change Owner to Writer throughout. Note that the parties are Producer and Owner, which matches most of the other contracts in this book. These defined parties must remain consistent throughout a contract.

EXPENSES: Producer shall reimburse Owner's actual, pre-approved, out-of-pocket expenses for all travel requested to be made by Owner to the extent pre-approved by Producer.

> *Comment:* This is usually a deal point. It shows up in virtually all contracts for personal services. This is the best language because it puts you in control. Studios usually spell out a specific dollar amount to be paid as per diems. **Per diem** is a specific amount paid to cover all expenses without any need to provide receipts or an accounting. Another approach is to say, "Owner shall receive expenses on a favored nations basis with Producer when asked by Producer in writing to travel more than fifty miles from home on behalf of the project."

NAME AND LIKENESS: Producer shall have the right to publish, advertise, announce and use in any manner or medium the name, biography and photographs or other likenesses of Owner in connection with the exhibition, distribution, advertising and promotion or other exploitation of any film created as a result of the exercise by Producer of its rights hereunder, including merchandising, if merchandising rights are granted herein.

> *Comment:* You must acquire these rights to advertise the picture with the name of the Owner. Otherwise, you cannot use the Owner's name in your advertising. What a strange poster that would be. Some Owners will want the right to approve photographs of themselves. If so, you should insist that they approve at least half of those presented to them.

MERCHANDISING: Owner shall be entitled to receive a royalty equal to ten percent (10%) of Net Merchandising Receipts attributable to the use of any character in the Work in Merchandise of any kind, it being the intent of the parties to create the broadest possible definition to Merchandise. Such amounts shall be reducible by the aggregate amount paid on account of all royalties to other performers for use of such other performers' names, likenesses or images or Producer's Logo or other intellectual property that receives a royalty on any given piece of Merchandise to not less than seven and one-half percent (7.5%) of Net Merchandising

Receipts. Net Merchandising Receipts are all receipts of any kind or nature received by Producer less only third-party sales commissions not to exceed 25%.

> **Comment:** *10% is a generous offer. Many producers would start with 2.5% for the underlying property and 2.5% for the writer for a total budget of 5%, leaving plenty of room to move to a 10% budget.*

PUBLICITY RESTRICTIONS: Owner agrees that, except as merely incidental to Owner's personal publicity endeavors, Owner shall not issue or authorize or permit the issuance of any advertising or publicity of any kind or nature relating to this Agreement, Producer, the material, any exercise of any rights in the Work or any versions or productions based in whole or in part thereon, without the prior written consent of Producer.

> **Comment:** *Studios like to control all publicity. These provisions are desirable. Studios will accept an assignment without these provisions in the agreement, but they are preferred.*

NO OBLIGATION TO PRODUCE: Nothing herein shall be construed to obligate Producer to produce, distribute, release, perform or exhibit any production based upon or suggested by the results of Writer's services hereunder.

> **Comment:** *Totally unnecessary from a legal point of view, this paragraph cuts off any claim or misunderstandings. Even if you think that you have the money lined up, this is a good paragraph to have in your agreement in order to avoid future disagreements.*

REVERSION: If Producer exercises the option and fails to commence principal photography within seven years thereafter, Owner may send Producer written notice that the rights will revert to Owner unless principal photography commences within ninety (90) days of such notice. If Producer fails to so commence principal photography, the rights shall revert to Owner. If a picture is subsequently produced by another producer, Owner shall reimburse Producer all out-of-pocket costs paid by Producer out of first monies received by Owner in connection with the Picture, but no later than the commencement of principal photography.

> **Hint:** *You can leave this paragraph out of your first draft and put it in when the Owner asks for it. (If you hire a member of the WGA, the member will obtain something very near to the above rights through the WGA Minimum Basic Agreement.) The length of time is, of course, subject to negotiation.*

REMEDIES: Owner acknowledges and agrees that Owner's sole remedy for any breach or alleged breach of this Agreement by Producer shall be an action at law to recover monetary damages. In no event shall any of the rights granted or to be granted and/or the releases made herein revert to Owner, except as provided herein, nor shall Owner have a right of rescission or right to injunctive or other equitable relief.

> *Comment: This sounds harsh, but it is absolutely necessary in a studio deal. You should have this protection so that you have maximum flexibility on how and where to set up your film for financing and distribution, because no studio will take on a project without it.*

FORCE MAJEURE: If the development or production of the Picture is materially interrupted or delayed by reason of epidemic, fire, action of the elements, walk-out, labor dispute, strike, governmental order, court order or order of any other legally constituted authority, act of God or public enemy, war, riot, civil commotion or any other cause beyond Producer's control, whether of the same or of any other nature, or if because of the illness or incapacity of any principal member of the cast, any unexpired portion of the term hereof shall be postponed for the period of such interruption or interference.

> *Comment: Things happen. When they do, your rights should be spelled out. This simple paragraph helps to avoid the basic issue of whether you have the right to extend your agreement if some catastrophe happens that delays your project. Smart Owners will want to put some limit on the time a contract can be extended before it is terminated.*

ASSIGNMENT: Producer has the right to assign this contract to any person or entity in Producer's sole discretion.

> *Comment: Unnecessary legally, but it makes it clear that you can do this. Even if you are going to pay for the production of the film yourself, you want this ability since the actual production entity might be a corporation or other company that you control rather than you as an individual. You may need it when it comes time to distribute the film.*

REPRESENTATIONS AND WARRANTIES: Owner represents, warrants and agrees that it has the right and authority to enter this agreement and that:

(a) The Work itself is original with Owner and no part of the Work is in the public domain;

(b) Owner has not and will not enter into any agreements or activities which will hinder, compete, conflict or interfere with the exercise of any of the rights granted to Producer. Owner has no knowledge of any claim or potential claim by any party which might in any way affect Producer's rights herein;

(c) The Work does not, and no use thereof will, infringe upon or violate any personal, proprietary or other right of any third party, including, without limitation, defamation, libel, slander, false light or violation of any right of privacy or publicity or any copyright law.

(d) The exercise of the rights herein granted to Producer will not in any way, directly or indirectly, infringe upon any rights of any person, or entity whatsoever.

> **Comment:** *We see these so often that we forget how important they are. Read them over. Of course, your deal is premised on these understandings, but without them in the contract, the other party could say otherwise.*

INDEMNIFICATION: Owner agrees to defend, indemnify and hold Producer, and Producer's employees, agents, successors, licensees and assigns, harmless from and against any and all claims, damages, liabilities, losses or expenses (including reasonable attorney fees and costs) suffered or incurred by Producer on account of or in connection with the breach of any of Owner's representations, warranties or covenants set forth herein.

> **Hint:** *This puts teeth in the Representations and Warranties paragraph. Some producers issue the initial contract without binding themselves to a similar indemnification. If you do that and the other party complains, put it in a paragraph that mirrors this one and binds you as Producer to indemnify Owner.*

PUBLIC INFORMATION: Producer, and Producer's successors, licensees or assigns, shall have no less rights by reason of this Agreement to material in the public domain than any member of the public may now or hereafter have.

> **Hint:** *This clause allows you to make a film in this milieu, even if you don't make a film based on this particular script or book or life story. Wise owners and writers resist such a clause in the agreement with the following argument: "If you want public domain information, go ahead, but I won't help you get started."*

ARBITRATION: Any claim, controversy or dispute arising hereunder shall be settled persuant to California law by arbitration before a single arbitrator in accordance with the rules of the American Film Marketing Association (AFMA) held in Los Angeles, California. The award of the arbitrator shall be binding upon the parties and judgment there may be entered in any court. The prevailing party shall be entitled to all arbitration costs and reasonable attorney fees.

> *Hint: This is very important to independent producers. Many studios, with their large legal staffs and deep pockets, like to avoid arbitration, but will not turn down a project based on arbitration provisions in the underlying contracts. Unless you designate arbitration, you are stuck with expensive, time-consuming litigation in the courts. Arbitrations avoid lawsuits. An arbitration is cheaper and faster. You can even present your evidence yourself and do all the paperwork yourself, although you would be well-advised to consult an attorney. The negative is that there is virtually no appeal from the decision of an arbitrator. An arbitration award can be confirmed in court in a very simple process, and then the award becomes a court judgment without taking many dollars and much time to obtain. I recommend AFMA arbitration because the arbitrators are all attorneys who specialize in independent films. If the other side does not want to use AFMA, try the American Arbitrator Association (AAA).*
>
> *Hint: There are other recognized arbitral agents besides AFMA. AFMA is my preference because the panel of arbitrators is particularly knowledgeable in independent filmmaking. AFMA arbitrations can be held anywhere in the world. The largest panel of AFMA arbitrators is in Los Angeles.*
>
> *Hint: The designation of a city can be important in an actual dispute. If you cannot agree on a city in advance, at least narrow the choices down to two cities, either one of which can be used. This way you do not have a surprise trip to Iowa when you least expect it.*

NOTICE: Any notice to be given hereunder shall be in writing and faxed and mailed to the party receiving notice at the address written above. Notice shall be effective on the date faxed or three days after mailing, whichever is earlier.

ADDITIONAL ASSURANCES AND DOCUMENTS: This Agreement is irrevocable, and applies equally to any and all motion pictures produced hereunder and is not only for Producer's benefit, but also for the benefit of any other party to whom Producer may sell, assign and/or license any or all of the rights, privileges, powers and/or immunities granted herein. Owner, to the best of Owner's ability, will prevent the use by others of the rights granted hereunder in a manner inconsistent with the grant of rights to Producer. Producer may prosecute, and Owner irrevocably grants to Producer full power and authority to do so, in Owner's name, and to take any and all steps as Producer, in Producer's sole discretion may elect, to restrain and prevent others from so using such rights. Owner further agrees to execute, acknowledge and deliver to Producer any and all further assignments and other instruments, in form approved by counsel for Producer, necessary or expedient to carry out and effectuate the purposes and intent of the parties as herein expressed. If Owner shall fail to so execute and deliver or cause to be so executed and delivered any such assignment or other instruments within ten (10) days of being presented, Producer shall be deemed to be, and Owner irrevocably appoints Producer, the true and lawful attorney-in-fact of Owner to execute and deliver any and all such assignments and other instruments in the name of Owner, which right is coupled with an interest.

> **Hint:** *Although this is standard, it gives you a lot of power. Sharp writers/owners are going to want to restrict this. Do not eliminate it all together. The following paragraph is acceptable as an alternative:*
>
> **OTHER DOCUMENTS:** *Owner agrees to execute such assignments or other instruments as Producer may from time to time deem necessary or desirable to establish, or defend, its title to any material created hereunder or rights granted hereunder. Owner hereby irrevocably appoints Producer the true and lawful attorney-in-fact of Owner (which right is coupled with an interest) to execute, verify, acknowledge and deliver any and all such instruments or documents which Owner shall fail or refuse to execute, verify, acknowledge or deliver within ten (10) days of receipt thereof. Producer shall provide Owner with copies of any such instruments or documents executed, verified, acknowledged and delivered by Producer on Owner's behalf hereunder.*

_____   _____
Producer   Owner

                                   _____
                                   Owner's Soc. Sec. #

> **Comment:** *Note that there is no requirement for date and address because they are covered in the introductory paragraph. Also, be sure to obtain the Owner's social security number at this point. You will need it for tax reporting, so obtain it early.*

PART III

DEVELOPMENT AND PRE-PRODUCTION

Some producers put off the copyright and clearance issues. They should be taken care of before the commencement of principal photography. The sooner you begin thinking about these issues, the easier things will be for you.

CHAPTER 9

REGISTERING COPYRIGHT
OF THE SCRIPT

You register your script, even though you are going to make changes to it, for several reasons. This chapter gives you the reasons and benefits to registration along with a step-by-step registration guide.

WHEN TO REGISTER

The latest you should register your script is commencement of pre-production. However, you will continue to rewrite your script during pre-production and even during principal photography. Most of you will continue to rewrite the script during post-production.

The most important reason to register your script as soon as you are sure you will commence principal photography is that SAG requires proof of copyright registration of the script before you can use a SAG actor in your film. A copy of the application and the signed registered-mail receipt is the minimum they require.

You might be thinking that you will not use SAG actors in your low-budget digital film. Think again. SAG has made it so attractive to use their members that even student films tend to use SAG actors. There are now special student film contracts, experimental film contracts, and low-budget contracts that virtually eliminate the financial considerations from the use of union talent. And let's face it: Any actor with any experience at all is going to be a member of the union.

Even if you do not use SAG actors, as hard as that is to imagine, the commencement of pre-production is still a good time to register your script with the copyright office.

To register earlier could be a waste of time because of substantial subsequent revisions. If you wait until later, you are spending an enormous amount of time, energy, and money to create a film without clearly and publicly stating your claim to do so. Many independent filmmakers mistakenly delay this important item. This is not a good practice, especially when it is so easy and cheap to register both the script and the chain of title documents. Don't delay.

Registering your script with the copyright office brings a number of other legal protections. They are discussed in the next section, in order to give you an overview of the legal benefits that still flow from copyright registration. None of these reasons is strong enough to cause you to register your script prior to the commencement of principal photography.

LEGAL BENEFITS FROM REGISTERING YOUR SCRIPT

The author of the script (either the writer himself or herself or the employer if it is a work for hire) owns the copyright to the script as it is being created. No registration is necessary. No declaration on the cover of the script is necessary. All of those formalities were done away with when the copyright law underwent a major revision in the late '70s.

However, formal copyright registration of the script with the Copyright Office provides additional protection to the copyright owner beyond that which is automatically granted as the script is being written. By registering your ownership of copyright, you gain several protections: You give notice to the world of your status as the copyright owner. You can file a lawsuit to protect your rights. If you register before an infringement occurs, you qualify for statutory damages and attorney fees when someone infringes your copyright.

You must register your copyright with the Copyright Office, before you can bring a lawsuit for infringement. If you want to file a lawsuit but haven't registered the copyright, it is easy to file for the registration so that you can proceed, but you do not receive the benefit of obtaining attorney fees if you did not register *before* an infringement occurs.

The most serious problem with registering your copyright after it has been infringed is the limit on damages. **Damages** is the money a court awards you at the end of your lawsuit if you win. Without copyright registration, you can only receive actual damages. Actual damages are the losses that you proved in court with witnesses and accounting statements. If you have registered your copyright, you are also eligible for statutory damages.

Statutory damages are awards granted by a court when a copyright owner's work has been infringed, but the owner cannot prove the actual losses or the losses are quite small. Under these circumstances, the court may feel that the amount of actual damages that an infringer would have to pay the copyright owner is not a satisfactory amount to pay for the infringement. Statutory damages give the court a stronger deterrent to use against infringers.

To be eligible for statutory damages, you must have registered the copyright in your property within ninety days after its publication or before it is infringed. If not, your recovery will be limited to actual damages. **Actual Damages** are the actual provable dollars you lost or the defendant gained on account of the infringement. Proving actual damages is very time-consuming and expensive.

An innocent infringement triggers statutory damages between $750 and $30,000. If the infringement is shown to be willful, statutory damages can be increased to $150,000. The impact of all this is clear. My freelance reporter client had shot some news footage as a freelance reporter that he licensed to a local television station for the six o'clock news. A service copied the news off air and offered to make copies for anyone interested for $89 apiece. My client knew this activity was going on, on a regular basis. People who were on the news, their publicists, and folks pursuing legal claims were all potential customers of this off-air copying service. One day my client sent a friend in to the service and purchased two copies of one of his reports for $89 each. The evidence indicated that there were probably a few more tapes made, but my client, the copyright owner, could not prove this claim. Considering that only two illegal copies were confirmed, an award of actual damages ($89 per tape) would have been an inappropriate remedy under the circumstances. The court awarded $10,000 in statutory damages plus attorney fees for each of two videotapes that were illegally copied off air. **Off air** means from a television set as the program is coming across the cable or over the airwaves.

IN WHOSE NAME DO YOU REGISTER THE SCRIPT?

You are about to start principal photography. The copyright to your script should be registered in the name of the production company that will be producing the film. This is done because it insures that the copyright ownership will clearly reside with the production company, which is exactly what SAG requires.

Generally speaking, that company is a single-purpose production company. A **Single-purpose production company** is a production company that is formed solely and exclusively for the purpose of producing a film and has not performed any other business before producing the film.

The preferred kind of company used to be a corporation. Today, most people use a limited liability company. A **Limited Liability Company** is a form of business entity—usually referred to by its initials, LLC—that was legislated into existence in the '70s and has grown very steadily in popularity with professionals and filmmakers since then. An LLC protects you from liability in the same way as a corporation protects you, but has the advantage of working like a partnership as far as passing profits and losses through to the members.

Generally speaking, the LLC will also exploit the film after it is completed and disburse deferments and profits to those who are to receive them. This function can be assigned to a CPA or some other company. If the film is produced as a negative pick-up, the completed film will be turned over to a studio or other financier when it is completed.

Script registration should be in the name of the LLC (the production company) to make it very clear to SAG that the company is the current title holder and to pave the way for easy assignment of the completed film to a distributor. Be sure that all of your chain-of-title documents are in order, as is more fully described in the next chapter.

INSTRUCTIONS TO FILL OUT COPYRIGHT FORMS

Overview

It is easy to register your script with the copyright office. Just follow these steps:

A. OBTAIN a copy of FORM PA from the Copyright Office website at www.copyright.gov.forms or by calling (202) 707-9100. They have many registration forms, each for a different type of work. Make several photocopies. **Form PA** is the correct form for the registration of a published or unpublished script or treatment or script outline. (PA stands for performing arts, which includes film and television.) You can print them out to your heart's content. If you use the old-fashioned way, be sure to copy this form exactly. Use $8\frac{1}{2}$ x 11 paper, front and back, with the top of the front and the top of the back on the same end of the paper (same direction, top to bottom either side). If you do not photocopy the form exactly, it will be sent back to you by the Copyright Office!

B. FILL OUT the form following the easy instructions in this chapter. (A sample form is included at the end of this chapter.)

C. Prepare a cover letter like the one at the end of this chapter. You can send your letter certified with a return receipt requested so that you know your letter was received or you can include a return postcard.

D. Include a CHECK or MONEY ORDER payable to the "Register of Copyrights."

E. Include one copy of your SCRIPT.

F. MAIL TO: Register of Copyrights
                 Library of Congress
                 Washington, DC 20559-6000

G. WAIT (be patient).

Eventually, you either receive your application back with a registration number stamped in the upper right-hand corner, or you receive a call or letter from someone in the Copyright Office who is reviewing your document. Answer their questions satisfactorily and your registration will show up quickly. If things get sticky, call your attorney.

Your Certificate of Copyright is a copy of the actual form you filed, with a number stamped in the upper right-hand corner. The registration number begins with the letters PA, followed by two digits identifying the year and a sequential number identifying your work.

Be sure that the copyright symbol "©" is affixed to every copy of the work, together with the year of creation and the owner's name as follows:

© 2003 Michael C. Donaldson

or

Copyright 2003 Michael C. Donaldson

In the United States, the copyright notice is no longer required, but it is still a good idea. People are used to seeing this notice, and if you do not include it, they may erroneously assume that you are not claiming copyright. It also gives them the name of a contact for your script.

Step-by-Step Guide

SPACE 1: TITLE OF WORK

You must provide a title. This information is important and permanent. The title must be in letters and/or numbers in the English language. If the script that you attach to your registration form has a title page (or an identifying phrase that could serve as a title), write those words *completely* and *exactly* in this space on the application. Indexing depends on the information you write in this space.

Previous or Alternative Titles

Complete this space if there are any additional titles for the script under which you could reasonably anticipate that someone searching for the registration might look, or under which a treatment or option or other document pertaining to the script might be recorded. If there are none, then write the word "none." Do not write down titles that you merely played with in your mind. (Note: Do not write down the name of an underlying property that your script is based upon. You are asked to give that information later in the form.)

Nature of the Work

Write this word in the space provided: "screenplay." The word works whether your script is for a feature film, a movie made for television, a short, or a documentary.

SPACE 2: Author(s)

While the answer is usually simple enough, there can be a variety of interesting issues raised by this deceptively simple question. Important legal rights are determined by the answer to this block. Answer these carefully because rights can easily last 100 years or more. Don't forget that you will have to record all the documents needed to show the transfer(s) from the author to the production company that is listed as the copyright claimant. This will create a good chain of title as explained in the next chapter.

a. Name of Author

First, decide who is or are the "author(s)" of this work. You may want to review the guidelines in Chapter 5, regarding Work for Hire. In the case of a "work made for hire," write the full legal name of the employer or person for whom the script was written. You may also include the name of the employee along with the name of the employer (for example: "Elster Production Co., employer for hire of John Ferguson") on the first line of this blank.

If someone helped create the work, be sure to read the next section to find out if that person should also be listed. If you wrote the script by yourself, this space has your full name alone. This tells the Copyright Office and the world at large that you were the sole and individual creator of the specific script that you are submitting to the Copyright Office.

Information about the author's date of birth is optional, but useful to identify the author further. If the author is dead, the year of death is *mandatory*. This is because the life of the copyright is measured from the death of the author.

Anonymous means that the author is not identified on the copies of the script. If the author is anonymous, state "anonymous" on the "name of author" line or, if you choose, reveal the author's identity on this form. Note that the identity of the claimant is revealed in Space 4. The claimant must always be revealed, even if an author is anonymous or pseudonymous.

Pseudonymous means that the author is identified on the copies of the script under a fictitious name. If the author is pseudonymous, either give the pseudonym and identify it as such (example: "Huntley Haverstock, pseudonym") or, at your option, reveal the author's name, making clear which is the real name and which is the pseudonym (for example: "Judith Baton, whose pseudonym is Madeline Elster").

Nationality or domicile *must* be given even if the author is anonymous or pseudonymous. Domicile is the place of permanent residency of the person(s) who wrote the script or the employer of that person in the case of a work made for hire. If only one of these is the United States, fill in that one. You do no harm by filling in both of these lines.

b. Nature of Authorship

Give a brief general statement of the extent of the original contribution the author made, such as: "Wrote the entire script." If this author contributed anything less than the entire script, give a brief, but accurate, description of that contribution, such as "added several scenes to the first draft" or "created the character WOODY" or "English translation of original Swahili script."

c. Name of Author (again)

Filling in this blank declares that the registered work has joint authors. Give the requested information about every author who contributed any copyrightable matter to this version of the work. A person becomes a joint author if the amount of the contribution is more than trivial. If you need further space for additional authors, use Continuation Sheets. Follow the same instructions as above for each additional author you list.

If a person is a co-author, that person has substantial legal rights. Unless there is a written collaboration agreement that says otherwise, the co-author has an equal right to control every aspect of the exploitation of the script. This is true even if the contributions to the script are highly unequal. See the section regarding collaboration agreements in Chapter 5 for more information on joint authorships.

SPACE 3: CREATION AND PUBLICATION

This information is required. A mistake as to the date does not invalidate your registration as long as there is no intent to deceive.

a. Do not confuse creation with publication. A script is created when it is written on paper for the first time. You must state the year in which creation of the script was completed. The date you give here should be the year in which the person who physically wrote the words completed the particular version you are registering, even if other versions exist or if further changes or additions are planned.

b. You will almost always leave this space blank. The distribution of copies of the script to the public by sale or other transfer of ownership, or by rental, lease, or lending is publication. Publication does not occur as a result of a private use of a script or even shopping a script, because that is private activity designed to ultimately sell the script. You do *not* have to amend the registration when and if publication ever occurs. Under certain circumstances, the court will consider a script published when the film based on the script is published. So it is easy to see why this blank is usually left blank.

SPACE 4: COPYRIGHT CLAIMANT(S)

a. Claimant(s)

Since I recommend registering in the name of the production company at the beginning of pre-production, this will rarely be the person who actually did the writing. By this time, the copyright claimant is a person or organization to whom the copyright has been transferred in order to produce the film.

b. Transfer

If the copyright claimant is not the author, write a brief statement of how ownership of the copyright was obtained. One of the following phrases covers almost all circumstances: "By written contract"; "Transfer of all rights by author"; "Assignment"; "By will."

The documents that evidence these transfers must be recorded with the Copyright Office so that they become public records. The next chapter covers the recording of these documents (Chain of Title).

SPACE 5: Previous Registration

Basically, only one copyright registration can be made for the same version of a particular work. That is why "no" is by far the most common answer, and you can skip the rest of this discussion of space 5. If there are other works out there that are tempting you to check "yes," read the next chapter about recording Chain of Title documents before you go further.

a. Why Re-Registration

If this version of the script is substantially the same as a script covered by a previous registration, a second registration is not generally possible. There are only three situations in which you can successfully file a second registration:

1. The work has been registered in unpublished form and a second registration is being sought to cover the first published edition. This would rarely apply to a film script. When it does, it is because the movie was made and becomes such a hit or such a classic that someone wants to publish the screenplay. If so, check box "a."

2. Someone other than the author is identified as copyright claimant in the earlier registration, and the author is now seeking registration in the author's own individual or corporate name. Such a situation indicates someone probably already has a lawyer. If you are in this situation, check box "b."

3. If the work has been changed and you are now seeking registration to cover the additions or revisions, check box "c" and complete both parts of Space 6. As you know, I recommend one registration at the commencement of pre-production.

b. Previous Registration Number

The number to be filled in on this blank is the number that appears on the top right-hand corner of the earlier registration certificate. If more than one previous registration has been made for the work, give the number and date of the latest registration.

SPACE 6: Derivative Work or Compilation

a. Derivative Work

Your script is a **derivative work** if it was based on one or more pre-existing works, such as a book, a play, or a magazine article. Sequels, prequels, and remakes are derivative works of the previous film. If there is a previously registered version of the script, the current version is a derivative work. Such a script would be an infringing work if the material taken from the pre-existing work had been used without the consent of the copyright owner. Do not disclose pre-existing works that merely influenced or inspired your script or served as a source of factual information if there has been no substantial copying from the pre-existing work. If you have obtained life story rights from someone, the script is still considered original, and not a derivative work.

If your script is a derivative work, be sure you listed the scriptwriter as author in Space 2, not the author of the underlying work. The year of completion in Space 3 is the completion of the script, not completion of the underlying work.

Complete both Space 6a and Space 6b for derivative works. In Space 6a, identify the pre-existing work that has been recast, transformed, or adapted. Include the copyright registration number if you know it.

b. Material Added

The copyright in a script that is a derivative work covers only the additions, changes, or other new material appearing for the first time in that script. It does not extend to any pre-existing material, such as the dialogue of characters first appearing in a book. Therefore, describe the new material broadly, such as "entire script, except selected story points and eight of the thirty characters, from the book" or "entire script except selected plot points."

c. Compilation

Though this form raises the issue, scripts are rarely a compilation. A **compilation** is defined as "a work formed by the collection and assembling of pre-existing materials." Even *The Civil War* by Ken Burns was not a compilation for copyright law purposes, although pre-existing photos comprised most of the footage. Thirteen authors working one after another or all in the same room do not make a compilation. A compilation is a gathering together of independent materials. The creative work is in the selection and arrangement. I cannot imagine how a screenplay could be a compilation. Therefore, do not check the box indicating a compilation without talking to a lawyer!

SPACE 7: DEPOSIT ACCOUNT

Leave this space blank. Lawyers and studios who do a lot of registrations deposit money in advance with the Copyright Office. Their accounts are debited for their individual registrations. You will send a check for total fees due with your application.

SPACE 8: CORRESPONDENCE

You *must* provide the name, address, area code, and daytime telephone number of the person to receive correspondence about this application. If you are registering this yourself, use your name or company name. If you want questions about your application to go to someone else, such as your lawyer, provide their name.

SPACE 8: CERTIFICATION

The application cannot be accepted unless it bears the date and the *handwritten signature* of the person filing the application. You must put an "x" or "√" in one of the four boxes to let the copyright office know your status. Because you will generally be registering the script at commencement of pre-production in the name of the producing entity, you will almost always check the second box. If you are the author, check the first box. If you are not the author but are the copyright claimant, check the second box. By the time pre-production starts, the author is rarely still paying for everything out of pocket, so this box will rarely be checked. The entity producing the film is the copyright claimant, so the second box is checked. Read the next chapter carefully to find out what documents need to be recorded at the copyright office in order to show exactly how the production company became the copyright claimant. As producer (or author), you will not check the third box for owner of exclusive rights. This would be a distributor in most cases. If you are signing on behalf of your corporation, because you were authorized to do so by the author or the copyright owner, check the "authorized agent of" box, which is the fourth box at the bottom of the list. (Note: You must be a corporate officer to sign on behalf of your corporation or the manager of an LLC to sign on behalf of a Limited Liability Company.) This is the box I always check when I sign these copyright registration forms for clients.

SPACE 9: ADDRESS FOR RETURN OF CERTIFICATE

This address block must be completed legibly. The Copyright Office uses a window envelope to mail back your application after the registration number is assigned.

Fees

Each individual application must be accompanied by a fee. At the time of this writing, the fee is set at $30. It increases every five years based on the Consumer Price Index.

The Deposit Requirement

Every application to register a copyright must contain a deposit of the materials being registered. It is the specific item attached to the application that is registered with the copyright office. Include a complete copy of the version of the script you are registering, even though there are many versions before the one you are registering and many more changes to come.

FORM PA

For a Work of the Performing Arts
UNITED STATES COPYRIGHT OFFICE

REGISTRATION NUMBER

PA   PAU

EFFECTIVE DATE OF REGISTRATION

Month   Day   Year

DO NOT WRITE ABOVE THIS LINE. IF YOU NEED MORE SPACE, USE A SEPARATE CONTINUATION SHEET.

1

TITLE OF THIS WORK ▼

PREVIOUS OR ALTERNATIVE TITLES ▼

NATURE OF THIS WORK ▼ See instructions

2

a

NAME OF AUTHOR ▼

DATES OF BIRTH AND DEATH
Year Born ▼   Year Died ▼

Was this contribution to the work a "work made for hire"?
☐ Yes
☐ No

AUTHOR'S NATIONALITY OR DOMICILE
Name of Country
OR { Citizen of _____
Domiciled in _____

WAS THIS AUTHOR'S CONTRIBUTION TO THE WORK
Anonymous?   ☐ Yes ☐ No
Pseudonymous?   ☐ Yes ☐ No
If the answer to either of these questions is "Yes," see detailed instructions.

NATURE OF AUTHORSHIP Briefly describe nature of material created by this author in which copyright is claimed. ▼

NOTE

Under the law, the "author" of a "work made for hire" is generally the employer, not the employee (see instructions). For any part of this work that was "made for hire" check "Yes" in the space provided, give the employer (or other person for whom the work was prepared) as "Author" of that part, and leave the space for dates of birth and death blank.

b

NAME OF AUTHOR ▼

DATES OF BIRTH AND DEATH
Year Born ▼   Year Died ▼

Was this contribution to the work a "work made for hire"?
☐ Yes
☐ No

AUTHOR'S NATIONALITY OR DOMICILE
Name of Country
OR { Citizen of _____
Domiciled in _____

WAS THIS AUTHOR'S CONTRIBUTION TO THE WORK
Anonymous?   ☐ Yes ☐ No
Pseudonymous?   ☐ Yes ☐ No
If the answer to either of these questions is "Yes," see detailed instructions.

NATURE OF AUTHORSHIP Briefly describe nature of material created by this author in which copyright is claimed. ▼

c

NAME OF AUTHOR ▼

DATES OF BIRTH AND DEATH
Year Born ▼   Year Died ▼

Was this contribution to the work a "work made for hire"?
☐ Yes
☐ No

AUTHOR'S NATIONALITY OR DOMICILE
Name of Country
OR { Citizen of _____
Domiciled in _____

WAS THIS AUTHOR'S CONTRIBUTION TO THE WORK
Anonymous?   ☐ Yes ☐ No
Pseudonymous?   ☐ Yes ☐ No
If the answer to either of these questions is "Yes," see detailed instructions.

NATURE OF AUTHORSHIP Briefly describe nature of material created by this author in which copyright is claimed. ▼

3

a **YEAR IN WHICH CREATION OF THIS WORK WAS COMPLETED** This information must be given _____ Year in all cases.

b **DATE AND NATION OF FIRST PUBLICATION OF THIS PARTICULAR WORK**
Complete this information Month _____ Day _____ Year _____
ONLY if this work has been published. _____ Nation

4

See instructions before completing this space.

COPYRIGHT CLAIMANT(S) Name and address must be given even if the claimant is the same as the author given in space 2. ▼

TRANSFER If the claimant(s) named here in space 4 is (are) different from the author(s) named in space 2, give a brief statement of how the claimant(s) obtained ownership of the copyright. ▼

DO NOT WRITE HERE
OFFICE USE ONLY

APPLICATION RECEIVED

ONE DEPOSIT RECEIVED

TWO DEPOSITS RECEIVED

FUNDS RECEIVED

MORE ON BACK ▶ • Complete all applicable spaces (numbers 5-9) on the reverse side of this page.
• See detailed instructions.   • Sign the form at line 8.

DO NOT WRITE HERE
Page 1 of _____ pages

DO NOT WRITE ABOVE THIS LINE. IF YOU NEED MORE SPACE, USE A SEPARATE CONTINUATION SHEET.

PREVIOUS REGISTRATION Has registration for this work, or for an earlier version of this work, already been made in the Copyright Office?

☐ Yes ☐ No If your answer is "Yes," why is another registration being sought? (Check appropriate box.) ▼ If your answer is No, do **not** check box A, B, or C.

a. ☐ This is the first published edition of a work previously registered in unpublished form.

b. ☐ This is the first application submitted by this author as copyright claimant.

c. ☐ This is a changed version of the work, as shown by space 6 on this application.

If your answer is "Yes," give: **Previous Registration Number** ▼   **Year of Registration** ▼

5

DERIVATIVE WORK OR COMPILATION Complete both space 6a and 6b for a derivative work; complete only 6b for a compilation.

Preexisting Material Identify any preexisting work or works that this work is based on or incorporates. ▼

a **6**

See instructions before completing this space.

Material Added to This Work Give a brief, general statement of the material that has been added to this work and in which copyright is claimed. ▼

b

DEPOSIT ACCOUNT If the registration fee is to be charged to a Deposit Account established in the Copyright Office, give name and number of Account.

Name ▼   **Account Number** ▼

a **7**

CORRESPONDENCE Give name and address to which correspondence about this application should be sent. Name/Address/Apt/City/State/ZIP ▼

b

Area code and daytime telephone number (   )   Fax number (   )

Email

CERTIFICATION* I, the undersigned, hereby certify that I am the

Check only one ▶
☐ author
☐ other copyright claimant
☐ owner of exclusive right(s)
☐ authorized agent of _____
Name of author or other copyright claimant, or owner of exclusive right(s) ▲

8

of the work identified in this application and that the statements made by me in this application are correct to the best of my knowledge.

Typed or printed name and date ▼ If this application gives a date of publication in space 3, do not sign and submit it before that date.

Date

Handwritten signature (X) ▼

x _____

Certificate will be mailed in window envelope to this address:

Name ▼

Number/Street/Apt ▼

City/State/ZIP ▼

YOU MUST:
• Complete all necessary spaces
• Sign your application in space 8

SEND ALL 3 ELEMENTS IN THE SAME PACKAGE:
1. Application form
2. Nonrefundable filing fee in check or money order payable to *Register of Copyrights*
3. Deposit material

MAIL TO:
Library of Congress
Copyright Office
101 Independence Avenue, S.E.
Washington, D.C. 20559-6000

Fees are subject to change. For current fees, check the Copyright Office website at www.copyright.gov, write the Copyright Office, or call (202) 707-3000.

9

CONTINUATION SHEET FOR APPLICATION FORM RE

INSTRUCTIONS

- Use this continuation sheet **only** in conjunction with basic Form RE.

- Use this sheet only if you need more space to continue the listing started in Space 1 and/or Space 5 of Form RE. Use as many additional continuation sheets as you need.

- Use the continuation of Space 5 on this sheet only for contributions to periodicals by the same individual author that were published in the same calendar year.

- Follow instructions accompanying Form RE in filling out this continuation sheet. Number each line in Spaces B and C consecutively.

- Submit this continuation sheet with the basic Form RE and the other continuation sheets, if any. Clip (do not tape or staple) and fold all sheets together before submitting them.

- Type or clearly print all information in **black ink**.

DO NOT WRITE ABOVE THIS LINE. FOR COPYRIGHT OFFICE USE ONLY.

⊘ FORM RE /CON

UNITED STATES COPYRIGHT OFFICE

REGISTRATION NUMBER

EFFECTIVE DATE OF RENEWAL REGISTRATION

| (Month) | (Day) | (Year) |

CONTINUATION SHEET RECEIVED

Page _____ of _____ pages

A

Identification of Application

IDENTIFICATION OF CONTINUATION: This sheet is a continuation of Space 1 and Space 5 of the application for renewal registration on Form RE, submitted for the following:

- TITLE AT SPACE 2 OR TITLE OF FIRST OF GROUP OF WORKS IN WHICH RENEWAL IS CLAIMED: Give first title as given in Space 5 of Form RE.

  ....

- RENEWAL CLAIMANT AND ADDRESS: Give the name and address of at least one renewal claimant as given in Space 1 of Form RE

  ....

B

Continuation of Space 1

RENEWAL CLAIMANT(S), ADDRESS(ES), AND STATEMENT OF CLAIM: See Instructions on basic Form RE.

☐ Name ....
Address ....
Claiming as ....

☐ Name ....
Address ....
Claiming as ....

☐ Name ....
Address ....
Claiming as ....

☐ Name ....
Address ....
Claiming as ....

☐ Name ....
Address ....
Claiming as ....

☐ Name ....
Address ....
Claiming as ....

Use the reverse side of this sheet if you need more space for continuation of Space 5 of the basic form.

158

☐ Title of Contribution: . . . .

Title of Periodical: . . . . Vol. . . . . . . No. . . . . . Issue Date . . . .

Date of Publication: . . . . Registration Number: . . . .

(Month)   (Day)   (Year)

C

Continuation of Space 5

☐ Title of Contribution: . . . .

Title of Periodical: . . . . Vol. . . . . . . No. . . . . . Issue Date . . . .

Date of Publication: . . . . Registration Number: . . . .

(Month)   (Day)   (Year)

☐ Title of Contribution: . . . .

Title of Periodical: . . . . Vol. . . . . . . No. . . . . . Issue Date . . . .

Date of Publication: . . . . Registration Number: . . . .

(Month)   (Day)   (Year)

☐ Title of Contribution: . . . .

Title of Periodical: . . . . Vol. . . . . . . No. . . . . . Issue Date . . . .

Date of Publication: . . . . Registration Number: . . . .

(Month)   (Day)   (Year)

☐ Title of Contribution: . . . .

Title of Periodical: . . . . Vol. . . . . . . No. . . . . . Issue Date . . . .

Date of Publication: . . . . Registration Number: . . . .

(Month)   (Day)   (Year)

☐ Title of Contribution: . . . .

Title of Periodical: . . . . Vol. . . . . . . No. . . . . . Issue Date . . . .

Date of Publication: . . . . Registration Number: . . . .

(Month)   (Day)   (Year)

☐ Title of Contribution: . . . .

Title of Periodical: . . . . Vol. . . . . . . No. . . . . . Issue Date . . . .

Date of Publication: . . . . Registration Number: . . . .

(Month)   (Day)   (Year)

☐ Title of Contribution: . . . .

Title of Periodical: . . . . Vol. . . . . . . No. . . . . . Issue Date . . . .

Date of Publication: . . . . Registration Number: . . . .

(Month)   (Day)   (Year)

☐ Title of Contribution: . . . .

Title of Periodical: . . . . Vol. . . . . . . No. . . . . . Issue Date . . . .

Date of Publication: . . . . Registration Number: . . . .

(Month)   (Day)   (Year)

☐ Title of Contribution: . . . .

Title of Periodical: . . . . Vol. . . . . . . No. . . . . . Issue Date . . . .

Date of Publication: . . . . Registration Number: . . . .

(Month)   (Day)   (Year)

☐ Title of Contribution: . . . .

Title of Periodical: . . . . Vol. . . . . . . No. . . . . . Issue Date . . . .

Date of Publication: . . . . Registration Number: . . . .

(Month)   (Day)   (Year)

☐ Title of Contribution: . . . .

Title of Periodical: . . . . Vol. . . . . . . No. . . . . . Issue Date . . . .

Date of Publication: . . . . Registration Number: . . . .

(Month)   (Day)   (Year)

Certificate will be mailed in window envelope to this address:

Name ▼

Number/Street/Apt ▼

City/State/ZIP ▼

YOU MUST:
- Complete all necessary spaces
- Sign your application in Space 7

SEND ALL 3 ELEMENTS IN THE SAME PACKAGE:
1. Application form
2. Nonrefundable $45 filing fee in check or money order payable to *Register of Copyrights*

MAIL TO:
Library of Congress, Copyright Office
101 Independence Avenue, S.E.
Washington, D.C. 20559-6000

D

As of July 1, 1999, the filing fee for form RE is $45.

December 1999–20,000
WEB REV December 1999

♻ PRINTED ON RECYCLED PAPER

☆U.S GOVERNMENT PRINTING OFFICE: 2000-461-113/89

9.03   **SCRIPT REGISTRATION COVER LETTER**

Date:

<u>**CERTIFIED**</u>
<u>**RETURN RECEIPT REQUESTED**</u>

160

Register of Copyrights
LIBRARY OF CONGRESS
101 Independence Ave., SE
Washington, DC 20559-6000

RE:

Dear Register:

Enclosed please find the following elements to register the above-referenced script:

1. Check in the amount of thirty dollars ($30.00) for the Copyright Registration

2. Completed PA Form

3. Script

4. Return postcard

Please register the above items immediately. We understand that the stamped original Form PA will be returned to this office.

Thank you for your assistance in this matter.

Very truly yours,

MICHAEL C. DONALDSON

Enclosures: as listed

You should type this letter on your letterhead.

9.04   RETURN POSTCARD FOR SCRIPT REGISTRATION

The copyright office will date-stamp and sign and return to you a self-addressed, stamped postcard (not a letter, a postcard). That is your proof of receipt. Use the following language on the back part of the postcard and you will have your proof.

BACK

This postcard shall act as a receipt for the following items:

Form PA to register the Script entitled:

_____

By: _____

together with a check in amount of $30.00 and a copy of the script for Registration of Copyright.

FRONT

Your Name
Address

Your Name
Address

CHAPTER 10

CHAIN OF TITLE

Sooner or later, everybody with a completed film has to deliver a good "chain of title." **Chain of title** refers to the contracts and other documents that show any change in ownership of a film project from its inception. The documents are a trail of transfers from the original author of a work through the final film (or whatever stage the project is at at the time).

WHAT IS CHAIN OF TITLE?

In some instances, the process is simple. The writer of an original screenplay based on his or her own original idea signs a Certificate of Authorship, which declares in no uncertain terms that 1) the writer wrote the script, 2) it was an original work, and 3) that no rights in the script have been previously granted. This one-page document is required of every writer who writes anything for a studio. It establishes ownership of the script and the right to sell it.

By the time you are an adult, the principle of ownership is well known. You cannot sell anything that you do not own. You cannot loan it, use it, or keep it without the owner's permission. When you own something, you are said to have good title to it. For most tangible things, the fact that you have possession is strong proof of ownership. You stop by a garage sale and look at all the articles the seller owns. You buy whatever *thing* attracts you and then you own it—you have good title to that *thing*. However, if there are 100 stereos for sale priced at $1.00 each, you might question whether the seller has legal ownership. If the stereos were stolen, then the "seller" does not have good title—the seller does not own them. If the seller does not own the stereos, you might get possession of a stereo for $1.00, but you will not own it, you will not have good title. If you ask how the "seller" came by so many stereos at such a good price, you would be questioning title.

For some things, more is required to prove good title than mere possession, free of suspicious circumstances. For instance, to sell an automobile, you must have the registration certificate. You must show that you own the automobile and then actually sign a form, supplied by your state, to transfer title of the automobile to another person. This is a simple process, but necessary to transfer ownership of the automobile to another person.

When you sell a piece of real estate, you have to do even more than sign a piece of paper in order for the transaction to be binding. You also have to show that you in fact own the interest that you are selling. This is accomplished through a title search. A **title search** traces the ownership records from an initial land grant—usually from the King of England on the East Coast or a Spanish Land Grant on the West Coast—through transfers from owner to owner by way of sale, death, subdivisions, marriages, divorces, and on and on, up to your ownership. This is the chain of title for a piece of real estate.

When you sell a script or try to enter into a distribution deal for a finished film, you have to show that you own the script (or film) that you are selling. The usual language is that the obligations (including payment) of the buyer, producer, or distributor with whom you are dealing is "subject to satisfactory proof of Chain of Title."

By proving your chain of title, you establish the fact that you have good title to a property. **Good title** means that you own that which you claim to own, free and clear of any encumbrances or liens. You must prove this at some point before your film is released. The bigger the producer you join up with, the earlier you have to prove your chain of title.

For example, let us assume that you wrote, directed, and produced your own film. Assume that a distributor asks you to prove your chain of title. This is straightforward, but still requires several documents. You need the following:

1. Certificate of Authorship, signed by you as the screenwriter

2. Copyright certificate for the script registered in your name

3. Copyright certificate for the film registered in your name

Often, even in this simple scenario, the film is actually produced by a partnership or some other entity other than the individual screenwriter. Let us assume that it was a partnership. The chain of title would look like this:

1. Certificate of Authorship, signed by you as the screenwriter

2. Copyright certificate for the script registered in your name

3. Assignment, sale, or other transfer of the right to make a film based on the script from you to the partnership

4. Copyright certificate for the film registered in the name of the partnership

Some lawyers would accept the four documents listed. Others would want a copy of the partnership agreement showing that the partnership is a real entity, who its members are, and what their respective rights are. The larger the studio or law firm where the lawyer works, the more likely you are to be asked for additional documents.

Let's consider a slightly more complicated example, but not an unrealistic or uncommon example, even in the community of independent filmmakers. In this example, you are asked to prove chain of title on a script you co-wrote based on a published novel. Suppose you contacted the author directly. He or she told you that the book was under option to a producer who had just delivered a script that everyone hated. You get on well with the author. You wait patiently for the option to lapse. As a precaution, you carefully avoid reading or even talking in great detail about the previous script.

As soon as the other producer's option lapses, you option the film rights to the book. You write two drafts but you are still not happy, even though you received significant help from a friend on the second of the two drafts you wrote. You finally do what you

have been resisting, because you did not want to lose control of
the project. You option your script to a studio with a piece of
paper that guarantees that you will be attached as a producer.

The deal isn't everything you wanted, but you sign the agreement and wait for the initial, paltry check. However, the whole
deal is subject to approval of the chain of title. That means that
having signed the agreement and therefore having tied up the film
rights, you have to submit a mountain of paper to be reviewed by
a lawyer whom you never met and who does not work for you.
Makes you wish you had taken care of this before signing the
agreement! If requested, this material is generally reviewed before
the deal is signed so that the project is not tied up while you jump
over hurdles to obtain more and more documents. Also, you can
generally negotiate an outside date by which this approval has to
be given, or the deal is null and void. About sixty days is a
standard length of time for this approval process.

Here is a drawing that shows what the above chain of title
would look like:

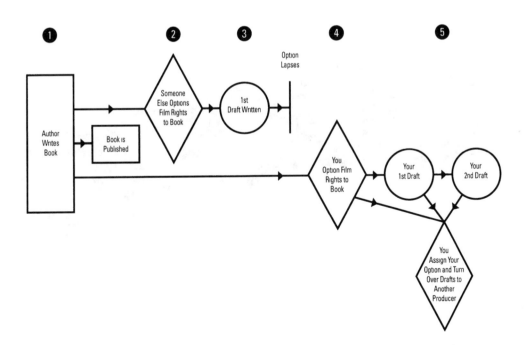

Here are the minimum documents you have to supply the distributor to establish the chain of title. The numbers refer to the numbers in the diagram above.

1. Certificate of Copyright on the book registered in the name of "Owner"

2. First Option Agreement that lapsed

3. The Writer's Agreement under which the first draft was created

4. Your Option Agreement

5. Your Agreement with Your Joint Author on your second draft

Here is what another drawing of what this chain of title looks like:

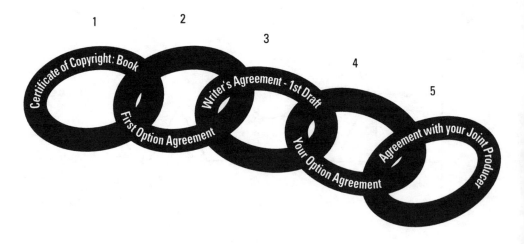

Here is the rub:

Many lawyers would agree that the list of documents set out above, assuming that they are internally correct, would establish a good chain of title. However, many lawyers would want more documents or might find your documents wanting. For instance, the reviewing lawyer might want to see the contract between the author of the book and the publishing company. This request would insure that the author did not grant the right to the publishing company to negotiate and/or sell the film rights in question. The lawyer also may require a Publisher's Release to be signed. Additionally, the reviewing attorney may require that the producing entity have the right to buy that first draft that neither you nor your friend ever saw. The purpose of such a request would be to reduce the risk of lawsuits.

The above example is about as simple as it gets. For instance, if the novel were based on a real person, most lawyers would want to see the release or agreement with that person on whom the author based the book.

Our office helped review all the documentation to prove chain of title for every film in a large library of films being considered for purchase by 20th Century Fox. The films included the *Rambo* series, *Cliffhanger,* and *The Doors*. About forty documents were required to prove the basic chain of title on most of the films. More documents were reviewed for the music. Security Agreements, which could cut off title, were even more voluminous. A **security agreement** is issued by a film's lender or financier to secure the repayment of their money by the producer. It is like a mortgage on your home. Banks who loan money to make a film can foreclose on a film much like the lender on your home can foreclose on your home if you do not pay off the loan when it is due.

Chain of title is a very important area. Ultimately, this is one area for which you want an experienced entertainment lawyer. Every link in your chain must be strong and tightly attached to the next link.

RECORDING CHAIN OF TITLE DOCUMENTS

If you are registering a script written by someone other than yourself or have transferred any rights, there should be some written agreement that shows how that happened. You need to register these contractual documents with the Copyright Office.

To record any document transferring ownership in a copyright, use the form called DOCUMENT COVER SHEET. You may copy the example at the end of this chapter, or you may create your own. Unlike the various forms used to register copyright in a script or film, this form does not have to be exactly like the one from the Copyright Office as long as the necessary information is there.

The person(s) submitting a document with a cover sheet are solely responsible for verifying the correctness of the cover sheet and the sufficiency of the document that is being registered. When the Copyright Office records a document submitted to it, it does not ascertain the document's validity or the effect of that document. The Copyright Office just records the document and Document Cover Sheet that comes with it. Only a court of law may determine the legal impact of the document you registered. However, this recording process gives notice to the world of how you came to have the right(s) that you claim to have in the copyright.

DOCUMENT COVER SHEET

Here is a simple guide to what to fill in on each of this form's blanks.

1. Name all of the parties to the document that you are seeking to record. For transfers, notices of termination, and other two-party documents, indicate the name of the person or company that is assignor, grantor, or seller as party one (1) and the name of the person or company that is assignee, grantee, or buyer as party two (2). If there are additional parties so that additional space is needed, use a white, 8½ x 11-inch

sheet of paper to list the parties. At the top of the additional sheet, type "these names are additions to Space 1."

2. Check the box that best describes the kind of document you are recording. This description is entered in the catalog record of the recordation. Check the first box if the document you are recording is an assignment, option, or purchase of a license of a copyright. This is the box that is almost always used for Chain of Title documents.

3. List the titles of all works that are mentioned anywhere in the document that you are seeking to record. List all titles, even if you are only interested in one of them. Include registration number, names of authors, and other information to identify the work(s) so that each one can be linked to its original registration. If you need more room, use an additional sheet of white, $8^1/_2$ x 11-inch paper. At the top of the additional sheet, type "these titles are additions to Space 3." Be complete. This is important to ensure that someone doing a future copyright search can identify the transfer, option, or other document that transfers the rights to you.

4. Any document you record should be complete. If a document is not complete, it is referred to as an "as is" document. **"As is" documents** are always open to question. However, so-called Section 205 documents must be complete by their own terms in order to be recordable. **Section 205 documents** include almost all of the documents you will record as a filmmaker. Examples of Section 205 documents include transfers of copyright ownerships and other documents pertaining to a copyright, such as exclusive and non-exclusive licenses, contracts, mortgages, powers of attorney, certificates of change of corporate name or title, wills, and decrees of distribution. Section 205 refers to that specific

section of the Federal Copyright Law that provides for the recording of these important documents. As a practical matter, there is almost nothing you will be able to record as a filmmaker on an "as is" basis.

5. Count the number of different titles mentioned in the document you are recording. The number of titles that are mentioned in the document determines the fee that you pay to the Copyright Office. The Copyright Office verifies your title count, so be accurate on your application or its processing time will be extended.

6. Calculate the fee from the information given in Space 5. The fee for a document of any length containing one title is, at the time of this writing, $80. No matter how long the document is that you are recording, you pay $20 for each group of ten or fewer additional titles mentioned in the document you are recording.

7. Ignore this blank. Send a check for the correct amount.

8. Give the date of the accompanying document. This can either be the date the document being recorded was signed or the date it became effective. If these dates are not the same, pick the one that best suits your purposes. This is usually the effective date of the agreement you are recording. Do not give the date that the Cover Sheet was executed!

9. This space must be completed. The party to the document submitting it for recordation or an authorized agent should sign the affirmation and authorization contained in this space. This affirmation and authorization is not a substitute for the certificate required for documents containing a photocopy signature. (See Certification, Space 10.)

10. Many people (including me) prefer to keep the document with the original signature if there is only one

such document. You may photocopy the entire document and record it. In that case, you complete this
section only if you are submitting a document that
does not bear the actual signature on the document
being recorded. That is, if the document contains only
a photocopied signature, fill in this space. If the
document you are sending to the Copyright Office
bears an original signature (even if the document itself
was photocopied before it was signed), do not fill in
this space.

The need for this certification is that copyright law
provides that any transfer of copyright ownership or
other document pertaining to a copyright (a Section
205 document) may be recorded in the Copyright
Office if the document bears the actual signature of
the person or persons who executed (signed) the
documents. If a photocopy of the original signed
document is submitted, it must be accompanied by a
sworn or official certification. A sworn certification
signed by at least one of the parties to the document
or their authorized representative (who is identified
as such) at Space 10 satisfies that statutory requirement. It follows, therefore, that copies of documents
that are taken from the files in a federal, state, or
local government office must be accompanied by an
official certification.

10.01 DOCUMENT COVER SHEET

Copyright Office fees are subject to change. For current fees, check the Copyright Office website at *www.copyright.gov*, write the Copyright Office, or call (202) 707-3000.

DOCUMENT COVER SHEET
For Recordation of Documents
UNITED STATES COPYRIGHT OFFICE

DATE OF RECORDATION
(Assigned by Copyright Office)

Month	Day	Year

Volume _____ Page _____

Volume _____ Page _____

FUNDS RECEIVED _____

Do not write above this line.

To the Register of Copyrights:

Please record the accompanying original document or copy thereof.

FOR OFFICE USE ONLY

1 Name of the party or parties to the document spelled as they appear in the document (List up to the first three)
_____
_____
_____

2 Date of execution and/or effective date of the accompanying document
(month)   (day)   (year)

3 Completeness of document
❑ Document is complete by its own terms.
❑ Document is not complete. Record "as is."

4 Description of document
❑ Transfer of Copyright
❑ Security Interest
❑ Change of Name of Owner
❑ Termination of Transfer(s) [Section 304]
❑ Shareware
❑ Life, Identity, Death Statement [Section 302]
❑ Transfer of Mask Works
❑ Other _____

5 Title of first work as given in the document _____

6 Total number of titles in document

7 Amount of fee calculated
$ _____

8 Fee enclosed
❑ Check
❑ Money Order

❑ Fee authorized to be charged to :
Copyright Office
Deposit Account number _____
Account name _____

9 **Affirmation*:** I hereby affirm to the Copyright Office that the information given on this form is a true and correct representation of the accompanying document. This affirmation will not suffice as a certification of a photocopy signature on the document.
(Affirmation *must* be signed even if you are also signing Space 10.)

Signature _____
Date _____
Phone Number _____ Fax Number _____

10 **Certification*:** Complete this certification in addition to the Affirmation if a photocopy of the original signed document is substituted for a document bearing the actual signature.
NOTE: This space *may not* be used for an official certification.
I certify under penalty of perjury under the laws of the United States of America that the accompanying document is a true copy of the original document.

Signature _____
Duly Authorized Agent of: _____
Date _____

Recordation will be mailed in window envelope to this address:

Name▼
Number/Street/Apt▼
City/State/ZIP▼

YOU MUST:
• Complete all necessary spaces
• Sign your Cover Sheet in Space 9
SEND ALL 3 ELEMENTS TOGETHER:
1. Two copies of the Document Cover Sheet
2. Check/money order payable to *Register of Copyrights*
3. Document
MAIL TO:
Library of Congress, Copyright Office
Documents Recordation Section, LM-462
101 Independence Avenue, S.E.
Washington, D.C. 20559-6000

Fees are subject to change. For current fees, check the Copyright Office website at www.copyright.gov, write the Copyright Office, or call (202) 707-3000.

*Knowingly and willfully falsifying material facts on this form may result in criminal liability. 18 U.S.C.§1001.

Rev: June 2002—20,000   Web Rev: June 2002   ♻ Printed on recycled paper

U.S. Government Printing Office: 2000-461-113/20,021

FORM 10.2 COVER LETTER TO RECORD AGREEMENTS

Register of Copyrights
Library of Congress
Washington, D.C. 20559-6000

Dear Register:

Enclosed please find the following:

1.   Document to be recorded entitled _____.

2.   Check in the amount of $_____ for Recording the Cover Sheet for Document Recording

3.   Completed Cover Sheet; and

4.   Return Post Card

Please record the cover sheet.

We understand that the stamped original Cover Sheet will be returned to this office.

Thank you.

Very truly yours,

_____

Enclosures

You should type this letter on your letterhead.

FORM 10.3 RETURN POSTCARD FOR RECORDING DOCUMENTS

The copyright office will date-stamp and sign and return to you a self-addressed, stamped postcard (not a letter, a postcard). If you fill it out properly, this postcard—worded for recording documents to show chain of title—can act as your proof of receipt. Use the following language on the back part of the postcard and you will have your proof.

BACK

This postcard shall act as a receipt for the following items:

Document Recordation Cover Sheet to record the following document:

_____

The Parties to the Document are: _____ and _____

A total of _____ titles are mentioned in this document.

Our check in the amount of $_____.

FRONT

Your Name
Address

Your Name
Address

CHAPTER 11

OTHERS WHO MAY HAVE RIGHTS IN YOUR FILM

Parts I and II discuss the rights of writers and those who create works on which films are based. Once principal photography begins, a myriad of other people will work on, invest in, give you opinions about, and generally "help" you on your film. They all make—or think they make—creative contributions to the total effort. Some of those contributions could be registered for their own separate copyright. This chapter discusses the most important among these people and provides the language you should include in your deal memos and agreements to be sure that you retain all the rights in your film that you need (and deserve).

WRITERS

The first and most obvious group of people who would have an interest in your film, absent some written agreement to the contrary, are the writers. The first two sections of this book deal almost exclusively in the written agreement between you, as the producer, and the writer. You must have a written agreement with the writer for a variety of reasons, not the least of which is that without a written agreement, the writer of the film would have a slam-dunk claim for copyright infringement against your film.

Fortunately, everybody is alert to the importance of having a written agreement with the writer of the screenplay before the commencement of principal photography. In fact, SAG will not allow their members to start work on your film until you can show them that the script has been registered with the copyright office and that you have an enforceable agreement with the writer and that you have paid the writer. Usually, a canceled check will do, but you have to satisfy SAG that the writer is under contract and fully paid whatever is owed as of that date, or your SAG actors will not be cleared to work on your film.

THE DIRECTOR

The primary person—besides you and the writer—who contributes creative efforts to the film is the director. In fact, in much of the world, the creation of the director is considered so major that the director has rights that cannot be taken away by any contract. These are called moral rights. Throughout Europe, they are known by their French name, *droit moral*.

The term **droit moral**, or **moral rights**, covers a group of rights that protect the work from being changed without permission of the person who holds droit moral or moral rights.

For example, John Huston's 1950 black-and-white film *Asphalt Jungle* was one of the greatest crime films of all time. Sterling Hayden and a near-perfect cast created one of the real gems in the MGM library. When Turner Broadcasting acquired the MGM films, the package included this Huston classic.

Shortly thereafter, Turner colorized the film. By then John Huston had died, but Huston's estate wanted to prevent the colorization. They didn't bother to sue in U.S. courts because the

U.S. doesn't recognize moral rights. The estate sued in French courts to prevent the exhibition of the film in France under the moral rights, which French law says cannot be waived by an artist. Even if the artist signs a contract saying that they waive their moral rights, the moral rights are not given up or waived. The Huston estate won. The colorized *Asphalt Jungle* cannot be exhibited or sold in France.

As a producer, you want to be sure that the contract with your director has language to minimize the impact of droit moral. You also want the contract to affirmatively grant to you all the rights that you need. Here is what you need:

> **Grant of Rights:** All of the results and proceeds of Director's services shall constitute a "work made for hire" for Producer. Accordingly, Producer shall be deemed the author and the exclusive owner thereof and shall have the right to exploit any or all of the foregoing in all media, whether now known or hereafter devised, throughout the universe, in all versions, in perpetuity as Producer determines at Producer's sole discretion. Director waives any so-called moral rights.

Note how the waiver of moral rights is at the end of the paragraph. Some producers like to have a separate paragraph so that there is no question about the waiver. Remember that under the law of many countries, the "author" of a work of art cannot waive moral rights. There is a substantial movement in this country, led by the Directors Guild of America and The Artists Rights Foundation, to lobby Congress for some movement toward the European model concerning artists' rights. Interestingly, at the time of this writing, Dreamworks, which was founded by Steven Spielberg, Jeff Katzenberg, and David Geffen, announced at its formation that it would not require artists to waive moral rights. However, Dreamworks—like everybody else—uses work for hire language, so the concession may not be of much value to the individual artists until the U.S. law is changed. It does make for good public relations, however.

ACTORS

If you use a Screen Actors Guild (SAG) actor, the Standard Day-Player and Standard Weekly contracts have a clause that incorporates the SAG Basic Agreement into each deal. The rights and responsibilities of that agreement include ownership by the production company of the performances rendered by the actors. If you are using non-union actors or are writing a more comprehensive contract, be sure to include the following language:

> **Rights:** Producer shall own all rights of every kind in the results and proceeds of Actor's services hereunder. Producer shall have the unlimited right throughout the universe and in perpetuity to exhibit the Motion Picture in all media, now or hereafter known. Actor's services are a work for hire.

COMPOSER

On independent films, the composer of the film's soundtrack often retains a financial interest in the copyright for the music composed for the film. Sometimes composers retain actual ownership of the copyright. This is fully discussed in Chapter 16. The only reason to make this sharp departure from the comprehensive grant of rights discussed here for everybody else is to pick up music for your film at a good price. Do not lightly give up ownership of the music in your film if you can avoid doing so. If you do, make sure you have a license in perpetuity throughout the universe to use the music in your film.

CREW

Many crew members create things that could be registered for copyright except for their agreement with you, the filmmaker. For instance, a propmaker, a set designer, the costume designer, and the cinematographer routinely create items that could be registered for copyright protection in their own name. Under current copyright, even choreography is protected by copyright.

Many crew deal memos fail to take this into account. This is particularly true with independent filmmakers. One very famous filmmaker working on a documentary said, "Hey, man, these guys are cool. We're all friends. They're not going to hassle me." He was *probably* right. Besides, this crew frequently worked on his high-visibility features. They weren't about to "hassle" him. The film was a labor of love by people who had known each other for a long time.

OTHERS
WHO MAY
HAVE RIGHTS
IN YOUR
FILM

179

However, consider the small Michigan filmmaker Hi Tech Video, who made a wonderful documentary about Mackinaw Island. When ABC ripped off thirty-eight seconds of their work for a network piece and refused to pay for it, even after they were asked nicely to do so, Hi Tech sued. Slam dunk, right?

Wrong! ABC defended itself on the grounds that there were no written agreements with crew members who worked on the documentary. Therefore, the crew who created the documentary were the authors under the copyright law, not Hi Tech Video. The crew would have to collectively sue, not the company that organized the shoot but did not create the film. ABC won.

Few crew members attempt to acquire an independent copyright on their work, but they could if they wanted to. Here is the language you need:

> **Services and Rights:** All of Employee's work performed hereunder shall be a work for hire. Producer shall be the sole and exclusive owner of all the results and proceeds of Employee's services, and Producer shall have the right to exploit said results and proceeds and all rights of every kind therein in all media throughout the universe in such manner as Producer elects.

INVESTORS

This group is the one that you have to be the most careful about. The investor(s) often seeks to own or co-own the copyright to your film. It's hard to argue against that effort because:

They are involved early, at a time when you have the rights to give away.

They can argue that you really are not losing anything since you wouldn't own the copyright if you made your film through the studio system.

You need them.

They have lawyers. In fact, most entertainment law offices represent a number of investors.

So what do you do? You argue against the request with the following:

As an investor, their real interest is a financial return. You can give them the exact same amount of money from profits as they would receive from the same percentage of ownership. Investors shouldn't have to take on the obligation of a copyright owner. The copyright owner can be sued for infringement of copyright. Investors don't need the worry of copyright ownership. If something happens to the investor, you don't want to co-own a copyright with heirs you don't know.

If you go through the hassle to make a film independently, of raising the money, of working without the safety net of a studio, of trying to sell it, of mortgaging your home to get it completed, you want to control the copyright. Copyrights last a long, long time. The copyright to film is your retirement. A copyright has the potential for throwing off income for the life of the copyright. By their statutory term, they will outlive you. Even though new films are made every year, the appetite of new media gobbles up more than the supply. Films are constantly being dusted off for re-release, remakes, video release, or sale to cable. As new media are coming on line in the next decade, more films will be needed. New production cannot fill this need.

Take the case of the original videotapes of the wedding of Nicole Brown and O.J. Simpson. When the company that shot that footage sold the business to a new owner, the new owner threw all the old master tapes of weddings into a trash bin behind the

OTHERS
WHO MAY
HAVE RIGHTS
IN YOUR
FILM

181

building without going through them. A passerby raided the bin for the tapes and used them to tape programs for his own pleasure at home. After viewing one such private home recording, he caught a glimpse of the wedding activities underneath, and recognized the participants as O.J. and Nicole Simpson. The murder trial had not begun, but he knew that he had something of value and was able to sell the master (not the copyright). The purchaser of the master also had to acquire the copyright to this film from the original photographer before it could be used, so the copyright owner received a substantial payment. (Even at the height of public interest in all things O.J., the "wedding tapes" did not sell well.)

In a more traditional scenario, Jack Hill produced a number of low-budget action films in the '60s and '70s. None of them was tremendously successful. In 1995, Hill discovered the negative to one of his films, *Switchblade Sisters*, in an old garage. Shortly thereafter, to Hills's amazement and surprise, he received a call from Miramax. The gentleman advised him that Miramax wanted to make *Switchblade Sisters* the initial release under Quentin Tarantino's banner, Rolling Thunder. Hill's shock turned to joy when he confirmed that he still owned the copyright and the print he found could be used by the lab to generate a negative from which release prints could be struck. The premier in Los Angeles was June 7, 1996—more than twenty years after its initial release. You'd better believe that Jack has since verified his ownership of the copyrights of other films he produced.

Be sure that you maintain ownership or control of your copyright. Let your investors participate to the full extent of your agreement in the cash generated by the film. You do not want to chase down co-owners in order to react to an opportunity for you to exploit your film. If you owe someone money as a result of the exploitation, you can always put that share into a savings account until you find that person's heirs. You don't have that leisure when opportunity knocks on your door. You need to answer the door!

The most common investment documents for independent films take care of this problem for you. The Limited Partnership (LP) has been the single most-used method for raising equity investment for an independent film. In the LP, investors are limited partners with limited liability that they can only hang on to if they do not exercise control over the business of the limited partnership. In this case, the limited partnership would own the film, and you or your corporation would be the General Partner. The General Partner exercises all the control over the assets of the limited partnership. This gives you what you need.

One reason for the popularity of the LP is that people who invest are used to the limited partnership. It clearly is the preferred form for investors in real estate and in legitimate stage productions. It gives them comfort to have a form of business that they are used to since many of them will not be familiar with how films are made and distributed.

Recently, the Limited Liability Corporation (LLC) has come into vogue. A **Limited Liability Corporation** is a hybrid entity that provides the shared responsibilities of a partnership with the protection from personal liability of a corporation. The allocation of control is contained in the Operating Agreement. If you use an LLC, be sure that your lawyer builds in the same amount of control for you that you would have if you used a limited partnership. The control provisions of the LLC should be written in clear English so that your investor knows that you will be calling the shots with regard to the exploitation of the film.

BANKERS

"Bankers? Bankers? We don't need no *!@#* bankers!", you might cry. But bankers—such as creditors, vendors, and investors—might well acquire an interest in your film through the mechanism of a security interest in your copyright. In order for someone to have a security interest in your film, you will have to have signed a specific document to that effect. A **security interest** is like a mortgage on your house in that it allows someone to foreclose on the copyright in your film if you don't do what you say you are going to do, which usually is pay money.

The name of the document you sign is **Mortgage of copyright**. People who obtain such interests have to file the papers correctly in all the right places. They usually know the ropes and get all their paperwork lined up correctly. Every bank that loans money in connection with a film will insist on obtaining a mortgage of copyright. If your film is partially financed through foreign sales contracts, a bank loan will almost always be involved.

A security interest in your film is also the way that the Screen Actors Guild (SAG) likes to insure that you keep your promise to pay residuals to actors. They will often ask you, as an independent filmmaker, for a security interest in your film to secure the payment of residuals. In this way, they act very much like a bank. Their security interest gives SAG an effective enforcement mechanism for those who slack on their payment of SAG residuals.

Investors could ask for a security interest also, to insure that any money due them is paid. However, most people who invest in independent film are not sophisticated enough to ask you for this particular piece of paper.

OTHERS
WHO MAY
HAVE RIGHTS
IN YOUR
FILM

183

NAME AND LIKENESS

In addition to being able to use the proceeds of the work of all of the above people, you also want the right to use their names and likenesses in the publicity and the advertising of your film. It would seem that most people involved in a film *want* credit, but sometimes how much credit, or credit for what, becomes an issue. Size, placement, and relative position are all hotly negotiated items that the cast and crew seek.

The credit provisions are so carefully negotiated that you might forget the flip side of the credit equation—you need permission to use names in advertising. Take the case of Stephen King's *Lawnmower Man*. The film was inspired by a short story by King. After script development and filming, King was convinced that the film was such a departure from his original short story that it was no longer "Based on the Short Story by Stephen King." So as not to mislead his fans, he sued to have his credit removed and to remove his name from in front of the title. He won a partial victory. The court was persuaded that the federal Lanham Act prevented attributing the film to King's story when it didn't relate. So King's name came off the title. The "based on" credit remained because there was a written contract that specifically provided for a "based on" credit, and the producer did start with King's short story.

Be sure to include the following in all of your contracts with creative personnel:

> **Name and Likeness:** Producer shall have the right to publish, advertise, announce and use in any manner or medium the name, biography and photographs or other likenesses of Owner in connection with the exhibition, distribution, advertising and promotion or other exploitation of any film created as a result of the exercise by Producer of its rights hereunder, including merchandising, if merchandising rights are granted herein.

CHAPTER 12

TITLE CLEARANCE

Hey, what a great title! It is the best title for a film that anyone ever heard of. But can you use it? Can you prevent others from using it? The *title* to your script or film is not protected under the law of copyright. Copyright protects the *work* you create, not the title you give to it. It is a natural instinct to think that the first few words you put at the top of the first page will be protected by copyright in the same way that all the words that follow are protected. Not so. Many filmmakers find this out—for the first time—when the distributor asks for a formal legal opinion about whether the title is useable.

HOW TITLES ARE PROTECTED

Commonly, people tend to be very protective of a title they have used, especially a title that has been very successful. Plenty of lazy folks out there would love to sell a few extra tickets on opening weekend by trading on the good will built up in the title of someone else's film. Many a filmmaker has been scared away by a "lawyer letter" telling them to "cease and desist" use of a particular title.

My favorite response to one of those letters explained the principles so well that I thought I would reprint the whole thing here with only a few deletions for space. The Marx Brothers made the film *A Night in Casablanca in 1946*, not too long after Warner Bros. had experienced great success with *Casablanca*. Here is the letter that Groucho Marx wrote to Warner Bros. after he received a warning not to use a title with the word "Casablanca" in it.

"... up to the time that we contemplated making a picture, I had no idea that the city of Casablanca belonged to Warner Brothers.

"However, it was only a few days after our announcement appeared that we received a long, ominous legal document warning us not to use the name 'Casablanca' . . . .

"I just can't understand your attitude. Even if they plan on re-releasing the picture, I am sure that the average movie fan could learn to distinguish between Ingrid Bergman and Harpo. I don't know whether I could, but I certainly would like to try.

"You claim you own Casablanca and that no one else can use that name without your permission. What about Warner Brothers—do you own that, too? You probably have the right to use the name Warner, but what about Brothers? Professionally, we were brothers long before you were.

"Even before us, there had been other brothers— the Smith Brothers, the Brothers Karamazov; Dan Brouthers, an outfielder with Detroit, and 'Brother, can you spare a dime?' This was originally 'Brothers, can you spare a dime,' but this was spreading a dime pretty thin. . . .

"... I have a hunch that this attempt to prevent us from using the title is the scheme of some ferret-faced shyster serving an apprenticeship in their legal department. I know the type—hot out of law school, hungry for success, and too ambitious to follow the natural laws of promotion, this bar sinister probably needled Warners' attorneys, most of whom are fine fellows with curly black hair, double-breasted suits, etc., in attempting to enjoin us.

"Well, he won't get away with it! We'll fight him to the highest court! No pasty-faced legal adventurer is going to cause bad blood between the Warners and the Marxes. We are all brothers under the skin and we'll remain friends till the last reel of *A Night in Casablanca* goes tumbling over the spool."

Not only is that letter clever, it correctly implies the governing rule of law: The test of the availability of a title is whether its use by a second person would mislead or confuse the public. Groucho argued that no one, but no one, would confuse the Marx Brothers' *Night in Casablanca* with Warner Bros.' *Casablanca*. And he did it long before the courts had clearly enunciated that rule of law in a case involving another small town a half a world away.

Amityville: One Small Town, Six Horror Movies, Three Production Companies

In 1974, Butch DeFeo murdered his entire family—his father and mother and two sisters and two brothers—at the family home in a small and obscure town, Amityville, New York. His defense? The devil made him do it.

A year later, the home was purchased and occupied by George and Kathleen Lutz. Twenty-eight days after moving in, the Lutzes and their three children fled in fear of their lives. The house was haunted. They and Jay Anson wrote about their experiences in a book entitled *The Amityville Horror*. It became a major best-seller. The authors sold the film rights, retaining the right to publish literary sequels to the book and to exploit motion-picture sequels after a holdback period of five years. American International Pictures (AIP) produced and released the film *The Amityville Horror*. It also was a major hit.

In 1981, the book *The Amityville Horror II* was published using the Lutz rights to do so. It also became a best-seller. Preparations were undertaken to film a motion picture based on the book. Screenplays were written. Budgets were prepared. In the meantime, Dino de Laurentiis produced a motion picture about a fictional family who lived in the Lutz house in Amityville prior to the Lutzes. Orion Pictures obtained whatever rights AIP had and released the film, which they said was based on a book about the real murder trial. Orion released it under the title *Amityville II: The Possession*. That film was so successful that Orion released another film in 1983 entitled *Amityville 3-D.*

Obviously, the Lutzes sued. You might think that this was a no-brainer for the Lutzes to grab a quick injunction. Actually, the defendants won at trial on a "judgment on the pleadings," no less. A **judgment on the pleadings** is the worst—it means that the plaintiff (in this case, the Lutzes) could not even state their case clearly enough to require the defendants to file an answer! Not good. But the court of appeals said, "Not so fast." The court of appeals agreed that the lawyers had not stated a good cause of action, but said that all the various theories stated in the complaint would be merged into a cause of action for unfair competition. The court of appeals went on to say that, as a matter of law, the unfair competition claim could not be dismissed so early because, "the status of **secondary meaning** can only be determined after an inquiry into the facts." The court found that: "Reduced to funda-mentals, secondary meaning is a shorthand phrase which describes the existence of a condition from which public confusion will flow if the defendant is permitted to pursue his deceptive scheme."

The court confirmed that unfair competition must be based upon public confusion and/or deception. Anyone may use a title so long as the title is "not used in such manner as to induce the public to believe that the work to which it is applied is identical with the thing which it originally designated."

So, here is what it takes to get into court on a title claim. You must allege all three of the following elements:

1. that you have created a secondary meaning in all or part of your title, so that a substantial segment of the purchasing public associates the title with a particular person or film or source, even if they can't identify the source. For the Lutzes, they would have to allege that the word "Amityville" equaled their film.
2. that the public was misled into believing that the film was the anticipated sequel to the first movie.

3. that the defendant had intentionally traded on and appropriated for themselves the valuable secondary meaning created by the plaintiffs' efforts and expense.

It is interesting to note the involvement of the public in this process. Titles are not property in the sense that copyright and patents can be property of an owner. Only the public develops the secondary meaning in its collective brain and then is misled to purchase tickets, which trigger the unjust enrichment of the defendant. The court focuses entirely on public confusion, not disclaimers, not technicalities, not the plaintiff's efforts to build up and protect a title. The only thing that matters is the public's reaction to all of this.

Mounting a lawsuit based on public confusion is expensive because of all the polling that is needed to find out if the public is confused. But it is expensive to defend such suits also, and you cannot get rid of them on the pleadings or summary judgment motion. If the parties don't settle, they have to go to trial.

That is why insurance companies remain real sticklers on title reports, which are discussed later in this chapter. Insurance companies are not in the business of going to trial. If they are called on to finance a defense at all, they want to get out of the suit as early as possible.

Why Copyright Doesn't Help Here

Titles are too short to be protected by copyright. No short phrase is subject to copyright protection. When you copyright a script or film as a whole, the copyright does not cover the title. The title is considered the label for the script or the film rather than an integral part of the script or film. Many times distribution companies change a title after the film is completed and copyrighted. Rarely are titles translated literally in every country in the world. This practice confirms the real-world truth of the legal theory.

Nevertheless, the fact that a title is not covered by the same copyright that protects the film often surprises people. It is not unlike obtaining a patent for an invention. The invention is marketed under a certain name. The name of the product is not protected by the patent. Similarly, the title of a script or film is not protected by the film's copyright. In that way, a title is like a product name.

The name of a product can be covered by a trademark. Unfortunately, the title of your film generally cannot be protected by a trademark. The reason is that the purpose of the trademark is to identify the source of a product. If you buy a soap and like it and want to buy another bar of soap just like it, all you have to do is to go to the store—any store—and find a bar of soap with the same trademark on it. The trademark (e.g., Dove) identifies the source of the soap. A studio trademarks its name, so the trademark *Disney* identifies films from a certain source. Individual film names are generally not able to be trademarked.

Trademark is difficult to obtain for the title of a single work, although it is available for a series of works that fall within a general unifying title, such as the line of business books known as "_____ *for Dummies.*" An individual book title within that series, such as *Negotiating for Dummies* (another book with my name on the cover), is not given its own trademark. Only the general title is trademarked. The trademark for the series protects the titles within the series.

TITLE PROTECTION

The way you protect the rights to a film's title is by using that title in the marketplace. Generally speaking, there is no basis for protection of a title other than the body of law involving unfair competition, which is embodied in the federal law called the Lanham Act. **The Lanham Act** covers a number of a business practices. The two themes throughout the Act are the twin principles of fairness as between businesses and protection of the public from being misled. If titles are confusingly similar, the public may believe that a film is connected to a property to which it has no relation. The courts say that you are passing off a film under false pretenses.

Even when you have a good lawsuit, you may decide that you can live with the competing title in the marketplace. For years, I represented Michael Landon. When the pilot of his last series, *Highway to Heaven*, was about to air, he discovered that a book by the same title was being released almost simultaneously with the airing of his pilot. Both sides decided that they could live with the competing titles in the marketplace. When both projects are films, the decision is tougher. But some people are still willing to put up with the confusion rather than finance a legal fight.

MPAA TITLE REGISTRATION

Litigation is expensive, and it can consume your time and energy. The Motion Picture Association of America, Inc. (MPAA) has established a title registration system. As an independent filmmaker, you need to read this entire section before registering your title with the MPAA.

The MPAA title registration service was set up to avoid litigation over identical or similar film titles intended for the theatrical marketplace here in the United States. Independent filmmakers may subscribe to the MPAA registration service by voluntarily signing one of their subscription agreements. Subscribers agree to abide by the rules and regulations of the title registration agreement. If there should be a conflict over title usage, the parties negotiate. If the title cannot be negotiated directly between the two parties, the MPAA provides arbitration to settle the conflict.

According to the MPAA Title Registration Bureau, there are about 3,500 new titles registered with their office each year, and there are also about 3,500 objections to title usage filed each year. However, there are only about fifteen to twenty MPAA title use arbitrations per year. The MPAA attributes this small number of arbitrations to successful negotiations directly between the parties to resolve conflicts. For the MPAA to resolve a dispute over title usage, both parties must be subscribers.

Whether or not a company protests the use of a specific title is completely up to the companies who are subscribers to the title service. The protection that the MPAA can give to subscribers of their service only extends to other registered subscribers to their service. The MPAA does not have jurisdiction over people who do not subscribe to this service. There are about 370 subscribers to the MPAA service, and they encompass all the major producers and distributors of United States theatrical product.

Consider the following example of a title conflict reviewed by the MPAA. Two different films, *Forget Paris* (starring Billy Crystal) and *Paris Match* (starring Meg Ryan), were scheduled to be theatrically released around the same time. The issue of title use went to arbitration because the similarity of titles. The arbitrator denied the producers of Meg Ryan's film the right to use the title *Paris Match* and the film was retitled *French Kiss* to avoid confusion. The MPAA does not make written opinions available to the public, so we will never know exactly why this result occurred.

Alternatively, Universal was convinced to allow Columbia to go forward with the title *Bram Stoker's Dracula*. Universal had the title *Dracula* in their 1930's film, but the studios concluded that the 1990's *Bram Stoker's Dracula* had a very different look, and so the public wouldn't be confused.

The reason an independent filmmaker should think twice before entering the MPAA system is because you are agreeing to be bound by the arbitration system that decides who has what rights. The "independent" arbitration panel is made up of a designee from each of three of the MPAA's member companies. These member companies—the major studios—fund the MPAA. These studios sign a "Member Title Registration Agreement." All the other independent producers and distributors that subscribe to the MPAA service sign a "Non-member Title Registration Agreement."

If the arbitration is between an independent filmmaker and a studio, the three arbitrators who, by definition, are from major studios may have a bit of bias. Further, the factors they consider are strangely foreign to the legal principles of protecting the public from being confused. The governing rules say that the "factors that may be evaluated include, but are not limited to, budget, status of scripts, investment already expended, proximity to principal photography or theatrical release, theme or plot, marketing campaign, and anticipated release pattern." You can see that these factors are in large part economic and heavily weighted toward the studio over the independent filmmaker. A studio can have a film in development for a relatively short period of time and spend more money than your entire production budget.

TITLE REPORT

A **title report** lists all the films, books, songs, and plays that bear the same or similar titles, together with press mentions of those titles. Before anyone distributes your film, whether through a theatrical release or television or videocassette sale, you must have cleared your title. It is a relatively easy process.

You merely send your title along with the appropriate fee to one of the following names. Either one of them will prepare a report on the title you want to use and similar titles that have been used in the past for films, plays, songs, books, and other works. The cost ranges from $350 to $750, depending on how quickly you need the report.

• Dennis Angel (New York), (914) 472-0820
dangel@aol.com
A firm that specializes in providing copyright information to the entertainment industry.

• Thomson and Thomson (Washington, DC), (800) 356-8630
(617) 479-1600
www.thomson-thomson.com
Thomson & Thomson is the leader in trademark and copyright services.

Experienced lawyers (including the above) can issue opinion letters based on these reports as to whether any given title is available for use as the title of your film. (A sample report and a sample opinion letter can be found at the end of this chapter.) Many lawyers prefer to send the title report to the insurance company and let the folks who work there decide for themselves.

12.01 OPINION LETTER

MICHAEL C. DONALDSON
JOSEPH F. HART

OF COUNSEL
FRANK M. LUNN
MICHAEL E. MORALES

WRITER'S E-MAIL ADDRESS

mcd@donaldsonhart.com

LAW OFFICES OF

DONALDSON & HART

9220 SUNSET BOULEVARD
SUITE 224
LOS ANGELES, CALIFORNIA 90069-3501
———
TELEPHONE: (310) 273-8394
FACSIMILE: (310) 273-5370

CORRESPONDENT FIRM
COWAN, DeBAETS, ABRAHAMS
& SHEPPARD LLP
41 MADISON AVE., 34TH FLOOR
NEW YORK, NY 10010
TEL: (212) 974-7474

WRITER'S DIRECT EXTENSION

23

July 21, 2003

**VIA FACSIMILE
AND U.S. MAIL**

Mr. Scott Kennedy
2464 Micheltorena Street
Los Angeles, CA 90039

RE: **KENNEDY, SCOTT/OT:OUR TOWN/FILM MOVEMENT/TITLE OPINION**

Dear Mr. Kennedy:

You have forwarded to our firm for an opinion a title report prepared by Thomson & Thomson dated July 8, 2003 on ***OT: OUR TOWN*** for use in connection with a documentary film. The Thomson & Thomson report included a search of the Copyright Office with 48 references, a search of the United States Patent and Trademark Office with 45 records, a search of State Trademarks with 28 records, a search of Internet Domain Names with 352 references and a search of Thomson & Thomson's Newspaper and Trade Notices with 2 records, one of which was about the above-referenced film.

Based upon my review and analysis of the July 8, 2003 Thomson & Thomson report, I am of the opinion that ***OT: OUR TOWN*** is available for use as the title of a documentary film.

Very truly yours,

MICHAEL C. DONALDSON

MCD/as

G:\WPDOCS\CLIENTS\Kennedy\Our Town\Legal Opinion Ltr.doc

11.01 TITLE REPORT

Thomson & Thomson®

July 12, 1996

<u>VIA OVERNIGHT MAIL</u>

Mr. Vince Ravine
Gemini Entertainment
10844 Burbank Blvd.
North Hollywood, CA 91601

Title Report - WORTH KILLING FOR

Dear Mr. Ravine:

We have conducted a search of the records of the Copyright Office, the Library of Congress, and Thomson & Thomson's common law sources with regard to your proposed use of the title **WORTH KILLING FOR** for a screenplay/feature film.

This title was searched using the following strategy:

WORTH KILLIN(G) FOR
WORTH KILLIN(G)

The following references were found:

Motion Pictures

No references found.

Television

No references found.

Multi-Media/CD-Roms

No references found.

Radio

No references found.

Books (Fiction and Non-Fiction)

No references found.

Stories and Articles

No references found.

Dramatic Works

No references found.

Screenplays

WORTH KILLING FOR: Unpublished screenplay by Corey Michael
Eubanks, registered for copyright in the name of the author,
August 27, 1992. "Worth Killing For" is an application title for
an unpublished screenplay entitled "Desperate Times" by Corey
Michael Eubanks, registered for copyright in the name of the
author, September 9, 1991.

Record Albums

No references found.

Musical Compositions

No references found.

Additional Uses

No references found.

Comments

We note the following references also of interest:

CAUSE WORTH KILLING FOR?: Article by Tamar Lewin, subtitled
DABATE SPLITS ABORTION FOES, published in New York Times, Late·
New York Edition, issue of July 30, 1994.

WORTH WINNING: **Film** in 102 minutes running time, produced by
Twentieth Century Fox-Film Corporation in 1988, directed by Will
Mackenzie, starring Mark Harmon and Lesley Ann Warren, and
described as a film about a popular television weatherman who
becomes engaged to three different women. Currently **available**
for television distribution to the export market through 20th
Century Fox Int'l Television and in video format through CBS/Fox
Video.

The records disclose uses such as WORTH IT, WORTH THE WAIT, THE KILLING, and GIRL TO KILL FOR for additional filmed titles, many of which are currently **available** for television distribution and/or in video format.

Trademark Search

We have conducted a search of federal and state trademark registrations in entertainment-related classes for the exact mark and closely-related similars. If expanded coverage is required, you may wish to order a Thomson & Thomson Full Trademark Search or Merchandising Search.

This search includes Active trademarks from the OFFICIAL GAZETTE up to and including the one dated 07/09/96 and applications filed at the U.S. Patent and Trademark Office through 05/21/96, except for a small number delayed by that agency. INACTIVE trademarks (expired, cancelled or abandoned) as far back as January 1, 1979 have also been examined.

U.S. Patent and Trademark Office Records Search

No references found.

State Trademark Registration Search

No references found.

Newspaper and Trade Notices

No references found.

Notes

If we may be of any further assistance, or if you have any questions regarding this report, please do not hesitate to call me at 1-800-356-8630 ext. 3326.

Sincerely yours,

Mary Pat Berkenbaugh

MPB/mpb

CHAPTER 13

E&O INSURANCE

E&O insurance is the shorthand name for **errors and omissions insurance**. This insurance is similar to that purchased by doctors, lawyers, and accountants to compensate others for damage caused by negligent mistakes. If you accidentally infringe a copyright, slander a trademark, invade someone's privacy, violate someone's right of publicity, or otherwise stub your toe on any of the many obstacles discussed in this book, E&O is the insurance policy that applies.

WHEN TO BUY E&O INSURANCE

Everyone whose film is exploited in any way must eventually purchase E&O insurance, so plan for it early. Because independent films are often made without distribution in place, independent filmmakers often put off purchasing E&O insurance until the last possible minute. Studios routinely have this insurance in place well before the commencement of principal photography. You must purchase such insurance prior to any domestic release of your film in any medium. (Practices vary in foreign territories.) Granted, cash flow does not always permit this luxury any more than a lot of other luxuries that the studios enjoy over guerrilla filmmakers.

Studios secure E&O insurance prior to the first big wave of publicity on a film because that wave of publicity often brings out the first claim. "That's my idea," someone hollers in pain. If the cry is first heard after the insurance is in place, the resulting claim is covered. If it is heard before the insurance is in place, the claim must be disclosed to the insurance company on the application— and may very well be excluded from coverage. You should always disclose known problem areas.

E&O insurance can be expensive. Typical premiums for independent films with no obvious legal problems are currently $6,500-$9,500 for a standard three-year policy with upper limits of $1,000,000 per claim and $3,000,000 total for all claims filed. The deductible amount for independently produced films is usually $10,000. Legal problem areas that are identified to the insurance company may trigger changes to the typical premiums as discussed below.

WHERE TO BUY E&O INSURANCE

Here is a list of a few of the agents who regularly sell E&O insurance and, therefore, are familiar with terms, rates, and the filmmaker's needs:

New York
DeWitt Stern Group, Inc.	(212) 867-3550
D.R. Reiff & Associates	(212) 603-0231
Near North Insurance Brokerage	(212) 935-7373
info@nng.com	

California
Infiniti Pacific Insurance Services	(619) 945-3333
Near North Insurance Brokerage	(310) 556-1900
Albert G. Ruben	(310) 234-6800
Truman Van Dyke Company	(323) 883-0012
Truman@TVDco.com	

Illinois
Near North Insurance Brokerage	(312) 280-5600
www.nnng.com	

Interestingly, all E&O insurance agents deal with the same small group of insurance companies that actually issue the policies. Fireman's Fund is the granddaddy firm. It is the one that has stayed in the field over the years and will probably continue to stay in the field. Other insurance companies enter the field for a few years and then stop writing such insurance because of the difficulty of predicting the losses. Unlike auto insurance or life insurance, it is hard to figure the actuarial likelihood of a suit being filed on any given film. This is of no real concern to the filmmaker. As long as the insurance company is strong, it honors claims under your E&O policy, even if it is no longer in the business of writing E&O insurance.

HOW TO BUY E&O INSURANCE

The procedure for obtaining a policy is not unlike buying health insurance. You select your insurance agent and call for an application, which you fill out and return as discussed below. (You must include your lawyer's name on this application.) The application is forwarded to the insurance company underwriters. **Underwriters** are the people who assess risk and decide whether to issue a policy and what it should cost. If there is any identifiable risk disclosed on your application—such as the depiction of a living person, the inclusion of written material that was not purchased, reliance on public domain material, or any other "flag"—the application is sent to a law firm that advises the underwriters. Usually it is Leopold, Petrich and Smith or Ted Gerdes, both of which are located in Los Angeles, California.

The reviewing attorney contacts you or your attorney with any questions. Based on the answers that are given to the reviewing attorney, a recommendation is made to the insurance company's underwriters, who, in turn, quote the price and terms very quickly thereafter. Because of the consequences of this relatively brief conversation, you want to have an experienced attorney listed on your insurance application. There is an element of negotiation for any adjustment to the norm that applies to a problem area, such as the price or exclusions or deductions to the policy. Let your lawyer handle these areas since they almost always involve nuances of law. It is the threat and cost of litigation and the merits of your position that will be discussed. It can be quite technical. The review process is very fast—this all occurs within two or three days.

Generally, attorneys for the underwriters try to assess the likelihood that a suit will be filed, and if filed, the likelihood of getting you out of the case on a motion for summary judgment. A **summary judgment motion** is heard by a judge who determines whether there are issues of fact that should be tried by a jury. If a case cannot be resolved at this level, it is going to be expensive. Only areas of settled law can be considered in deciding if a motion for summary judgment is likely to be successful. **Settled** as used as an adjective for the law means that the law is not likely to change because of the number of courts that have issued decisions in the area over a long period of time.

Even if the underwriter's lawyers agree with your position, they cannot recommend taking the risk to their client (the insurance company) if there is not a clear case that decides the legal point in your favor. Insurance companies do not want to be on the cutting edge of the law. They look for the protection of settled law or they do not issue the policy.

TIPS ON FILLING OUT YOUR E&O APPLICATION

Filling out the application form is not difficult, although its length is occasionally daunting to some filmmakers. You will find a reprint of a typical form at the end of this section. Your application may be slightly different based on the company you are using as agent, but the enclosed form is close enough to be a very helpful guide. There are some common questions that many filmmakers have when filling out this form. The answers for the more commonly asked questions are addressed below.

The following notes apply to the example application at the end of this chapter. The application you will receive may not look *exactly* like the one in this book, but it should be very, very similar.

1-5, 7, 9, 12, 13. Each of these questions calls for straightforward factual information. Answer each question precisely.

6. Your effective date will be before the first date of
release, broadcast, cablecast, or distribution by Internet.
The effective date of the policy should be as early as
possible. Remember, claims before the effective date
have to disclosed and may not be covered. The term
depends on your needs, but most domestic distributors
require E&O for a three-year term.

8. The answer to this question is a simple factual
report. However, refer to Chapter 12 for details on
Title Reports. Generally speaking, your policy will
not cover title without a title report.

10. Most independent filmmakers purchase insurance
after they have an agreement to exploit the film and
a contract that sets out coverage requirements. If you
don't have this, go with the standard $1,000,000 and
$3,000,000 in coverage and $10,000 in deductible
when you answer these questions.
    Often, insurance companies ask you if you want
coverage for merchandising activities. This is additional,
special coverage for which there is an additional
charge. Documentary filmmakers never need this.
Independent fictional filmmakers rarely need this
coverage. If you know that your film is going to spawn
a major merchandising effort beyond T-shirts and caps,
you might want to inquire about this coverage.

11. Give the underwriter an honest feel for your project,
but never, ever use more than the space allotted. It is
simply not necessary.

14. This is important, because the insurance company's
attorney routinely calls this person. The attorney you
choose should be completely knowledgeable on the
law of copyright and clearance. She or he must also
have sufficient knowledge about your project to

dispose of any questions in a brief telephone conversation. This may take a couple hours of preparation.

15 and 16. You almost always have to answer these
   questions "yes" to have your application approved.

17-22. These are very specific questions regarding clearance that must be answered accurately. If you have
   made an affirmative decision not to obtain one or
   more clearances for some reason, your attorney needs
   all the details so that the insurance company can be
   persuaded to provide coverage without the clearance.
   Under some circumstances, you may want to provide
   a pithy explanation right on the application.

23a. Again, this is a factual response. You will need a
   copyright report sooner or later to establish for sure
   that you have the right to make your film.

23b. This question was put in the forms after the U.S.
   Supreme Court decided the *Rear Window* case, which
   was discussed in Chapter 2. For the reasons you
   learned in Chapter 2, you have to make a deal with the
   heirs of the author if you check the "yes" box indicating that the music or underlying work was written in
   the time period that raises the renewal issues of *Rear
   Window*. You also have to give detailed answers as to
   exactly what material falls into this category.

24. This question is a short checklist for your clip
   clearance procedure set out in Chapter 19.

25-27. These questions reveal the care you took in your
   music clearance as discussed in depth in Chapter 15.
   Sometimes, you fill out your application before you
   actually perform these steps. If so, just say so and
   follow proper procedures when you do clear your
   music.

28-29. These are simple factual questions to be
   answered honestly.

30-33. These are your personal representations and must be filled out with brutal honesty. The notice at the top of the form underscores the importance of these final four questions. Each of these blocks must be initialed by you. If anything is written in the line after the words "Except as follows," a question is raised. Of course, if you have or expect a claim, you are required to disclose it on the line after "Except as follows." Specific claims known to the producer are the subject of specific negotiations between the production attorney and the insurance company. The following sections discuss these negotiations. Being less than honest is not a good option.

CONSEQUENCES OF A FAILURE TO DISCLOSE

Beware of friends who fudged on their insurance application and tell you, "We got our insurance. Everything was okay." They were telling you the truth, but before you follow their lead, stop and think. The reason that "everything was okay" is that no claims came in on the area where they fudged. Occasionally, someone fudges and a claim comes in and the insurance company does not catch it, but that is very, very rare. One of the first things an insurance company does when a claim comes in is to review the policy carefully. If there is any question about the non-disclosure of prior claims, they like to investigate further. That may result in a denial of coverage, or worse. Hmmmmmmmmmmmmm. Not a pleasant thought. All those adjustors hunched over the fine language of the insurance contract you did not even read, but they know very well . . . and their sole purpose is to figure out if they should or should not pay a claim and their salaries are paid by the insurance company. Scary!

There are three possible responses of an insurance company when an applicant has been less than forthcoming about a potential claim and the claim that was only potential at the time of the application becomes a reality. The most draconian option is rescission of the policy, meaning the policy is void from inception. It never existed! This will invalidate the entire insurance agreement. That would only happen in an extreme case. The two more common responses to untruthful or incomplete responses to the last questions on the application are still draconian if you are on the receiving end of a claim. Here are the other two concepts:

1. There is no coverage for this particular claim at all (no defense and no indemnity);
2. A reservation of rights to recover the costs of defense and indemnity from you, the insured.

You will not have this problem because you have read this chapter and you know to fill out your application completely and honestly. If you must err, err on the side of full disclosure.

Basically, if the insurance company says that the policy does not cover a particular risk because the insured knew about it and did not disclose it, then the insurance company will not pay to defend or settle the claim. Somewhere deep in the fine print of the application or the policy it says that you are covered for a variety of copyright claims and claims of personal injury (invasion of privacy, slander, libel, misrepresentation, false light, and such things as are covered in chapter 4) AS LONG AS you have fully disclosed all the facts known to you about the potential risk. The notice at the top of the application makes this crystal clear—at least, as crystal clear as anything that you are ever likely to receive from an insurance company. And, the law implies a duty on you, the applicant, of good faith and full disclosure.

The "Reservation of Rights" is a variation on the same theme. Basically, the insurance company says, "The applicant fudged on the facts here. Normally, the policy would cover this claim, but the insured wasn't honest with us, so we may not have a duty to defend [or pay] the claim." The insurance will provide the legal defense you need under a reservation of rights to recoup the money paid to the lawyers from you, the insured. That means that after the case is over, the insurance company may come after you for the costs of defense and any indemnity or settlement paid to the claimant. Given the high cost of litigation, legal talent, and the fact that you have little or no control over those bills, this can be a very expensive result indeed.

WHEN FULL DISCLOSURE REVEALS A POTENTIAL CLAIM

When filmmakers fudge on their applications, it is usually out of fear that they will be denied an insurance policy. Oops! You have already signed a distribution agreement that requires you to supply an E&O insurance policy. You can't possibly risk not being able to buy one. But wait, the insurance company is in the business of selling policies. They don't want to take on any unknown risks. Surely, this is a situation ripe for compromise.

So here are the alternatives you can negotiate—in descending order of attractiveness to you—in order to avoid the dreaded and unacceptable "no E&O insurance policy available."

1. Have your lawyer convince the insurance company that the risk is quite low.
2. Make some creatively acceptable modifications to your film.
3. Obtain an appropriate release or other clearance.
4. Allow a higher deductible with regard to that risk only.
5. Agree to a sub-limit for that risk only.
6. Pay a higher premium.
7. Exclude that particular risk from coverage.

Let's discuss each one of these alternatives and how you might go about negotiating them to your advantage. I put numbers next to the explanations that match the list above.

1. Obviously, you want to try to convince the insurance company that the risk is acceptable. In this regard, the standing of your attorney and the facts themselves are of considerable importance. Your lawyer will act as an educator to the insurance company lawyer. You should arm your lawyer with a fully annotated script and all of the facts. Your lawyer will try to convince the insurance company that you have enough independent sources for the material in your script that there should be no serious threat of suit and even less of a threat of losing.

Remember that insurance companies don't like lawsuits, even if they think that they can win them. Therefore, you not only want sources, but you want sources that are likely to have been seen by the objecting party. The argument then is that this very same material has been published before and no one complained, so there should not be any complaints when it shows up in your film. When independent filmmaker David Jacobson was writing *Dahmer*, based on the life of serial killer Jeffrey Dahmer, he imagined the potential claims and carefully double-sourced everything in order to convince the insurance company that this horrific story would pass legal muster in spite of the fact that the adults who most influenced Dahmer were all still alive and that the families of the victims were still around, as were the police officers who visited Dahmer, even with corpses in his apartment and a new victim pleading for help. The trick was to locate true double sources as opposed to the same source quoted in two different newspapers. Court records helped a lot. In fact, court testimony—preceded as it is with solemn oaths, enforced by perjury laws, and verified by cross-examination—is always a source of particularly high value.

2. The mention of making creative changes always runs counter to the basic instincts of independent filmmakers. If you liked taking notes from studio execs, you wouldn't be fighting the fierce battles to make a film independently. And then to take notes from lawyers in order to satisfy insurance coverage, well, that is just too much. You would be surprised at the number of times that minor changes of no consequence to the creative team have saved a project from the prospect. Perhaps a few stories will help put your mind at ease. By way of example of how this works, let's stay with the Dahmer story of the above paragraph. The one area where our double sourcing did not persuade the lawyer for the insurance company was the police officers. The reason was that insurance companies want to avoid litigation rather than win litigation. The police officers had already fought the charges against them. The officers had been called out to Dahmer's place, and one of his victims tried to get the police to step in. Neighbors tried to get the police to step in. They eventually left with the victim "in the care of" Dahmer. Needless to say, they are sensitive about any allegations surrounding these events. The screenwriter, who was also to be the director, was comfortable in toning down this scene. Overall dramatic effect of this elimination: zero. We would not have agreed to make a change if the overall impact weakened the storytelling. Use your creative talent to avoid future problems.

3. Obtaining releases after the fact is not always possible, but always worth exploring. When you are at the point in the process that insurance is being obtained, your picture is a reality. Sometimes people would rather be left in a picture than cut out, even if they are not all that happy with the depiction. You might think seriously about this one. There are many creative approaches. How you make the approach is important because you do not want to invite a claim where none might have been otherwise made. Better yet, get all your releases in advance.

4. Deductibles for a specific risk can be raised, sometimes as high as $50,000 in order to obtain coverage. Again, this is a negotiation. You don't want the deductible to go up at all, but if there must be an increase, your attorney negotiates for the smallest possible amount based on how early a motion for summary judgment can be filed and an appropriate sharing between insurer and insured of the increased risk. This is a highly technical negotiation. Also, a higher deductible overall may mean more money out of your pocket in the event of a claim, but could also lower your premium. It's all a negotiation.

5. A sub-limit for the problem risk means that the insurance company has a cap on what it will have to pay for that potential claim. That makes it more attractive to insure. The lower the risk to the insurance company, the more likely they will agree to provide some coverage. Of course, once your sub-limit is exhausted, the rest of the costs are on you. You probably have agreed to such policy limits in your auto insurance. This is all part of the negotiation.

6. Paying a higher premium is also a highly technical discussion involving risk assessment and exposure. Exposure in this case refers to the potential costs that could be incurred. You don't want to go down this road unless you absolutely have to.

7. Excluding the risk entirely is generally unacceptable, although it is your ace in the hole if the insurance company wants to raise your premium too high. You can eliminate the premium problem by agreeing to exclude the particular risk that is troubling them. Unfortunately, it is the risk that the insurance company is most worried about that is usually the risk that you are most worried about . . . and probably every distributor and broadcaster. Some E&O insurance coverage is invariably a requirement of any broadcaster or distributor. No exceptions. So excluding the risk rarely solves all your problems.

12.01 E&O INSURANCE FORM

APPLICATION FOR
MOTION PICTURE AND TELEVISION PRODUCERS LIABILITY INSURANCE
(Libel, Slander and Infringement of Copyright Cover)

NOTICE: This is an Application for a "NAMED PERILS" CLAIMS MADE POLICY. Except to such extent as may be provided otherwise herein, any insurance Policy which may issue hereafter will be limited to liability for only those CLAIMS THAT ARE FIRST MADE AGAINST THE INSURED AND REPORTED TO UNDERWRITERS DURING THE POLICY PERIOD. Please read and review this Application carefully and discuss the coverage with your insurance agent, broker or representative.

1. Name of Applicant: _____

2. Street & Mailing Address: _____
_____

3. Applicant is a: ☐ Corporation ☐ Individual ☐ Partnership ☐ Joint Venture

4. Names and Title of Principal Officers, Partners or Individuals:_____
_____

5. Name of Producer (Individual): _____
Executive Producer (Individual): _____

6. Desired Effective Date: _____ Desired Term of Policy: _____ years

7. Title of Production to be Insured: _____

8. Has Title Report been obtained from any one of the Title Clearance Services?: ☐ Yes ☐ No

If "Yes," Name the Clearance Service: _____
(Attach Copy of Report)

9. Estimated Dates for:

(a) Completion of Principal Photography: _____

(b) First Release or Air Date:_____

10. Limits of Desired Coverage: For any one claim: $_____

In the aggregate: $_____

Deductible amount: $_____

11. Synopsis of Production: _____
_____
_____
_____

VD 90 (1/88)

APPLICATION FOR MOTION PICTURE AND TELEVISION PRODUCERS LIABILITY INSURANCE (Cont'd)

12. Names of Authors and Writers:

    (a) Of Underlying Works: _____

    _____

    (b) Of Screenplays, etc.: _____

    _____

13. Production is:

    ☐ Motion Picture for Initial Theatrical Release   Running Time: _____

    ☐ Motion Picture for Initial Television Release   Running Time: _____

    ☐ T.V. Pilot   ☐ T.V. Special   ☐ Radio Program   Running Time: _____

    ☐ T.V. Series   Number of Episodes: _____   Running Time: _____

    ☐ Radio Series   Number Each Week: _____ Number of Weeks: _____   Running Time: _____

    ☐ Videocassette

    ☐ Theatrical Stage Presentation

    ☐ Other (e.g. Cable, Pay-TV, Subscription, etc.) Describe: _____

    _____

14. Name & Address of Applicant's Attorney: Individual: _____

    Firm: _____ Phone: _____

15. Has Applicant's Attorney read the "Clearance Procedures" included within this Application? ☐ Yes ☐ No

    If "No," Explain: _____

16. Has Applicant's Attorney approved as adequate the steps taken for Clearance Procedures used in connection with th

    Production?   ☐ Yes ☐ No   If "No," Explain: _____

    _____

17. Is the name or likeness of any living person used or is any living person portrayed (with or without use of name or likeness

    in the Production? ☐ Yes ☐ No If so, have clearances been obtained in all cases? ☐ Yes ☐ N

    Is the name or likeness of any deceased person used or is any deceased person portrayed (with or without name o

    likeness) in the Production? ☐ Yes ☐ No   If so, have clearances been obtained in all cases from Person

    Representatives, Heirs or other Owners of such rights? ☐ Yes ☐ No

18. Is there a plausible risk that a living person could claim (without regard to the merits) to be identifiable in the Production

    whether or not the person's name or likeness is used or the Production purports to be fictonal?

    ☐ Yes ☐ No   If so, has a release been obtained from such person? ☐ Yes ☐ N

19. Are actual events portrayed in the Production? ☐ Yes ☐ No

APPLICATION FOR MOTION PICTURE AND TELEVISION PRODUCERS LIABILITY INSURANCE (Cont'd)

. Has Applicant or any of its agents bargained for (a) any rights in Literary, Musical or other material; or (b) releases from any persons in connection with the above Production, and been unable to obtain or refused an agreement or release?

☐ Yes ☐ No   If "Yes," Please Explain: _____

_____

. Is the Production: ☐ Entirely Fictional   ☐ True Portrayal of Events or Happenings   ☐ Entirely Fictional but inspired by specific Events or Occurrences ☐ Portrayal of actual facts, but which includes significant fictionalization

☐ Based on another Work   If so, Please Specify:_____

☐ Other: _____

. Is the Production: ☐ Quiz or Panel   ☐ Interview or Forum   ☐ Variety   ☐ Musical

☐ Dramatic   ☐ Children's Show   ☐ Documentary   ☐ Mini-Series   ☐ Docudrama

☐ Other: _____

. (a) Has a Copyright Report been obtained?   ☐ Yes ☐ No   If "Yes," the Copyright Report must accompany this Application.

(b) Is there any literary, musical, or other material whatsoever in the Production that was copyrighted before January 1, 1978? ☐ Yes ☐ No   If "Yes," the Supplemental Application must be completed and submitted with the Primary Application.

. Will any Film Clips, Photographs or Artwork be used in this Production?   ☐ Yes ☐ No

If "Yes," Please answer each of the following:

Have all Licenses and Consents been obtained as follows?:

From Copyright Owners?	☐ Yes ☐ No	Have Musical Rights been obtained? ☐ Yes ☐ No
From Music Owners?	☐ Yes ☐ No	Recording & Synchronization Rights? ☐ Yes ☐ No
From Writers and/or Others?	☐ Yes ☐ No	Performing Rights? ☐ Yes ☐ No
		From Performers or Persons appearing in the Film? ☐ Yes ☐ No

If "No" to any of the foregoing, Explain: _____

_____

_____

. Have Musical Rights been cleared?   ☐ Yes ☐ No

(a) Recording and Synchronization Rights?   ☐ Yes ☐ No

(b) Performing Rights?   ☐ Yes ☐ No

. If Original Music was commissioned, has a Hold Harmless been obtained from the Composer?   ☐ Yes ☐ No

If "No," Explain: _____

. Will the Production be distributed to the public on Videotapes, Videocassettes, Videodiscs or other new technology?

☐ Yes ☐ No

If "Yes," has Applicant acquired necessary Music and other Licenses and Consents therefor?   ☐ Yes ☐ No

. Has Applicant had prior Copyright, Libel, etc. (Producers' Liability) Insurance on the Production to be insured?

(If "Yes," Attach a Copy of prior Policy.)   ☐ Yes ☐ No

29. Has Applicant or any Officers. Directors or Partners ever been refused similar Insurance for this Production or any other Production? ☐ Yes ☐ No If "Yes," Explain: _____

30. Applicant represents and warrants that neither it, nor any of its Officers, Directors or Partners, or their Counsel, have any knowledge, actual or constructive:

  (a) of any claims or legal proceedings made or commenced against the Applicant, or any Officers, Directors, Partners, or subsidiary or affiliated corporations within the last five (5) years for invasion of privacy, infringement of copyright (statutory or common law) defamation, unauthorized use of titles, formats, ideas, characters, plots or other program material embodied in this or any other Production, or breach of implied contract arising out of alleged submission of any literary or musical material. If no exceptions, Please Initial [____]

  ☐ Except as Follows: _____

  (b) of any threatened claims or legal proceedings against the Applicant or any Officers, Directors, subsidiaries or Partners, or against any other person, firm or corporation arising out of or based upon the Production including title thereof, or any material upon which the Production is or will be based, that would be covered by the Policy sought to be obtained by the Applicant. If no exceptions, Please Initial [____]

  ☐ Except as Follows: _____

  (c) of any facts, circumstances or prior negotiations by reason of which they, or any of them, believe that a claim might reasonably be asserted or legal proceedings instituted against the Applicant that would be covered by the Policy sought to be obtained by the Applicant. If no exceptions, Please Initial [____]

  ☐ Except as Follows: _____

31. Applicant agrees to obtain from third parties from whom it obtains matter, material or services from the Production written warranties and indemnities against claims arising out of the use of such matter, material or services. Please Initial [____]

32. Applicant agrees that it will use due diligence to determine whether any matter or materials to be used in the Production are protected by law and, where necessary, to obtain from parties owning rights therein the right to use the same in connection with the Production. Please Initial [____]

33. Applicant also understands that there will be special provisions in the Policy (General Condition E.) covering the respective obligations of the Company and Applicant to provide DEFENSE and SETTLEMENT where coverage issues or conflicts of interest are or may be present.

Applicant acknowledges that claims and lawsuits may be brought which may combine covered and uncovered claims or forms of relief and that conflicts of interest may arise as between one Insured and another Insured under this Policy or as against the Company. In all such circumstances. Applicant recognizes that, under this Policy, the Company's obligation is only to provide one (1) counsel for defense of all claims and if any further counsel are desired by Applicant, they may be retained at the Applicant's own cost and expense in accordance with the terms of the Policy. Applicant understands that the premiums set forth herein, the deductible, and the balance of the terms of this Policy have been specifically set and determined with the foregoing provisions in mind and acknowledges that he is waiving his right to separate counsel paid for by the Company but shall retain the right to such counsel paid by himself. Please Initial [____]

4.   **THIS APPLICATION IS SUBMITTED WITH THE FOLLOWING SPECIFIC UNDERSTANDING:**

(a)   Applicant warrants and represents that the above answers and statements are in all respects true and material to the issuance of an Insurance Policy and that Applicant has not omitted, supressed or misstated any facts.

(b)   If any claims, threatened claims, or other matters which might affect issuance of a Policy come to the attention of Applicant after execution or filing of this Application with the Underwriters but before a Policy issues, Applicant must notify the Underwriters immediately.

(c)   All exclusions in the Policy apply regardless of any answers or statements in this Application.

(d)   Applicant understands that the limit of liability and deductible under any Policy to be issued in response hereto shall include both loss payment and claim & defense expenses as defined in the Policy.

(e)   Defense Cost Provision - Please note that the Defense Cost Provision of this Policy stipulates that the limits of liability may be completely exhausted by the cost of legal defense, and any deductible or retention shall apply to investigation expenses and defense costs as well as indemnity.

5.   This Application shall be attached to and become a part of any Policy, should a Policy be issued as a result of this Application, which shall then be deemed a schedule to such Policy as well, but the signing hereunder does not bind the Applicant or the Underwriters to complete the Insurance unless and until a Policy of Insurance is issued in response to this Application.

Date Signed: _____

pplicant's Signature: _____

y: _____

tle: _____

Brokerage Firm: _____

Address: _____

Phone:_____TELEX:_____FAX:_____

(SEE ATTACHED FOR CLEARANCE PROCEDURES)

CLEARANCE PROCEDURES

The Clearance Procedures below should not be construed as exhaustive and they do not cover all situations which may aris
in any particular circumstance or any particular Production.

1. Applicant and its counsel should continually monitor the Production at all stages, from inception through final cut, wit
    a view to eliminating material which could give rise to a claim.

2. The script should be read prior to commencement of Production to eliminate matter which is defamatory, invades privac
    or is otherwise potentially actionable.

3. Unless work is an unpublished original not based on any other work, a copyright report must be obtained. Both domesti
    and foreign copyrights and renewal rights should be checked. If a completed film is being acquired, a similar review shou
    be made on copyright and renewals on any copyrighted underlying property.

4. If the script is an unpublished original, the origins of the work should be ascertained - basic idea, sequence of even
    and characters. It should be ascertained if submissions of any similar properties have been received by the Applica
    and, if so, the circumstances as to why the submitting party may not claim theft or infringement should be described in deta

5. Prior to final title selection, a Title Report should be obtained.

6. Whether Production is fictional (and location is identifiable) or factual, it should be made certain that no names, face
    or likenesses of any recognizable living persons are used unless written releases have been obtained. Release
    unnecessary if person is part of a crowd scene or shown in a fleeting background. Telephone books or other source
    should be checked when necessary. Releases can only be dispensed with if the Applicant provides the Company wit
    specific reasons, in writing, as to why such releases are unnecessary and such reasons are accepted by the Compan
    The term "living persons" includes thinly disguised versions of living persons or living persons who are readily identifiab
    because of identity of other characters or because of the factual, historical or geographic setting.

7. All releases must give the Applicant the right to edit, modify, add to and/or delete material, juxtapose any part of th
    film with any other film, change the sequence of events or of any questions posed and/or answers, fictionalize person
    or events including the release and to make any other changes in the film that the Applicant deems appropriate. If
    minor, consent has to be legally binding.

8. If music is used, the Applicant must obtain all necessary synchronization and performance licenses from composers c
    copyright proprietors. Licenses must also be obtained on prerecorded music.

9. Written agreements must exist between the Applicant and all creators, authors, writers, performers and any other person
    providing material (including quotations from copyrighted works) or on-screen services.

10. If distinctive locations, buildings, businesses, personal property or products are filmed, written releases should be secure
    This is not necessary if non-distinctive background use is made of real property.

11. If the Production involves actual events, it should be ascertained that the author's sources are independent and primar
    (contemporaneous newspaper reports, court transcripts, interviews and witnesses, etc.) and not secondary (another author
    copyrighted work, autobiographies, copyrighted magazine articles, etc.).

LEARANCE PROCEDURES (Cont'd)

2. Shooting script and rough cuts should be checked, if possible, to assure compliance of all of the above. During photography, persons might be photographed on location, dialogue added or other matter included which was not originally contemplated.

3. If the intent is to use the Production to be insured on Videotapes, Videocassettes, Videodiscs or other new technology, rights to manufacture, distribute and release the Production should be obtained, including the above rights, from all writers, directors, actors, musicians, composers and others necessary therefor, **including proprietors of underlying materials.**

4. Film clips are dangerous unless licenses and authorizations for the second use are obtained from the owner of the clip or party authorized to license the same, as well as licenses from all persons rendering services in or supplying material contained in the film clip; e.g., underlying literary rights, performances of actors or musicians. Special attention should be paid to music rights as publishers are taking the position that new synchronization and performance licenses are required.

5. Aside from living persons, even dead persons (through their personal representatives or heirs) have a "right of publicity," especially where there is considerable fictionalization. Clearances should be obtained where necessary. Where the work is fictional in whole or in part, the names of all characters must be fictional. If for some special reason particular names need not be fictional, full details must be provided to the Company in an attachment to the Application.

6. Consideration should be given to the likelihood of any claim or litigation. Is there a potential claimant portrayed in the Production who has sued before or is likely to sue again? Is there a close copyright or other legal issue? Is the subject matter of the Production such as to require difficult and extensive discovery in the event of necessity to defend? Are sources reliable? The above factors should be considered in your clearance procedures and recommendations.

MOTION PICTURE AND TELEVISION PRODUCERS LIABILITY INSURANCE
(Libel, Slander and Infringement of Copyright Cover)

NOTICE: This Supplemental Application must be completed in detail whenever Question No. 23(b) on the Primary Application is answered "Yes."

1. For any literary, musical, or other copyrighted material used in the production, and copyrighted before January 1, 1978, list the Title of any such material and the date of initial and renewal copyright for each such copyrighted matter.

Title of Material Used	Date of Copyright (Mo./Day/Yr.)	Date of Renewal (Mo./Day/Yr.)
_____	_____	_____
_____	_____	_____
_____	_____	_____

   a. As to each of such materials, does the license or assignment grant renewal rights?

   ☐ Yes   ☐ No

   b. Was the copyright for all such material renewed during the lifetime of the author?

   ☐ Yes   ☐ No

   If No, Explain: _____

   _____

2. Name of Applicant's Attorney verifying the above Copyright information, if different than the Attorney shown on Question 14 of Primary Application.

   Individual _____   Firm _____

   Phone: _____

3. A current Copyright Report must be submitted with this Application.

4. This Supplemental Application shall be attached to and become a part of any Policy, should a Policy be issued as a result of this Application, which shall then be deemed a schedule to such Policy as well, but the signing hereunder does not bind the Applicant or the Underwriters to complete the Insurance unless and until a Policy of Insurance is issued in response to this Application.

   Date Signed: _____

   Applicant's Signature: _____

   By: _____

   Title: _____

TVD 90-A (6/90)

PART IV

PRINCIPAL PHOTOGRAPHY AND POST PRODUCTION

Often you will have to make quick decisions about the clearance issues that come up on the set during principal photography. To aid you in these decisions, a handy list of rules follows. Of course, post-production problems carry their own unique problems and strict time pressures.

RULES TO LIVE BY ON THE SET

RULES TO LIVE BY ON THE SET

1. Think before you ask. Remember, if you ask permission, it is proof positive that on the date you asked, you believed that you needed permission. Even a request loaded with hedge-words and disclaimers is a request.

2. If you need a specific permission or agreement, you must get it in writing—or, if not, at least on film.

3. Always have alternatives in mind when you ask for a permission.

4. Once you obtain a release, keep the original in your permanent file and have a copy at the set.

5. All music—even a riff—must be cleared.

6. All clips from copyrighted films must be cleared, together with the music and, often, various recognizable persons in them, plus the clip's directors and the writers.

7. You have every right to make a realistic film. Therefore, all the trademarks and product names that show up in a realistic scene are fair game. As long as the products are used properly and safely, as the manufacturers intended, you may use them without obtaining permission.

8. If you cannot obtain a permission needed, create your own original object. Do not create a knock-off of the copyrighted object.

9. Private persons have a right to remain private. You do not have a right to use the name of a living person in an identifiable way. For the same reason, never, ever use an actual phone number, address, or license tag available in the service area where your film is set.

10. When in doubt, consult with an experienced clearance attorney.

CHAPTER 14

ALL THE THINGS THAT THE CAMERA SEES

Finally we turn our attention to a number of other legal concepts that are necessary to make snap decisions on the set about clearance. This chapter pulls together a wide variety of legal concepts—trademark, unfair competition, trade libel, and infringement—and applies them to everyday situations that you face as a filmmaker during principal photography. Use this chapter in conjunction with Chapter 4 on Personal Rights and Chapter 17 on Fair Use.

CLEARANCE

To clear or not to clear, that is the question. It is probably the question that led Shakespeare to say, "Kill all the lawyers."

It is always safest to clear. To **clear** means to obtain written permission from the proper individual to use a certain item in your film or to obtain a written legal opinion that permission is not necessary. Young lawyers, anxious to protect their newly licensed necks, always opt to clear as opposed to not clear a work. The problem is that to clear every little thing is expensive, time consuming, and could be quite disruptive if you are not able to clear something in time to continue your shoot.

Keep in mind that studios are very conservative in this area and tend to get releases from many people who would *seem* to be exempted from that need by the fair-use concept or the rules set out at the beginning of this section. This is particularly true in the areas of clearing trademarks and copyrighted books, magazines, and newspapers used as set dressing. It is also true when someone's name or likeness appears in a film. One reason for the studios' conservatism is their institutional size. Corporate size always tends to inhibit risk-taking urges. Another reason is that studios are wealthy, which makes them an appealing target to those who feel wronged. Also, wealth creates it own conservative attitude. Finally, studios—with their large and stable legal departments—know things that you may not know. They are reservoirs for bad experiences that they do not want to repeat.

The practice has grown up with studio legal departments to clear every piece of copyrighted material that appears in a film. They do this out of an understandable self-defense mechanism: The studios are what is known by plaintiffs' attornies as a target defendant. A **target defendant** is anyone who looks as though they have the capacity to pay big bucks to avoid being sued. Interestingly, you may also look like a target defendant if your movie is released to good reviews or enjoys even a modicum of success. Being a target defendant is in the eyes of the beholder.

The attitude of the studios is that it is cheaper to clear in advance than defend after the fact. If you can afford the time and effort, this conservative advice is sound advice. Few independent filmmakers believe that they have the resources to do that and so must take some chances that the studios do not have to take and do not want to take. Unfortunately, the studio practice has led some people to believe that such items have to be cleared as a matter of law.

POSTERS, PAINTINGS, SCULPTURES, AND MAGAZINE COVERS

The subjects under this heading were appropriately grouped together in the first edition of the book. Since then, the law has been clarified with regard to the rights controlled by the holder of the copyright to something that was created as decorative art. I like to think of this description as being for works created for display. The most obvious things that you might want to use in your film that are created specifically for display are posters, paintings, sculptures, and photographs. Basically, the courts have held that showing these works on television or in a movie is displaying them publicly, so they have to be cleared if they are clearly recognizable. The right is called the Right of Public Display. That only applies to artwork that was created with the intention to have it displayed publicly and does not apply to magazine covers and newspapers, so we will discuss the artwork first.

Decorative Works— Art work intended for Public Display

The price for not clearing a piece of art that has to be cleared can be very high. Frederick E. Hart and the National Cathedral in Washington D. C. sued Warner Bros. over the use of the bas-relief sculpture *Ex Nihilo* that is over the cathedral's main entrance. The film was *Devil's Advocate*. A bas-relief that was strikingly similar to *Ex Nihilo* hung behind the desk of the satanic character played by Al Pacino, head of an ungodly successful New York law firm. It was on screen for about twenty minutes, and in a climatic scene in the third act, the figures in the bas-relief began writhing around. Hart is a devout Catholic. He sued. The church joined in. They asked the court to stop distribution!

The suit was filed just after the film went into wide release. The trial court immediately indicated that it was inclined to issue a preliminary **injunction. An injunction** is when the court says you can or can't do something. In our world, that usually means that you can't distribute your film. Not good news when you are in the middle of a wide release.

An injunction is always bad news for someone. Warner's settled immediately. They agreed, among other things, to major changes in the video version of the film, in case you are wondering why you didn't see all that writhing that I described above when you rented the movie.

In a similar case, the inventive architect Lebbeus Woods sued Universal Studios because a set in *12 Monkeys* copied one of Woods' drawings. Bruce Willis was suspended on a chair and interrogated. The scene was on screen for about five minutes. The trial court concluded that the set copied "substantial portions of Woods'" drawing and issued a preliminary injunction against showing the film.

Surprise! Universal settled. There is a backstory to all of this. Woods had launched a career separate from his teaching and architectural career by designing fanciful sets for films that never saw the light of day, so he was particularly upset at getting ripped off in this fashion. He wasted no time. It paid off.

Bedspreads as Art—Yes!

This category of decorative arts can also include things that one would normally think of as utilitarian such as a quilt or a ceramic plate, but that because of its design, construction, value, or some other reason is clearly a work of art created for display rather than a household item created for a purely utilitarian purpose.

The **leading case** in this area involves a story quilt. **Leading case** refers to a case that was the first case to clearly state a certain conclusion of law. Prior to the case, the law was either unclear or untested or both. Non-quilters don't usually think of quilters as fighters. But then they probably haven't met Faith Ringgold. Neither have I, but read on. She single-handedly—along with her hired guns—set things straight in the area of clearance for set-dressing involving "decorative" works.

Faith created a quilt called Church Picnic Story Quilt. It's no ordinary quilt. It has a painting of a 1909 church picnic and twelve panels of text incorporated into the quilt. High Museum in Atlanta owns the quilt. Faith owns the copyright.

Faith licensed the right to create a poster to the High Museum, which sold thousands of them in their gift shop. One of those posters found its way onto the set of the final scene in an episode of *Roc,* a half-hour television sitcom about a middle-class African-American family in Baltimore produced by HBO Independent Pictures. The scene took place in a church hall. The poster (sans identifying wording) hung on the back wall of the set. It was never shown in its entirety. It was not always in focus. In nine shots, it was seen a total of 26.75 seconds.

But Faith knew it was a poster of her quilt. Faith sued.

She lost in the federal trial court in News York. The court said that the use of quilt as set dressing was **de minimus. De minimus** is a fancy way the courts have of saying that the injury is too trivial for the court to bother with. And just in case that didn't work, the court also said that the use as set dressing was Fair Use.

On appeal, Faith won. First, the court found that 26.75 seconds was not de minimus. Next, the court found that it wasn't Fair Use. In part, the appellate court relied on a regulation issued by the Librarian of Congress that says public broadcasting entities have to pay a license fee when a copyrighted visual work is used, even if it is displayed "less than full-screen" for more than three seconds. I bet you didn't know about that regulation. Few people do. The Librarian of Congress issues a lot of pesky, little regulations. Many of them, such of this one, are more in the nature of an advisory regulation since the Librarian has no direct enforcement mechanism.

But the same appellate court reached the opposite result just a few weeks earlier in considering ten un-cleared photographs used in a short scene in the film *Seven* for "less than thirty seconds." In the majority of the shots, actors or furniture obstructed the photographs and the camera did not focus on the photos. In fact, they were out of focus for much of the time. Even the plaintiff artist needed "careful scrutiny" to identify the photographs.

In both of these cases, prominence played a part. The unstated rule seems to be that if a normal viewer can see the artwork in an identifiable way (even if they don't know the name of the artist or the title of the work), then you better clear it or find something else or shoot it in a different way.

But prominence is in the eye of the beholder. For a case that might be decided the other way today, consider what happened when Columbia made a delightful movie called *Immediate Family* about a family anxious to adopt a baby. The family builds a nursery with a mobile suspended over the crib. The mobile contained a collection of little baby bears. The mobile also contained a copyright notice.

When Carola Amsnick saw the film, she had a mixed reaction. She was pleased that her artwork, which she had licensed to the makers of the copyrighted mobile, was used in the film and shown off in such a positive light. Exactly what the copyright holder would have wanted—if she had been asked. She wasn't asked, so she wasn't pleased. She paid a visit to a lawyer. (The phrase *paid a visit* must be short for *paid for a visit*.) The lawyer, in true professional style said, "We'll take them for every dime. I'll sue the bastards . . . and I will do it on contingency. You do not pay me unless we win."

They lost.

The court held that indeed the mobile was copyrighted, and no permission had been sought or received for the use of the mobile in the film. The court then concluded that this use would *not* require permission because such depiction in a film was not the kind of copying contemplated by the authors of copyright law. Specifically, the court stated that Columbia's "display of the mobile . . . is different in nature from her copyrighted design . . . [it is] not a mechanical copy . . . [it] can be seen only by viewing the film."

If this language is adopted by appellate courts, it could be one of the clearest statements (in my own personal view) that such items do not have to be cleared as matter of copyright law. The court was saying that a copyrighted artistic creation (other than a photo, poster, or piece of film) would never have to be cleared according to the copyright law. Other laws have to be considered, but as a matter of copyright law, no clearance is necessary because a film of such a creation being used does not form a "copy" of the work under the law. Rather, the film constitutes a picture of someone using the article. Note well that this logic does not apply to a film clip that you might want to use, because that is exactly the kind of copying that the copyright law was designed to prevent.

To be safe, the court added "and if this was copying, this use was a fair use." In fact, most of the opinion discussed fair use. The court went through the statutory tests: Yes, this was a commercial use that would cut against fair use. Yes, the entire mobile was used. Yes, it was used in shots throughout the film for a total of one minute and thirty-six seconds. But it was still held to be a fair use because there was no likelihood—in the court's view—that the mobile appearing in the film would in any way diminish sales of the mobile to parents. If anything, the court reasoned, the sales of the mobile would only be helped.

If contacted in advance, the copyright owner probably would have sent several mobiles to the set for free. If not, the producer could have gone on to the next mobile. One factor that triggered the lawsuit was a feeling of being ripped off when the artist learned that the studio had contacted other copyright holders and cleared their works. "Why not me?" is a question that inspires many lawsuits. This is exactly the problem with the studios' current practice of clearing so many items.

Copyright holders who might well be flattered if asked become uniformly angry when their creation is used without being asked. Unfortunately, lawyers and their letters in response to claims often make spontaneous apologies and genuine expressions of remorse difficult if not impossible. Posturing sets in. Lawsuits follow. Guess what? The lawyers win—and profit—again. A little time up front can save you a lot of time and money after the fact.

All of this raises serious questions for people who make documentary films. The courts have not yet been presented with the opportunity to address the difference between a documentary filmmaker who does not control what is on the walls being photographed and a feature fictional film producer who affirmatively selects set dressing. There is clearly a difference, and the court should cut some slack for people who make documentaries and just happen to catch a piece of art in the background.

State Law Protection—Moral Rights

The appellate court also said that Faith Ringgold, our feisty quilt-maker discussed above, had a claim under New York state law. The law is called the New York Artists' Authorship Rights Act, and it includes "the right of the artist to have his or her name appear on or in connection with such work as the artist." The producers of the television show in question took off the museum's name and also took off Faith's name. At least you could not see her name on screen. The court did not discuss the details of her rights other than to say that trial court had to look into the matter. Presumably, an end-roll credit would work just fine in fulfilling this obligation, but keep in mind that New York gives artists that right as a matter of state law.

New York isn't the only state that has laws to protect artists. Other states are granting visual artists a limited form of moral rights through various state laws. Since these artists do not work for the producer, they don't waive their moral rights. That is the opposite of what happens to writers. Writers routinely waive their moral rights. Studios insist on it. It has become the norm in the industry, and writers oblige because they do not have moral rights under the copyright laws of the U.S. anyway.

Buildings and Their Architectural Appointments

The copyright in architectural drawings does not prevent you from including the building in a shot. You do not need the permission of the architect (or whoever else) who owns the copyright in the drawings from which the building was built. You do not need the permission of the owner of the building as long as all you do is photograph the building as it normally appears from places where it is ordinarily visible from a public place. Obviously, if you go tramping around the building with your cameras, you will need a location agreement as discussed in Chapter 14. There is a handly location agreement in that chapter for you to use.

In modern buildings, there is often a fine line between what is a separate decorative sculpture and what is architecturally part of the building. Artwork that is commissioned to decorate a building can also serve as architectural features of the building.

Andrew Leicester sued Warner Bros. for using a copy of his sculpture *Zanja Madre* in *Batman Forever*. Worse, the sculpture showed up in a lot of the advertising for the picture. Warner's had obtained permission from the owners of the building where the sculpture was installed to film the location, but did not obtain permission from Leicester to film his work.

Zanja Madre was created for a building in downtown Los Angeles. It consists primarily of four sculpted towers. You might remember them from the advertising for *Batman Forever*. However, the court found that of the towers were part of a larger piece of work that defined the open space and helped direct the flow of foot traffic through the area. The court put this work on the architectural side of the architecture/decorative art divide. If that decision had gone the other way, Warner Bros. would have been looking at very large damages. Because this particular piece of sculpture was considered architectural, Leicester lost. You can photograph architectural works (from public places) to your heart's delight . . . without permission . . . and without payment. The problem is that it is not always easy to tell the difference between an architectural feature and decorative artwork.

Magazines, Newspapers, Books and Other Works that are not Decorative

The cover of every magazine and book and the front page of every newspaper is a creative work protected by copyright. Yet, these items are frequently used in movies. As long as the use shown in your film is the normal use and you use an actual copy of the article and not a derivative work that you did not have permission to create, you should be on solid ground. None of these items are decorative items. The law does not set out a list of what is and what is not a piece of decorative art and therefore protected by the cases discussed above. However, there are committee hearings and debates that take place before a piece of legislation is passed, and those contain a lot of specifics that are helpful in deciding exactly what is intended by the wording of the laws that are passed. Those documents informed both of these sections.

So strew your sets with as much authentic reading material as you like. It is protected by copyright, but this is not the kind of copying that is protected by the Copyright Act for these particular items. As long as the use is pure set dressing and not a plot point or visual focus of a scene, it is my opinion that you do not have to clear these items. No case holds to the contrary.

WHO TO TALK TO

As with other areas, sometimes the hardest part of the clearance process is finding out who should give you the permission you are seeking. Most of the objects you photograph do not need to be cleared. However, if you decide to clear the object, you have to reach the person who owns the copyright.

Typically, the person who sells the poster or picture rarely has any rights other than the right to sell you the single item you purchased. Homeowners rarely have any copyright interest in a painting or sculpture they "own." If the artist did not sign the work, inquire as to who created it. In most instances, the creator controls the copyright to the work. If you cannot determine the name of the artist, find out the name of the work. You can always do a copyright search to discover the name of the artist and the address, at least as of the time of registration. If the creator has died, you will have to identify and locate the heirs. As you can see, this is often a lot more troublesome than creating your own work.

If you still believe that you need a release, the one-page form at the end of this chapter should suffice. As with music agreements, the exact description of what you are licensing and how you are going to use it in your film are of the utmost importance.

If a jeweled dagger of exotic design is the murder weapon and is frequently photographed and handled and discussed and helps to twist (pun intended) the plot of a film, be sure to create it yourself or clear it. If the theft of a figurine of great value forms the basis of a film's plot, and is frequently photographed and discussed by the characters in the film, create it or clear it. There is no case to support this. This advice is based on my experience. The more important the use of a work, the more likely the owner of a copyright is going to press forward with a claim.

Be sure that anything you have created as a prop or piece of set decoration for your film is either a work for hire or you have a complete assignment of all the rights you need, in perpetuity, throughout the universe. In such a case, use the work for hire agreement for the writer of a script set out in Chapter 5 (except in Paragraph 3, use substitute language that describes the *exact* work you are having created).

TRADEMARKS

Trademark is an entire, separate, and distinct area of law, as is copyright. However, trademark protection contrasts sharply with the above discussion on copyrighted works.

A filmmaker's right to include trademarks within a film is clear. **Trademarks** are used by a manufacturer to identify the source of products: Coca-Cola, Infinity, IBM are all trademarks, and you have a right to include them in your film as long as the product bearing the trademark is used as it was intended to be used without any consequences of its use being abnormal or out of the ordinary.

There is one caveat: You do not have the right to commit trade libel in the name of entertainment. **Trade libel** occurs when a product or service is falsely accused of some bad attribute. You do not have the right to hold the product up to ridicule or do anything that harms the reputation of the product.

The law is developing regarding a true parody of trademark. A true trademark parody has not found its way to the U.S. Supreme Court. Federal appeal courts have written opinions on the subject that reflect very different attitudes ranging from strong trademark protection to strong protection for the right to make social commentary about a product and its trademark.

The clearest example of the protection a trademark enjoys is the familiar Dallas Cowboy cheerleader outfit. The distinctive white vest decorated with three blue stars on each side of the front and white fringe around the bottom, white vinyl boots, white shorts, a white belt decorated with blue stars, and a blue bolero blouse is their trademark. The trademark is owned by Dallas Cowboy Cheerleaders, Inc.

The year was 1979. The Dallas Cowboys were headed to the Super Bowl again. They were having a great year. The cheerleaders were not having such a great year. The Pussycat Cinema was playing the self-rated XXX *Debbie Does Dallas*. An outfit almost identical to the trademarked outfit appeared in key parts of the film, either on or off the actresses featured in this now-famous film. The sport was purely sexual.

The Dallas Cowboy Cheerleaders, Inc. sued. They had spent a lot of money and effort to create a certain image of the Dallas Cowboy Cheerleaders. The girls in the film did not fit that image.

The Cheerleaders won.

As the court correctly pointed out, "Trademark law not only serves to avoid the likelihood of public confusion, but also serves to protect the right of a trademark owner to control the product's reputation."

The court stopped Pussycat Theaters from all further showings of the film.

Pussycat appealed.

Pussycat lost again. The result was that the entire movie was worthless to Pussycat. There was no way to save it. The trademark was infringed throughout the film, even if the entire outfit was not worn in every scene. Interestingly, the cheerleaders failed to ask for an injunction against video distribution, so the film is still available to the persistent video aficionado.

Corporations live and die by their trademarks. A filmmaker has every right to dress sets with real products, but no right to disparage a trademark. If the movie does not misrepresent the source of the product and does nothing that would have a negative impact on the value of the trademark, there is no prohibition of the use of a trademark in a film. Remember, if anybody on Earth could consider your use damaging to a trademark, you'd better believe that the owner of the mark will move swiftly to correct the perceived wrong.

Trademark protection has exploded in the last decade well past the traditionally protected graphic labels such as Coca-Cola, Texaco, and Visa. The distinctive green-gold color of pads for dry cleaning presses was given protection. The theme songs used for Merrie Melodies® and Looney Tunes® are registered trademarks that create additional legal rights for the owners and potentially longer lives than the copyright law grants to owners. The meteorite shower passing behind the "N" in the logo for Netscape Communication has been registered by the Patent and Trademark Office.

PRODUCT PLACEMENT

The fact that you can include trademarks without receiving permission or paying compensation has an interesting effect. As in other areas of life, the largesse follows the law. As a filmmaker, you can dress your set with any products you like. Therefore, you can charge the owner of a trademark for the privilege of being selected for use in your film. This has grown up to be known as product placement. **Product placement** is the practice of receiving some consideration from the company that owns the trademark for using the product in a film. For independent films, it is often the supplying of drinks for a cast and crew, if the actors drink that brand on-screen. For larger films, cash payments might be made.

Airline or hotel rooms are often supplied in return for their logos or trademarks appearing on the screen.

In such cases, there usually are specific requirements about use and screen time for the product that are negotiated in advance. Ten seconds of screen time is a common minimum requirement. (Next time you see an airline logo in a film, count the number of seconds that it appears on the screen.) The value received by the filmmaker is directly related to screen time. Favorable lines from a lead actor are also valuable. Budget, cast, and projected distribution are also considered.

Most studios have someone on staff to help obtain product placements. At a minimum, the trade-outs help to hold down costs. There are companies that help independent filmmakers obtain product placement deals. Good Unit Production Managers have a list of product placement companies, such as International Promotions, (818) 755-6333.

If you are making a movie for television, product placement is not allowed without clear disclosure to the viewing audience. The FCC has provided very specific rules to cover the use of products on television. The payments and considerations discussed here for feature films are tightly regulated on programming designed for initial exhibition on television. However, once your theatrical movie is completed, the fact that you may have had one product placement deal (or two or more) does not in any way disqualify your film from television exhibition. If all this seems a bit illogical, fear not. Other areas of legislative conduct are even more difficult to bring within logic's steely discipline.

Knock-offs

Making a knock-off doesn't help. **Knock-off** is a slang term for something that has been created especially to appear very similar to another, often notable, thing. In fact, you have created new violations of the Copyright Act: You have created a derivative work without obtaining the permission of the owner of the copyrighted work from which your work derived. You might win your case if you had used the original, but you will certainly lose the portion of the case that charges you with crafting a derivative work without the permission of the copyright owner.

No matter what you are tying to knock off, there are inherent dangers. If it is an item protected by copyright, the law looks at a knock-off as a derivative work. The right to make derivative works is one of the absolute rights that the copyright holder controls. Creating one without permission is a great big "no-no" under the copyright law. If the item you want to knock off is a trademark, there are problems under the Lanham Act, which is the federal anti-trust legislation. If it is someone's voice, persona, or performance that you want to knock-off, there are problems involving the misappropriation of name and likeness.

The lesson is that you should create your own wonderment. Do not mimic others. It is lazy. It is frequently unlawful. And it is almost always less interesting than what you would come up with if you let your own creative juices flow.

DISTINCTIVE LOCATION

You should have a location agreement for each and every location you use. If it is a public street, park, or building, you may also need a permit from the appropriate governmental authority. As a threshold issue, these location agreements serve as your permission to be there and do what you are doing.

If you are using a distinctive location, the location agreement also serves as a release so that you can use the trademark or trade name associated with such a location and your own signage to create a new identification for the location. There are no appellate cases directly addressing the exact situations under which you need permission to use a real location in a film, but the copyright law has an explicit statement that copyright of a building's design does not preclude photographing the building from a public location.

The general principles of law would allow you to film anything visible to the general public so long as you do not defame or disparage it. However, if you depict a business location using its real signage, be careful about trade libel. For instance, if you show a real retail store that defrauds its customers in your movie, you need a release or you are committing trade libel against the store. Every Unit Production Manager worth their salt has a location agreement that grants the necessary permission to film at a certain location during certain hours and leave the place neat and clean when they finish. The location agreement at the end of this chapter also covers all the clearance issues we have been discussing in this book. It is a safe document for you to use. If a landlord balks at granting one of the permissions, you can then evaluate whether you need that specific permission. Simply line through those rights that you do not need. For instance, a landowner may say that you cannot use the real signage or that you must use the real signage. If that is all right with you, just change the agreement accordingly.

Finally, be sure that you are asking the right person for the permission you need. Virtually all the location disputes I have encountered grew out of, or were complicated by, obtaining permission from the wrong person. For instance, if you want permission to film in a certain generic location without any special identifiers, you probably can obtain valid consent from a tenant in possession. If you need to clear the use of signage, you need to talk to the owner of the sign, since it is the owner who has the right to withhold or grant that permission. If the signage is of a trademark that you plan to malign in some way, you have to have permission from the owner of that trademark, in addition to permission from the owner of the sign on which the trademark is located.

You are the filmmaker. It is your responsibility to think through these problems. You cannot expect a busy location manager to be as completely informed as you are. You cannot expect a location manager to be familiar with all the nuances of the multi-layered law of clearances. If you suspect a problem, just tell your location manager, "Please, get the owner to sign a location agreement also."

Always beware of crew members who say that they did things a certain way last time and nothing bad happened. That kind of experiential wisdom is exactly what gets a lot of people into trouble. People say, "We used this form on the last film and it worked." More often, the truth is that the form was not tested. Let's face it, 90% of the people in the world are not jerks, and you can talk through any questions that arise. Further, the famous "last film" might not have transgressed anybody's rights. They came, they shot, they left. In those situations, the particular form that was used "worked" because everything on the set worked. This book is focusing on what rights people have, how you can avoid transgressing those rights, and how you can get those rights waived if necessary.

SCRIPT CLEARANCE

There are a number of businesses and individuals who are in the business of script clearance. **Script clearance** is really a misnomer since no permissions are gained. Rather, these businesses and individuals provide the very useful service of flagging all the potential clearance problems contained in the script.

It is particularly helpful with matters that seem to have nothing to do with copyright. For instance, the script clearance service checks phone books in the locale where your film is supposed to be set to see if you are inadvertently using the name of a real person or a real business. They also check the area for real phone numbers. If a car's license number is readable on screen, they can check with the state's Department of Motor Vehicles to be sure that it doesn't belong to anybody.

Big problems arise when the phone number of an unknown person is used. The annoyance is minimal: You draw a nuisance suit that won't involve a lot of money, but . . . it is a nuisance. Even a number that is unassigned today may belong to some super sensitive soul tomorrow. You should use a number that will never be assigned to an individual or a business. They are 555-0100 to 555-0199 and (800) 555-0199. There are no 900 numbers that have been reserved for use in films.

The same is true for business names and individual names. Some people even seem to mind when you present the character in a totally positive light. You can imagine the reaction when the character is in any large or small way despicable or the business is engaged in anything mildly nefarious. Again, if you do not have someone do this checking for you, be sure to do it yourself. The safest thing is not to use a real name, or if you do, make sure that the name is of a friend or family member and that that person signs a release. The fact that another person with the same name might surface is of less concern if you are using the name of a specific living person who has given you permission to use it.

Clearance begins with a review of the script itself. A script clearance service provides a report that sets forth everything that could possibly need to be cleared. However, the report merely points out which items might have to be cleared—leaving the responsibility of deciding what to clear or change, what to leave, and when to accept the risk or obtain permissions to you or your attorney. The report alone does not protect your production company should a subsequent lawsuit be levied against it. It merely alerts you to possible problems.

The principle of clearance is equal to that of preventive medicine: Pay a little bit now for a check-up and avoid a major hospital bill later. It is beneficial to your production company to be fully covered by script clearance to reduce the risk of settlement costs, litigation, or judgments.

Many individuals and businesses are available to write script clearance reports. The studios generally do this work in-house. Here are three places to go for script clearance:

Joan Pearce Research   (213) 655-5464
Los Angeles, CA
http://home.earthlink.net/~jpr
jpra@pearceresearch.com

Marshall Plumb Research   (818) 848-7071
Burbank, CA
www.marshall-plumb.com
info@marshall-plumb.com

An excerpt from a typical script clearance report is attached at the end of this chapter. You can see from that report that it just lists the potential problems. A script clearance report for a feature film generally runs ten to twenty pages and costs about $1,500. It can be completed in a couple of weeks, unless you want to pay more for a rush job. Dealing with the issues raised by such a report is the subject of much of this chapter.

After you review the excerpt, you can understand why many makers of low-budget films decide to do this work for themselves, especially on films with a contemporary setting. With this book, you can decide what response you should have to each and every entry in the report.

As you look over the actual script clearance report, you will notice that everything possible is pointed out. Nothing is left to chance. Now that you have read this chapter, you know that the trademarks that are pointed out are not things to be concerned about so much as they are opportunities to hustle some product for your film. The buildings all have their own rules that are set out in this chapter under the location section. People and phone numbers raise issues as set out here also. Use the information in this chapter in conjunction with a thorough script clearance service to achieve maximum protection for your film.

14.01   **INDIVIDUAL RELEASE**

> *Note:* This has been prepared in the form of a letter to you the
> Producer to make it less formal and therefore less intimidating.

[date]

To: [your name]
      [your address]

This letter shall confirm that I, the undersigned person, for good
and valuable consideration, the receipt and sufficienty of which is
hereby acknowledged, has granted permission to you, the producer
and your successors, assignees and licensees to use my name and/
or likeness as such name and/or likeness appears in motion picture
photography shot in connection with the motion picture tentatively
entitled _____ and in connection with advertising,
publicizing, exhibiting and exploiting the Picture, in whole or in
part, by any and all means, media, devices, processes and technology now or hereafter known or devised in perpetuity throughout
the universe. I hereby acknowledge that you shall have no obligation to utilize my Name and/or Likeness in the Picture or in any
other motion picture.

> *Comment:* Many individuals will not authorize the use of their
> likeness in your advertising without substantial extra payment.
> It is generally not worth the extra money, so you may have to
> take out that provision.

Your exercise of such rights shall not violate or infringe any
rights of any third party. I understand that you have been induced
to proceed with the production, distribution and exploitation of
the Picture in reliance upon this agreement.

I hereby release you, your successors, assignees and licensees
from any and all claims and demands arising out of or in connection with such use, including, without limitation, any and all claims
for invasion of privacy, infringement of my right of publicity,
defamation (including libel and slander), false light and any other
personal and/or property rights.

Very Truly Yours,

[Releaser's signature]
[Releaser's name]
[Releaser's address]
[Releaser's Social Security no.]

> *Note:* If you are paying this person more than $600, you need
> the releaser's social security number so that you can fill out a
> W-2 tax form. Otherwise, leave it off.

Location of Property: _____

Description of Property: _____

Dates of Use: _____   Fee for Use: $_____

PICTURE: _____   PRODUCER: _____

In consideration of the payment of the above-indicated fee, the undersigned hereby grants to Producer, its successors and assigns the right to enter the area located as described above (hereafter "Property") on or about the dates listed above, for the purpose of photographing by motion picture, videotape, and still photography and to make sound recordings and to otherwise use for so-called "location" purposes (the results of which are hereafter collectively referred to as "Photographs"). If such photography is prevented or hampered by weather or occurrence beyond Producer's control, it will be postponed to or completed on such date as Producer may reasonably require. Said permission shall include the right to bring personnel and equipment (including props and temporary sets) onto the Property, and to remove the same therefrom after completion of work.

The undersigned hereby grants to Producer, its successors, assigns and licensees the irrevocable and perpetual right to use the Photographs of the Property taken by Producer hereunder in connection with motion picture, television photoplays or otherwise, and all the ancillary and subsidiary rights thereto of every kind and nature in such a manner and to such extent as Producer may desire. The rights granted herein include the right to photograph the Property and all structures and signs located on the Property (including the exterior and interior of such structures, and the names, logos and verbiage contained on such signs), the right to refer to the Property by its correct name or any fictitious name and the right to attribute both real and fictitious events as occurring on the Property and to fictionalize the Property itself. The undersigned hereby agrees and acknowledges that any and all Photographs made or to be made by Producer shall be Producer's sole and exclusive property and the undersigned shall have no claims thereto or rights therein or to the proceeds hereof.

Producer agrees to use reasonable care to prevent damage to the Property and to remove any and all property which Producer may place upon the Property in connection with its use thereof. Producer agrees to restore the Property as nearly as possible to its original condition at the time of Producer's taking possession thereof, reasonable wear and damage not caused by Producer's use excepted.

Producer hereby agrees to indemnify and hold the undersigned harmless from any claims and demands of any person or persons arising out of or based upon personal injuries and/or death suffered by such person or persons resulting directly from any act of negligence on Producer's part while Producer is engaged in the photographing of said Photographs upon the Property.

The undersigned hereby releases Producer and its licensees, successors, assigns, all networks, stations, sponsors, advertising agencies, exhibitors, cable operators and all other persons or entities from any and all claims, demands, or causes of action which the undersigned, its heirs, successors or assigns may now have or hereafter acquire by reason of Producer's photographing and using the Photographs taken of the Property, including, but not limited to, all buildings (exterior and interior), equipment, facilities and signs thereon.

The undersigned hereby represents and warrants that the undersigned is the _____ (fill in: owner, lessee or agent for the owner) of said Property and has the full right and authority to grant the license herein contained. The undersigned hereby indemnifies and agrees to hold Producer free and harmless from and against any and all liability, damages, claims, costs or fees, including but not limited to attorney fees, arising from, growing out of or concerning any breach by the undersigned of this warranty.

• • • • •

Go to Chapter 8, Provisions Common to Most Agreements, to finish up this contract. You should include the Arbitration paragraph and the Signature Block. Be sure to have this form countersigned by both the landlord and the tenant, if possible. Remember, there may be signage that presents separate issues.

14.03   EXCERPTS FROM A SCRIPT CLEARANCE REPORT

Client: **Vince Ravine**

Date: **July 31, 1996**

Research on: **"WORTH KILLING FOR,"** draft dated **5/4/96**

Type of Project: **motion picture**

We presume that this script is a work of fiction, is not based on any pre-existing work and does not reflect any data pertaining to actual persons (living or deceased) or events, unless otherwise noted.

<u>Locale</u>: **Santa Barbara, California**

<u>Time</u>: **Present**

<u>CAST</u>	<u>COMMENT</u>
Victor Chavez, p. 1	We find one listing for this name at Santa Barbara High School. Advise a change to avoid conflict.
Rick Turner, p. 1	We find one listing for this name in Santa Barbara. Advise a change to avoid conflict.
Troy Michaels, p. 1	We find no conflict.
Randy Chavez, p. 1	We find no conflict.
Jose, p. 4	Given name only. Not possible to check.
Chris, p. 4	Given name only. Not possible to check.
Angel, p. 56	Sobriquet use only.
Danton, p. 59	Surname use only; we find no conflict.
Moore, p. 68	Surname use only; we find one listing for this surname with the S.B. Police Dept. Advise a change to avoid conflict.

CLEARANCE	PAGE	COMMENT
AND COPYRIGHT	1	***A patrol car...TWO YOUNG COPS*** - Advise avoid identification of actual law enforcement agency through the use of protected badges, patches, logos, vehicles, motto, etc., without the express written permission of said agency.
244	1	***Charlie two seven*** - We find no conflict.
	1	***3727 Carrillo St.*** - We find no conflict for this address in Santa Barbara.
	6	***an ABANDONED BUILDING*** - Possible location agreement. Presume any names to be visible for signage will be checked through Research.
	6	***4107 Carson St.*** - We find a listing in the Santa Barbara area for Carson Street. Research is unable to verify street number; a change would be prudent.
	8	***overflowing with boxes*** - Advise do not identify any copyrighted or protected material, or any data pertaining to actual persons, firms or organizations.
	13	***Seaside Cantina*** - We find one listing for a Seaside Gallery & Cafe; a change would be prudent.
	17	***punches the button on his remote [car alarm]*** - Advise do not identify any copyrighted or protected material, or any data pertaining to actual persons, firms or organizations.
	17	***the radio dial*** - Advise do not identify any actual radio station, network or cable/satellite source by name, call sign or frequency, channel number, logo, etc. Permission advised for copyrighted or protected program material identifiable on screen or audio track. Advise check music clearance.
	20	***8 x 10 surfing pictures*** - Presume created especially for production and will not reflect any copyrighted or protected material. Permission is advised from any living photo subject identifiable on screen who is not a cast member.

PAGE	COMMENT

23   ***spray bottle of Binaca*** - Commercial identification in prop use.

24   ***Aloha Burger*** - We find one listing for a restaurant by this name in Santa Barbara; a change would be prudent.

29   ***Pelican's Nest*** - We find no conflict.

33   ***distinct-looking key chain*** - Advise avoid proprietary design.

33   ***music is softly playing*** - Advise check music clearance.

42   ***a PATROL CAR*** - See note above for p. 1 re: law enforcement.

43   ***Did you run the plates*** - Research can provide cleared license plate numbers if desired.

43   ***corner of Pine and Clayborn*** - We find no listing for a street named Clayborn in Santa Barbara. We find one listing for a Pine Drive and one listing for Pine Avenue. Do not find use here to conflict.

43   ***News crew unloads equipment*** - Advise avoid identification of actual newspapers, magazines, wires or news services, radio or TV stations or networks, or other media firms or organizations.

44   ***Paramedic holding a one-year-old*** - Advise do not identify any actual hospital, care facility or ambulatory service by name, uniform, logo, badge, design, etc.

45   ***High school yearbook*** - Advise do not identify any copyrighted or protected material, or any data pertaining to actual persons, firms or organizations.

45   ***another photo...INSERT - ON PHOTO...other photographs*** - See note above for p. 20 re: photographs.

46   ***INSERT - ON PHOTO*** - As above.

46   ***Olive Oil*** - Reference in dialogue to character "Olive Oyl" from Popeye cartoon.

CLEARANCE AND COPYRIGHT	PAGE	COMMENT
	68	***EXT. ANTONIO'S CAFE*** - We find one listing in the Santa Barbara area for a restaurant called Antonio's; to avoid possible conflicts, suggest change.
	81	***loud music blasting*** - Advise check music clearance.
246	86	***a small VIAL*** - Advise do not identify any copyrighted or protected material, or any data pertaining to actual persons, firms or organizations.
	86	***rocks to the music*** - Advise check music clearance.
	88	***her computer screen*** - Advise avoid commercial identification of computer hardware and software, particularly screen design and sound effects as generated by any copyrighted software. Advise do not identify any data pertaining to actual persons, firms or organizations on computers or peripherals.
	92	***EXT. A PARKING LOT*** - Possible location agreement. Presume any names to be visible for signage will be checked through Research.
	93	***EXT. DENNY'S RESTAURANT*** - Location agreement. NOTE: We find no listing for a Denny's restaurant in Santa Barbara; a change would be prudent.

CHAPTER 15

CLEARING ALL THE MUSIC IN YOUR FILM

This chapter discusses clearing pre-existing music for use in your film. After reading it, you will probably be convinced that you do not want to clear the music yourself, so I will provide a list of reputable businesses that will clear such music for you. Using a composer to write original music throughout your film avoids the music clearance problems discussed in this chapter (as discussed in the next chapter).

CLEARING PRE-EXISTING MUSIC

Unless you only show your film in a classroom, clearing the music you are going to use in your film is an absolute necessity. No exceptions. Be absolutely confident that Murphy's Law exists. If only one person ever sees your film in a theater or on television or at a festival, the writers (or the owners) of the music contained in your film will hear about it. As soon as they hear about it, they call their agent. Their agent then calls you if you have not cleared the music. It happens every time!

Clearing pre-existing music involves a procedure that sounds simple, but has many pitfalls. To clear music means to obtain the permissions you need to use the music in your film. Your film cannot be exhibited publicly without a specific grant to do so from the owners of the music that can be heard in your film. This applies to the music that is intentionally included in your film, as well as that music which is merely part of the ambient noise picked up during a location shoot. Either way, the music must be cleared. Music clearance is the producer's responsibility.

You must pay very close attention to the legalities of music clearance. The consequence of not properly clearing a song is that the rights holder can obtain a speedy and virtually automatic injunction against further exhibition of your film until the music is removed or the music rights are cleared (and paid for). At that point, the cost of those rights almost always skyrockets, because you have eliminated a lot of choices. You either pay the owner of the music rights whatever punitive price is being asked, or you take the music out of your movie. You also may be working under tremendous time pressure at that point, especially if your film is actually in release or scheduled to play an important festival. This is a situation in which you never want to find yourself.

The steps to clearing pre-existing music sound simple enough. However, the process is so difficult and frustrating that most people use the services of someone else to perform this task. Even if you use an outside service for music clearance, you should be familiar with what they do and how they do it. It's as easy as 1, 2, 3 . . . and then you pay the fee.

STEP 1: Locate the Rights Holder(s)
STEP 2: Negotiate the Deal
STEP 3: Send Out or Request the Contract (Licenses)

This may seem mighty simplistic. Read on. Each step can be a daunting task. And keep in mind that this process only obtains the right to use the music and does NOT include the right to use a specific recording of the music. That is covered later in the chapter.

STEP 1: Locate the Rights Holder

The first step is bewildering to most filmmakers. Actual ownership of music rights can be a very complex question, since several people can collaborate to create a single composition. Further, a copyright can be divided into separate parts with each owned individually or by several parties.

Generally, a writer sells or assigns the copyright in his song to a music publisher. A **music publisher** manages the right to reproduce the music and collects the money for the writer from the royalties derived from its exploitation (less a fee, of course). A music publisher may be a lawyer, a manager, a person who does nothing but manage such rights for others, or a company owned by the songwriter and set up to manage a catalogue of music as a separate business. The songwriters themselves (acting as music publishers) may license their own works in their own names. You must contact the music publisher(s) of the music you wish to use in order to obtain the rights you need. One of the things that makes this process difficult is that publishers frequently buy and sell entire catalogues. The owner of the publishing rights one year may have passed them along to another company the next year. Tracking this ownership can be like following a trail of breadcrumbs.

For publisher contact information, you can try one of the three performing rights societies. A **performing rights society** is an organization that monitors the performance of music and collects royalties from performances on radio and television, concert arenas, in restaurants, lounges, even bars, hotels, and retail stores playing music on a radio, and workout/dance studios playing music for aerobics classes. Representatives of one of three performing rights societies visit all these entities to collect a fee for the performance of music in their establishment. In Europe, similar societies (usually allied with U.S. societies) collect royalties for music performance, including performances that occur when a film is shown in the theater. In America, those societies are:

ASCAP:	Los Angeles: (323) 883-1000
	New York: (212) 621-6000
	www.ascap.com
	licensing@ascap.com
BMI:	Los Angeles: (310) 659-9109
	New York: (212) 586-2000
	www.bmi.com
	LosAngeles@bmi.com
	NewYork@bmi.com
SESAC:	Los Angeles: (310) 393-9671
	New York: (212) 586-3450
	Nashville: (615) 320-0055
	www.sesac.com
	sjungmichel@sesac.com

These societies do *not* have anything to do with licensing the rights you need for feature films, even though they are at the heart of collecting the royalties for performances of music. They collect royalties for music included in films when it is performed during a broadcast of the film on worldwide television, or in foreign movie theaters in Europe. They could tell you who the publisher is for most songs you want to use in your film because they mail royalty checks to these publishers. However, helping filmmakers is not their business. Such information can only be extracted with finesse and diplomacy. Ask for the "Research Department" and be nice to the person who answers the phone, or go online and search the database yourself.

It is most often the publisher, not the writer, who has the authority to grant permission to use music in a film, even though the publisher may have to ask for the writer's approval. Be forewarned: Obtaining all the rights you need is not necessarily one-stop shopping. There may be several publishers involved, even on a single piece of music, because each person who wrote on the song enough to co-own the copyright could have his or her own publisher.

If none of the above works out, your best bet is to contact one of the music clearance houses listed later in this chapter. They have data on many publishers, and, if they don't have data on the one who controls the rights to the music you wish to use, they have the proper contacts to find the person who controls these rights.

STEP 2: Negotiate the Deal

This section deals with obtaining the right to use the music itself, whether you arrange to have it performed or you license a specific recording of it. If you want to use a specific recording of a song, you must go through all these steps for the song itself, and then go through a similar process for the specific sound recording of the song that you want to use. Be sure to review the next section of this chapter if you also want to use a specific recording of pre-existing music.

If you are clearing the music yourself, start your search for the music publisher. They will ask you to send a request on your letterhead describing your film and listing the music you wish to use, including how you intend to use it and the approximate length of that use. Then they will provide a quote that is good for ninety days. Be sure to obtain this written quote *before* the final mix. Usually, you don't sign the actual contract until after the final mix.

Remember that you are asking permission to use something that is owned by someone else. Most copyright owners want to maximize income from their music. That involves protecting it, in a certain sense, from any use that would lower its value. Sometimes that can result in a very unreceptive attitude. For instance, the rights to *Porgy and Bess* are very closely controlled by George Gershwin's heirs. The property is very close to their hearts, and the music from it is not necessarily available to you. The heirs are very protective. At the other extreme, a motivation to maximize income may cause the negotiation to focus purely on money demands, and the copyright holder hits you for everything they think that they can get. A very popular and much-used song such as "Happy Birthday" usually has a rate card with prices that depend on the budget of the film.

Your task, then, is to convince the publisher that you are making a good film, but that you do not have a lot of money. It is also important to determine the music's role in the film: whether it's playing in the background, performed in the movie by one of the characters, performed over the credits, or—like *Pretty Woman*—used as the title of the film. Each one of these uses is progressively more expensive to obtain. If you specify background music and end up using the song as a featured song, you will be in trouble. You must specify the length of the piece of music you want to use and describe the scene or scenes in which the music is to be used. Be accurate. The contract includes this information. This information defines the limit of the permission that is granted. Disclose the scenes as accurately as possible. Some owners may not want their music used as the background for certain kinds of scenes such as a suicide or a sexually explicit scene.

If you have not found your distributor, you may not be able to afford to license the music for the broad use that you want. In this case, you can obtain a much cheaper "Festival License" that grants synch licenses for limited festival exhibition. This is usually a few hundred dollars instead of a few thousand dollars. Be sure to obtain a quote for full rights and mention it specifically in your festival license agreement. That way you know exactly what your licensing budget will be if a distributor is interested in your film. You may meet resistance on this point, but press on. You don't want to be held up if you obtain distribution. Having this information is good business, and it makes you look more professional to potential distributors.

Take care in obtaining all the rights you need. Generally speaking, the rights that you want to obtain from the publisher or copyright owner can be divided into the following two broad categories: Public Performance Rights and Reproduction Rights. These are the rights contained in a standard synch license agreement, such as the one at the end of this chapter (Form 15.01). You may want to look over that form now to learn about the various elements you will be negotiating.

Public Performance Rights

Public performance rights cover the right to perform a piece of music in public. Licensing this right allows you to recite, play, sing, dance, or act out a piece of music. (Performance of a song or other piece of music by itself, apart from a play or a film, is referred to as **small rights**. Performance of a song or other piece of music as an integral part of a play or a film is called **grand rights**.) When your movie is run in a theater, the music in your film is being performed for the paying audience that is present to watch the film. In almost all of the world, except the United States, the owner of the publishing rights in the music receives a royalty payment for these public performances independent of any money received from the producer of the film.

In the United States, because of a specific court decree, the performing rights societies do not collect performing fees from motion picture theaters. You must secure the United States theatrical performance license directly from the publisher or agent when securing a synchronization license. Outside the United States, local performing rights societies collect a percentage of the box office receipts from theaters exhibiting your film and remit it to the proper person, usually the publisher, who turns it over to the composer or splits it between the composer and the producer depending on the agreement between the two.

Reproduction Rights

The publisher/copyright owner has the right to control who, how, when, where, and for how much money a piece of music is reproduced. These rights to reproduce a piece of music are again divided into two categories: synchronization rights, which you always need, and mechanical rights, which are commonly—but not always— needed. You must obtain synchronization rights, which are most often referred to as synch rights. **Synch rights** are the rights to record music as part of your film. The name of this right comes from the fact that the music is synchronized to visual images. It always excites me to watch a studio orchestra feverishly playing music to a projected film. The conductor stares at the images on the screen. The musicians stare at the conductor. The concentration is intense. The process of synchronizing the music with the moving image is one of the most exciting parts of the whole filmmaking process. **Mechanical rights** are needed when the music is to be reproduced on audio records, CDs, or tapes. You definitely need mechanical rights if a soundtrack album is released. Mechanical rights are automatically granted. However, few independent films are able to support a soundtrack album, so you may decide to forego the extra expense of obtaining these rights.

Out-of-Context Rights

These are not really separate rights. They are just the above two rights when the music is used in a trailer in a way different from its use in the film. If you wish to use music from your film in the trailer for your film, you need to get specific permission to do so. You usually have to pay extra for this permission, because you are using the music to advertise your film. That tells the publisher with whom you are negotiating that the music in question has unusual importance to the success of your film. Many producers find it is cheaper and more effective to have the music for the trailer composed especially for that purpose.

Adaptation Rights

If you are going to change or add to the music or lyrics you license, you need permission to do that also. When it comes to music and lyrics, the rights holder almost always wants to see your adaptation before giving final approval. Without written permission from the owner, you do not have the right to change a note of the music or a word of the lyrics, or to add either notes or words. It's not your music. You don't own it. Therefore, you can't change it—without permission.

Other Deal Points

The price for the rights you need covers a wide range. Songs are unique, but you should make a list of acceptable alternative pieces so that you are not stuck with only one choice. You are always in a better negotiating position if you have alternatives. There are many barriers to obtaining a particular song for your film besides money: There may be a contest over ownership. Exclusivity may have been granted to someone else. You may not be able to find the publisher quickly, or the person who can negotiate the deal may be on vacation. Always, always have other choices for the music in the film.

As you negotiate, be sure that you are obtaining all the necessary film rights—worldwide—in perpetuity. Unless you are *sure* that you are going to give the film only a limited release, obtain all rights. Because of the use of satellites for transmission and the possibility of permanent space stations, many people like to use the phrase "throughout the universe" instead of "throughout the world."

The phrase "in perpetuity" suggests the possibility of obtaining permission to use the music for more than the life of the copyright. The current length of copyright is the life of the author plus seventy years, which could put copyright ownership into the next century. An increasing number of people believe that since most countries have a longer copyright life than we do, the copyright life in the United States ought to be lengthened. You seldom save any money on the feature film rights by obtaining a shorter license than perpetuity. In spite of the use of the word "perpetuity," such a grant cannot give you a license any longer than the license granted by the words "for the full term of the copyright, including any and all renewals and extensions," because no one can sell or license more than they own. The copyright owner does not own anything after the copyright has lapsed.

You also need to obtain television rights for eventual domestic and foreign syndication, cable, and home video. Interactive and multimedia rights are highly desirable but may be too expensive. A lot of producers chuckle at a phrase commonly used by entertainment lawyers: "all media whether now existing or hereafter invented." That phrase didn't exist in very early contracts. Increasingly, the potential value of newly invented media—often called new technologies—is being appreciated. For instance, the courts have ruled that television rights do not include videocassette rights. If the filmmaker did not have a specific grant of videocassette rights or the very broad grant of rights created by that catchphrase, the filmmaker is out of luck. That fine print and those silly-sounding phrases can mean big bucks in the future.

STEP 3: Send Out or Request the Contract

Remember, you are dealing with rights flowing from copyright. You *must* have a signed agreement for your permission to have legal meaning. This is not an area in which an oral understanding can be enforced. Almost all other aspects of human conduct can be effectuated through an oral agreement. That is *not* true for rights that flow through copyright.

Many publishers have their own agreement. If you do this yourself, you want to use the agreement in this book. You have plenty of time now to read it over and understand it. It is fairly short, but it is complete. It does the job.

Fortunately for you, this signed agreement with its airtight indemnity clause is all that the insurance company requires. They do not require the person who grants the music license to prove their chain of title. If the custom and practice required such proofs, your task as producer would be much more difficult.

CLEARING THE USE OF A SPECIFIC RECORDING

You want to use a specific recording of music. You do not want to hire musicians to play the song. You have a specific favorite recording in mind and that is what you want to use. This situation usually occurs for specific vocalists, but it can also arise for a recording without vocals. Note that a specific sound recording of a song has its own copyright dating from the creation of the recording. This means that even though the music itself may be in the public domain, the recording of that song still may be protected by copyright. It also means that even though you have just gone through all the steps to obtain permission to use the music in your film, you still need to obtain the right to use the master recording in your film.

The song "Thriller" (written by Rod Temperton and controlled by Almo/Irving Music) and the recorded performance of "Thriller" (by Michael Jackson and owned by SONY Music Entertainment, Inc.) are two separate copyrights, each of which requires individual prior clearance if you want this specific recording in your film. In that case, you have to negotiate with the persons who own the copyright to the song and the copyright to the specific sound recording you want to use.

STEP 1: Locate the Rights Holder

Usually the correct entity to contact is the recording company. The recording company is almost always listed on the record jacket, the tape box, or the CD sleeve. This usually makes it easier than locating the holder of the publishing rights to the underlying music. Remember that compilation CDs are third-party licenses, so you have to read the liner notes to discover the correct contact for your purpose.

STEP 2: Negotiate the Deal

Generally, this negotiation is commenced as soon as you think that you are able to close the deal to use the song. The record company often has to get the artist's approval in order to grant these rights.

All the rules and comments about negotiating for songs apply to the process of negotiating for a specific sound recording. However, you are more likely to face an inquisition about your film when you are asking for the right to integrate a specific sound recording into your film than when you are seeking the music only. Owners of the copyright of a specific recording of a song tend to be much more protective. This may be especially intense in the case of a well-known vocalist or band. Also, the holders of master-use rights do not receive performance royalties. That is why their prices are sometimes a bit higher.

STEP 3: Send Out or Request the Contract

A typical contract to license a recording is called a **master use license**. This name refers to the fact that you are licensing the use of the master recording of a song. A short but satisfactory license can be found at the end of this chapter if the rights holder does not issue their own license agreement.

The specific description of the recording, the length of use, whether the recording will be edited, and the scenes in which it is to be used are set out in the contract. This description defines exactly what you have the right to use. You cannot use the recorded music differently from the way you describe it being used in the contract. You cannot use a different recording of the music, no matter how similar the sounds.

In *9 1/2 Weeks*, there was a seductive food scene that is credited for making Kim Basinger a star. It contains the song "Bread and Butter" by the musical group The New Beats. Although the filmmakers had permission to use this song, the album they intended to use had a scratch, so they went to the store to get another album. They bought a K-tel album with the song "Bread and Butter" and used this track. When the band heard the song, they were angry because the K-tel version was not the recording for which the rights were granted. K-tel produces collections of various artists' hit songs, but does not always use the original recording. K-tel may have a soundalike band perform the hit or have it re-recorded. **Soundalike** is filmmaker slang for one group legally recording a song in the manner and style of another group. In response to claims by artists such as Bette Midler and Tom Waites (see Chapter 4), courts are beginning to move against vocal soundalike recordings in advertising but have not ruled against soundalike band music in such non-advertising uses of music as film and television.

The filmmakers mentioned above did not notice an audible difference after listening to the two recordings of the song "Bread and Butter." Nevertheless, as a matter of law, they had to correct the mistakes. They had to pay for the master they did use. They had to fix the credits. They had to mollify The New Beats (probably with cash).

Note that the innocence of the filmmaker was not much help in this scenario. Accidental or not, the uncleared sound recording was a part of the film. The choice was simply to take it out or pay whatever the owner demanded.

Music clearance is one of the most technically exacting aspects of all the clearance issues that are presented in the making of films. It is also one of the most unforgiving. You must get it exactly right or you face a claim that is usually pretty clear-cut in favor of the claimant.

Sometimes this can be used to advantage. The film *It's a Wonderful Life* fell into the public domain. Republic Pictures forgot to renew the copyright under the old law, which required renewal after twenty-eight years. But they hired a copyright clearance house and a team of clever Los Angeles lawyers, who contacted the copyright holders of five songs on the soundtrack of *It's a Wonderful Life* and obtained the exclusive synchronization rights to that music. They also obtained the right to bring suit on behalf of the music's copyright owners. They used those rights to control the licensing of the film. You could still broadcast *It's a Wonderful Life*, but you would have to broadcast it with no music or create a brand-new soundtrack that does not have some of the songs contained in the original film. Not an easy task.

MUSIC CLEARANCE HELP

It is easy to understand why so many people use music clearance houses to do all the above-mentioned chores. Because they handle a volume of business, professional music clearance people can accomplish the necessary tasks in a fraction of the time that you would take. Sometimes they can even negotiate a better price, based on their ongoing relationship with licensors. Therefore, the net costs of their services are quite reasonable.

In Los Angeles:

The Music Bridge, LLC www.themusicbridge.com thebridge@aol.com	(310) 398-9650
The Copyright Clearing House, Ltd. www.musicreports.com	(818) 558-3480
Diane Prentice - Music Clearance	(818) 830-1270
Suzy Vaughan Associates, Inc. www.suzyvaughan.com svaughan@suzyvaughan.com	(310) 556-1409

Evan M. Greenspan Inc. (EMG)   (818) 762-9656
www.clearance.com
emginc@clearance.com

Other:

B.Z. Rights (New York)   (212) 580-0615
www.bzrights.com
info@bzrights.com

Diamond Time Ltd. (New York)   (212) 274-1006
www.diamondtime.net
info@diamondtime.net

Clearance Quest (Tennessee)   (615) 356-3345
photogal1@prodigy.net

Copyright Music & Visuals (Canada)   (416) 979-3333
www.copyrightmv.com
info@copyrightmv.com

There are also many twists in music clearance that the professionals know about and are beyond the scope of this book. Consider the so-called "*Rear Window*" case from Chapter 2. In general terms, songs copyrighted in the United States before January 1, 1978, are entitled to two terms of copyright protection: a first copyright term of twenty-eight years and a renewal term of forty-seven years—for a total of seventy-five years. If the composer died while the song you want to use was still in the first term of copyright, your licenses may be unenforceable unless you deal with the person who renewed the copyright. Furthermore, in other cases where the copyrighted work was in its first term of copyright after January 1, 1978, certain authors are entitled to a renewal and extension of the copyright in such work for the further term of forty-seven years, which is a total of seventy-five years.

Clearance houses also prepare contracts, collect the necessary fees from you, and forward these fees to various rights holders. Finally, the clearance service (for an additional fee) prepares and distributes the music cue sheet. A **music cue sheet** is a very important document that lists, in order of performance, each song or portion of a song and each underscore cue used in the film along with the composers, publishers, performing rights affiliations (ASCAP or BMI or SESAC), usage, and timing of each piece of music. The Performing Rights Societies use music cue sheets to determine who receives royalties for the public performance of the music on television stations and in theaters outside the United States.

THE MUSIC SUPERVISOR

If music is going to be an important part of the film, you may want to hire an experienced music supervisor to help you achieve the right sound. A **music supervisor** is the person who helps select music, supervise the clearing of music, hire a composer, and supervise the recording of the score. Often this person is also a composer or musician. The music supervisor can sometimes help obtain a soundtrack album deal.

A good music supervisor, such as David Powell of MusicBridge or Nic Harcourt, perform many more functions than can be included in this book.

15.01   SYNCHRONIZATION AND PERFORMANCE
RIGHTS AGREEMENT

1.   The musical composition (the "Composition") covered by this license is: _____ and was written by: _____ (the "Writer").

2.   The motion picture (the "Picture") covered by this license is: _____.

[Include other identifying details in addition to the title.]

3.   The type and number of uses of the Composition to be recorded are: _____. [Be very specific and complete in describing how the music is going to be used in your film. Be sure to include the maximum length you want to use.]

4.   The "Territory" covered hereby is: _____. [the world or the universe]

5.   Provided the Composition is included in the Picture, Producer shall pay Publisher the sum of $_____ upon the earlier of thirty (30) days after the Producer enters a distribution agreement for the Picture or upon first commercial exploitation, _____ ("Publisher") hereby grants to _____ [Production company], its successors and assigns ("Producer") the non-exclusive, irrevocable right, license, privilege and authority to record, dub and synchronize, in each country of the territory, the aforesaid type and use of the Composition in synchronization or in timed relation with the Picture, but not otherwise, and to make copies of such records and import said recordings and/or copies thereof into any country in the Territory and exploit, market and perform said Picture perpetually throughout each country in the Territory in all media and by all devices, whether now known or hereafter invented, including, without limitation, videocassettes, videodiscs and other audio-visual devices, all in accordance with and subject to the term and limitations hereinafter set forth.

> **Note:** Fees are negotiable. Most publishers will require payment with this agreement _before_ they countersign. What you get is a non-exclusive license. Other filmmakers can use the same music.

> **Comment:** This is also where the language should be inserted if you can't afford all of the above rights and are just obtaining a festival license. Language such as the following should suffice, although many publishers have their own version of a festival rights license that they prefer to use. Obviously, you will have to fill in the proper amount, but in your negotiations start with the $100 that I inserted the form.

> *"For twelve (12) months from the date of this agreement, Producer may exhibit the Motion Picture in the Territory at film festivals and private-invitation screenings for which the Producer receives no compensation for the purpose of promoting the Motion Picture and/or obtaining distribution for the Motion Picture for a flat fee of $250, payable upon execution hereof."*

6.   Publisher hereby grants to Producer the non-exclusive, irrevocable right and license to publicly perform for profit or non-profit and authorize others so to perform the Composition in the exhibition of the Picture to audiences in motion picture theaters and other places of public entertainment where motion pictures are customarily exhibited in the United States and its possessions (the "U.S."), including the right to televise the Picture into such theaters and such other public places, with the understanding and upon the condition that the Picture shall not be exhibited in the U.S. by means of television for any other purpose whatsoever, except according to the next paragraph.

7.   The right to perform the Composition in the exhibition of the Picture in the U.S. by means of television (other than as described in Paragraph 6 hereinabove), including by means of "free television," "basic cable television," "pay television," "subscription television," "satellite," "CATV" and "closed-circuit into home television" is and shall be available only under the following circumstances:

(a) The public performance of the Picture may be made by means of television by networks, local stations or closed-circuit systems having valid performance licenses from the American Society of Composers, Authors and Publishers ("ASCAP") or Broadcast Music, Inc. ("BMI"), as the case may be.

(b) The public performance of the Picture by means of television by networks, local stations or closed-circuit systems not licensed for television by ASCAP or BMI is subject to clearance of the performing rights either from Publisher or ASCAP or BMI or from any other licenser acting for or on behalf of Publisher.

> **Note:** *This insures that the composer gets paid for U.S. television exhibition. Television networks in the U.S. generally pay blanket licenses for music. A* **blanket license** *is a license obtained by the periodic payment of a flat fee for the right to perform various pieces of copyrighted music. Logs of the music played during each quarter of the year are sent to the performing rights societies, where the fees are divided up among the various publishers.*

8.   It is understood that clearance by performance rights societies in such portion of the Territory as is outside of the U.S. will be in

accordance with their customary practices and the payment of their customary fees.

9.   Publisher hereby further grants to Producer, in each country of the Territory, the non-exclusive right to cause or authorize the fixing of the Composition in and as part of the Picture on audio-visual contrivances now or hereafter known such as Video Records (including videocassettes, videotapes, DVDs and similar compact audio-visual devices) and:

(a) To utilize such Video Records for any of the purposes, uses and performances hereinabove set forth; and

(b) To sell, lease, license or otherwise make such Video Records available to the public as a device intended primarily for "home use" (as such term is commonly understood in the phonograph record industry).

The foregoing rights granted in this Paragraph may be exercised by Producer without any additional fee or royalty to Publisher.

Producer shall accord the following end-roll credit on all prints of the Picture, together with a similar credit for other music used in the Picture, substantially as follows:

_____

_____

10.   This license does not authorize or permit any use of the Composition not expressly set forth herein and does not include the right to alter the fundamental character of the music of the Composition, to use the title or subtitle of the Composition as the title of a motion picture, to use the story of the Composition or to make any other use of the Composition not expressly authorized hereunder.

> **Note:** *This form is designed for producers. Expect the publisher to strike "the fundamental character of." Also, this paragraph specifically confirms that this synch license does not grant "film rights to the song's story" or to the title of the song as the title of your film.*

11.   The recording and performing rights hereinabove granted include such rights for screen, video and television trailers for the advertising and exploitation of the Picture.

> **Note:** *Expect to pay extra—up to 25%—for this right. It is not always worth extra to independent filmmakers but try the above language in your first draft.*

12. The recording and performing rights hereinabove granted shall enure for the periods of all copyrights in each country of the Territory in and to the Composition, and any and all renewals or extensions thereof in each country of the Territory that Publisher may now own or control or hereafter own or control without Producer having had to pay any additional consideration therefor.

13. Producer agrees to furnish Publisher a cue sheet of the Picture within thirty (30) days from the first public exhibition of the Picture at which admission is charged (except so-called "sneak previews").

14. No failure by Producer to perform any of its obligations hereunder shall constitute a breach hereof, unless Publisher gives Producer written notice of such non-performance and Producer fails to cure within sixty (60) days of receipt of such notice.

> **Note:** *Cure periods are good, but you'll be lucky to get thirty days to cure. Only an unattentive publisher will allow sixty days.*

15. Any dispute between the parties shall be settled by arbitration before a single arbitrator according to the rules of the AFMA. In no event will Publisher have a right to enjoin or restrict the exploitation of the Picture.

The parties agree to the above effective as of _____, 200__.

Publisher: _____   Producer: _____

_____   _____

_____   _____
(address)   (address)

> **Note:** *Go to Chapter 8 to finish up this document by adding the Representation and Warranty, the Indemnification paragraph and the Remedies paragraphs.*

THIS AGREEMENT is made and entered effective _____, 200__ by and between _____ ("Producer") located at _____ and _____ ("Owner") located at _____.

1.   The musical composition (the "Composition") covered by this license is: _____ and was written by: _____ (the "Writer").

2.   The recording of the Composition (the Master) covered by this license is: _____

3.   The motion picture (the "Picture") covered by this license is: _____.
[Include other identifying details in addition to the title.]

4.   The type and number of uses of the Composition to be recorded are: _____.
[Be very specific and complete in describing how the music is going to be used in your film. Be sure to include the maximum length you want to use.]

5.   The "Territory" covered hereby is: _____.
[the world or the universe]

6.   (a) Owner hereby grants Producer, Producer's successors and assigns, the non-exclusive worldwide right, license and authority to use the Master solely in synchronization or in timed relation with the Picture in any and all media now known or hereafter devised and by all devices including, without limitation, videocassette, videodiscs and other audio-visual devices embodying substantially the entire Picture, all in accordance with and subject to terms hereinafter set forth; provided, however, that Producer shall not be permitted to use the Master in any device which allows the viewer to manipulate the images and/or audio program material in a non-linear (i.e., non-sequential) progression. Owner reserves the rights not expressly granted to Producer hereunder.

> **Note:** *This grant does not allow you to use the music in the trailer or advertisements for the film. If you want that you will have to ask for it and pay for it. This is the right to use the master out of the context of the movie you are making.*

   (b) In consideration of the rights granted to Producer hereunder, Producer shall pay to Owner the sum of $_____, payable upon execution of this license.

> *Note:* You might want to do the step deal described in the Synch license. If so, be sure to set out the step payments for the festival license and then for the broader use required here. In that case, you will only have to pay a small fee to run the film at festivals and a larger fee only if you obtain distributors.

7.   Producer shall accord Owner and Artist appropriate credit on all prints of the Picture, together with similar credit for other recordings used in the Picture, substantially as follows:

---

8.   Owner shall provide Producer with all the necessary information to enable Producer to pay all reuse fees which may be required by the applicable unions, in accordance with said unions' contracts and regulations. Producer hereby agrees to pay all such reuse fees and any and all pension and/or welfare payments required with respect to Producer's use of the Master as provided herein. Producer hereby agrees to defend, indemnify and hold Owner harmless from and against any and all claims, demands or actions with respect to such fees and payments.

> *Note:* Be sure to figure this out ahead of time. This is extra money you may have to pay to performers who are members of the American Federation of Musicians.

9.   Producer shall be solely responsible for obtaining the appropriate synchronization and performance license from the copyright owner or controller of the musical composition embodied in the Master and for paying all fees with respect thereto. Producer hereby agrees to defend, indemnify and hold Owner harmless from and against any and all claims, demands or actions with respect to such fees and payments.

10. The term of this Agreement is for the remainder of the current term of the United States copyright in the Master of the sound recording (and in the renewal term thereof, if any).

11. **NO OBLIGATION TO PRODUCE:** Nothing herein shall be construed to obligate Producer to produce, distribute, release, perform or exhibit any production based upon or suggested by the results of Writer's services hereunder.

12. **REPRESENTATIONS AND WARRANTIES:** Owner represents, warrants and agrees that it has the right and authority to enter this agreement and that:

(a) The Work itself is original with Owner and no part of the Work is in the public domain;

(b) Owner has not and will not enter into any agreements or activities which will hinder, compete, conflict or interfere with the exercise of any of the rights granted to Producer. Owner has no knowledge of any claim or potential claim by any party which might in any way affect Producer's rights herein;

(c) The Work does not, and no use thereof will, infringe upon or violate any personal, proprietary or other right of any third party, including, without limitation, defamation, libel, slander, false light or violation of any right of privacy or publicity or any copyright law.

(d) The exercise of the rights herein granted to Producer will not in any way, directly or indirectly, infringe upon any rights of any person or entity whatsoever.

> **Comment:** *We see these so often that we forget how important they are. Read them over. Of course, your deal is premised on these understandings, but without them in the contract, the other party could say otherwise.*

13. **INDEMNIFICATION:** Owner agrees to defend, indemnify and hold Producer, and Producer's employees, agents, successors, licensees and assigns, harmless from and against any and all claims, damages, liabilities, losses or expenses (including reasonable attorney fees and costs) suffered or incurred by Producer on account of or in connection with the breach of any of Owner's representations, warranties or covenants set forth herein.

> **Hint:** *This puts teeth in the Representations and Warranties paragraph. Some producers issue the initial contract without binding themselves to a similar indemnification. If you do that and the other party complains, put it in a paragraph that mirrors this one and binds you as Producer to indemnify Owner.*

14. **REMEDIES:** Owner acknowledges and agrees that Owner's sole remedy for any breach or alleged breach of this Agreement by Producer shall be an action at law to recover monetary damages. In no event shall any of the rights granted or to be granted and/or the releases made herein revert to Owner, except as provided herein, nor shall Owner have a right of rescission or right to injunctive or other equitable relief.

Comment: *This sounds harsh, but it is absolutely necessary in a studio deal. You should have this protection so that you have maximum flexibility on how and where to set up your film for financing and distribution, because no studio will take on a project without it.*

15. **ARBITRATION:** Any claim, controversy or dispute arising here-under shall be settled pursuant to California law by arbitration before a single arbitrator in accordance with the rules of the American Film Marketing Association (AFMA) held in Los Angeles, California. The award of the arbitrator shall be binding upon the parties and judgment there may be entered in any court. The prevailing party shall be entitled to all arbitration costs, and reasonable attorney fees.

Owner: _____   Producer: _____

_____   _____

(address)   (address)

Note: *This agreement is complete as it stands. You do not need to consult Chapter 8 to finish up this document.*

CHAPTER 16

HIRING A COMPOSER TO WRITE ORIGINAL MUSIC

Given the hassle and expense involved in clearing pre-existing music, it is no wonder that so many independent filmmakers decide to use nothing but original music in their films. Add to this the fact that you will undoubtedly hire a composer anyway to write some underscore for your film, and hiring a composer to write original music for the entire film may be just too good to pass up.

WHEN TO START

One of the most important aspects of a film—the music—is frequently neglected during most of the filmmaking process. The specifics of music are too often addressed at the very last moment. Money, time, and creative energy are assigned to it on an "as available" basis. My strong recommendation is that music be considered carefully, very early in the process.

The kind of music and whether it is original or pre-existing music are both very important questions. Many financial and legal considerations flow from those basic creative decisions. Personnel issues must also be decided. You must decide whom to hire to do what with respect to the music in the film. If you make this decision during pre-production, your music supervisor can go through the script with you and perhaps enrich the script with musical references once clearance is verified.

A WORTHWHILE SEARCH

Finding the right composer is not a simple task. Listen to lots of music. If the composer has scored other films, look at them and listen carefully. Talk to other producers and some directors with whom the composer has worked to find out as much as you can about costs, work methods, and compatibility. (Silman-James Press has an excellent book on the subject—*Getting the Best Score for Your Film* by David Bell.)

There are also a few talent agencies in Hollywood that specialize in representing composers for film and television. Here are three:

Gorfaine-Schwartz Agency
(818) 461-9600
gsamusic.com/index

The Carol Faith Agency
(310) 274-0776
carolatcfa@aol.com

The Robert Light Agency
(213) 651-1777
rlatalent@aol.com

As your list of potential composers gets shorter and shorter, it is common to have the candidates screen the film and discuss their musical concepts for the film. Your basic concern is whether the composer is going to write that perfect score that will help move the story along. Don't get caught up in soundtrack album fantasies at this initial stage.

NEGOTIATING THE DEAL

HIRING
A COMPOSER
TO WRITE
ORIGINAL
MUSIC

271

Generally speaking, you will be able to choose from a wide range of composers based on their style, talent, and experience. As an independent producer, you will not be able to pay what the studios pay up front, so you may have to share the publishing rights to the score and revenues from soundtrack albums. (In the old days, the studios hired composers on long-term contracts to compose and to conduct orchestras that were also made up of employees of the studios.)

The entire music budget can range from 2% to 5% of the film's total budget for studio pictures. Often, independent producers are running out of money at this point and have to appeal to composers on non-financial terms and back-end terms to get the one they want on their film. What follows is just enough information to make you dangerous, but at least you will know the primary areas of potential back-end income for the composer, so you can at least "talk the talk."

Here are the main income sources for the composer. The first three categories listed are called performance royalties and are the composer's main source of back-end income.

1. Theatrical exhibition. When your film plays in a theater, the music is being "performed." Normally, a performance royalty would have to be paid. Because of an old court case, no royalties are paid for the music for theatrical play dates in the United States. However, in other parts of the world, royalties are paid to the performance royalty societies who forward the money (less a handling fee) to their counterparts in America: ASCAP, BMI and SESAC. The royalties range from about 2.5% to 5% of the ticket price, so they can be quite substantial. Half of that amount is called the writer's half and automatically goes to the composer, the other half is called the publishing half. Most producers try for all the publishing. However, the publishing half typically is shared 50/50 between the composer and producer for independent films, but you may have to give more to get the composer you want.

2.   Videocassettes and discs. Most studios don't allow royalties to be paid to composers on these sales. You will probably have to split the income on these sales with your composer.

3.   Cable, pay, and free television. When your film plays on television, the music is "performed" and performance royalties have to be paid. These royalties are paid by the television entity to the performance royalty societies (ASCAP, BMI, and SECSAC), which negotiate blanket royalties for all the music that is played on television. The performance royalty societies divide the money up according to the composers and publishers listed on the cue sheets for your film. That is why cue sheets are so important. **Cue sheets** are a listing of all music in a film, including where it appears and for how long, with identifying information about the composer and the society to which they belong. Historically, free network television has paid the highest royalties, but the differences among cable and pay television are diminishing every day as the audience for the various types of television shifts and changes. If your movie goes into syndication, the same kind of royalties arrangement exists with the local syndication station and the performance royalty societies.

4.   Sheet Music. Not a big source of income. The composer gets a negotiated rate.

5.   Mechanicals. This amounts to about 7 cents per cut on what used to be a record and now includes the audio tapes and CDs.

It is easy to create an agreement based on the principle of work for hire so that you own all rights to the work from the beginning. Income flows to the music's copyright holder from performance royalties generated when the film is played on television, in theaters outside of the U.S., or when the music is played apart from the film on radio, for example. Half of such income always goes to the composer, if the composer is a member of ASCAP, BMI, or SESAC. The other half is called **publishing income**. To hold down your front-end costs, some or all of the publishing income may be retained by the composer. Among independent producers, it is common to split publishing income 50/50 between the composer and the producer. Publishing income can be as much as $50,000-$100,000 for a film with a limited theatrical release, plus some television play and foreign sales. It can be well into six figures for a major release. This money is paid directly to the holder of these rights by such organizations as ASCAP and BMI (discussed in the next chapter), which collect royalty fees from theaters outside the United States or television and radio anywhere in the world. Because the future income for the composer is tied to the number of times and places the film is screened, as opposed to the profits of the film, composers are often willing to write on spec (or near spec). They do not have to worry about the integrity or bookkeeping methods or financial strength of the producer or distributor. If the film plays in theaters outside the U.S. or on television anywhere in the world, checks are forthcoming to the composer. They do not flow through the producer or the distributor.

At the end of this chapter is a simple composer's agreement. Notice that it assumes that half the publishing income will go to the composer and that only a nominal fee is paid to the composer up-front. Again this contract is generic. It only has the deal terms for the composer.

THE PACKAGE DEAL

You can take the notion of putting all your musical eggs in one creative basket one step further. Often, if you are sure that you have the composer you want, you negotiate a so-called package deal. The composer in this **package agreement** composes all the music, hires the musicians, records the music, and delivers all the fully recorded music to the producer for a fixed fee. This is the way most independent films are scored.

Basically, you are contracting out all the music in your film to one person. You had better be sure that this is the right person. If you have found the right person, there is nothing cleaner and neater than the package approach to film scoring. If you miss, it's a big miss because all your musical eggs are in one basket—and some of your legal eggs are there also, because the package is responsible for acquiring rights from all the musicians.

16.01   **COMPOSER AGREEMENT**

This Agreement, dated as of _____, 200___, is entered into by and between _____
("Producer"), located at _____,
and _____
("Composer"), located at _____.

> ***Date:*** *By using an effective date right at the beginning of the contract, you eliminate disputes over when a contract was signed and therefore when a contract begins and ends.*
>
> ***Producer:*** *You, as the filmmaker, are the Producer, so fill in your name and address or the name and address of your production company before that word.*
>
> ***Composer:*** *Fill in the name and address of the Composer. From here on, capitalize those words that refer to yourself and the Composer, and the Picture.*

1. **Engagement:**

    1.1 Producer hereby engages Composer to furnish Composer's services as a work for hire to compose and arrange the complete musical score ("Music") for use in the soundtrack of the motion picture currently entitled _____ ("Picture"), and Composer hereby accepts such engagement, upon the terms, covenants and conditions set forth herein on the following schedule.

    1.1.1 Start Date: _____

    1.1.2 Completed Score: _____

    1.2 Composer's services hereunder shall include the "spotting" of the picture for the placement of music, and consulting on an ongoing basis with Producer and/or persons designated by Producer. Composer shall render all services on an exclusive basis. Composer shall deliver the Music to Producer per Producer's reasonable technical requirements.

> ***Spotting*** *is picking the points in the film where music will be heard. The company and director and music team do this together.*

2. **Compensation:**

    2.1 Producer agrees to pay Composer the sum of $_____, payable as follows:

HIRING
A COMPOSER
TO WRITE
ORIGINAL
MUSIC

275

2.1.1 $_____ upon commencement of services.

2.1.2 $_____ upon delivery of full orchestra score satisfactory to Producer.

2.2 With respect to the exercise of publishing rights in the music, Composer shall be entitled to fifty percent (50%) ownership of the "Publisher's share."

> *Hint:* 50/50 of Publishing is a common split if you are getting an experienced composer and you want to keep the initial fee down. Studios often keep 100% of Publishing. You may have to give up more than 50% to get an experienced composer if you have limited funds to pay up front. Once the split is determined, the issue arises of whose publishing company will administer the publishing rights. Usually the Composer already has a publishing company. Not many independent film producers do, but sometimes you may want to set up your own publishing company.

2.3 In the event Producer exploits a recording of the soundtrack containing the Music, Composer shall receive a performer's royalty of ___% and a producer's royalty of ___% of the suggested retail price of such album or Compact Disc with respect to records sold through normal retail channels of record distribution worldwide.

3. Rights: Composer hereby grants Producer rights to synchronize the Score provided to the Picture and thereafter to exploit the Picture, including the Score in all media whether now known or hereafter created in perpetuity throughout the universe.

> *Hint:* This language is the core of your agreement. Accept no less!!

4. Credit: Provided the Music is used in Picture, screen credit shall be accorded Composer substantially in the following form:

Music composed by: _____

which credit shall appear in the main titles on a separate card or frame, or its equivalent in the event of a roll. Composer shall be accorded this credit in all paid advertising, including posters, videocassette jackets and all other media, except congratulatory and team ads.

> *Hint:* The extent of credits is always negotiable.

• • • • •

*Go to Chapter 8, Provisions Common to Most Agree-
ments, to finish up this contract. The Indemnification
paragraph is so important to the Composer Agreement
that generally you cannot obtain E&O insurance if
you do not include it. Use the signature block, changing "Owner" to "Composer," and the following paragraphs:*

*Representations and Warranties (except subparagraph c
unless the composer is also a lyricist)*

Indemnification

No Obligation to Exploit

Notice

Cure

Remedies

Arbitration

16.02   **MUSIC PACKAGE AGREEMENT**

HIRING
A COMPOSER
TO WRITE
ORIGINAL
MUSIC

This Agreement, dated as of _____, 200___, is entered into by and between _____ ("Producer"), located at _____, and _____ ("Composer"), located at _____. located at _____.

> **Date:** *By using an effective date right at the beginning of the contract, you eliminate disputes over when a contract was signed and therefore when a contract begins and ends.*
>
> **Producer:** *You, as the filmmaker, are the Producer, so fill in your name and address or the name and address of your production company before that word.*
>
> **Composer:** *Fill in the name and address of the Composer. From here on, capitalize those words that refer to yourself, the Writer, and the Picture.*

1. **Engagement:**

    1.1 Producer hereby engages Composer to furnish Composer's services as a work for hire to compose, arrange and record the complete musical score ("Music") for use in the soundtrack of the motion picture currently entitled _____ ("Picture"), and Composer hereby accepts such engagement, upon the terms, covenants and conditions set forth herein on the following schedule.

            1.1.1 Start Date: _____

            1.1.2 Completed Score: _____

            1.1.3 Completed Recording of Score: _____

    1.2 Composer's services hereunder shall include the "spotting" of the picture for the placement of music, and consulting on an ongoing basis with Producer and/or persons designated by Producer. Composer shall render all services on an exclusive basis. Composer shall deliver the Music to Producer per Producer's reasonable technical requirements.

> **Spotting** *is picking the points in the film where music will be heard. The company and director do this together.*

1.3 The fee set forth in paragraph 2.1 below shall be inclusive of all costs related exclusively to the production of the music soundtrack. These costs do not include transferring 1/4-inch audio tape or DAT masters to 35mm magnetic film or any other media. It is understood that Composer shall [pick one of the following] hire an orchestra or ensemble of any size OR will not be requested to hire an orchestra or ensemble, but will create the music by synthesis or by any method Composer deems appropriate OR will hire at least ___ musicians to record the music.

> **Comment:** *Select the language in the last sentence that best describes your agreement with the composer. Four different choices are offered for the three most common situations.*

2. Compensation:

2.1 Producer agrees to pay Composer the sum of $_____, payable as follows:

    2.1.1 $_____ upon commencement of services.

    2.1.2 $_____ upon delivery of music master recording satisfactory to Producer.

2.2 With respect to the exercise of publishing rights in the music, Composer shall be entitled to fifty percent (50%) ownership of the "Publisher's share."

> **Hint:** *50/50 of Publishing is a common split if you are getting an experienced composer and you want to keep the initial fee down. Studios often keep 100% of Publishing. You may have to give up more than 50% to get an experienced composer if you have limited funds to pay up front.*

2.3 In the event Producer exploits a recording of the soundtrack containing the Music, Composer shall receive a performer's royalty of ___% and a producer's royalty of ___% of the suggested retail price of such album or Compact Disc with respect to records sold through normal retail channels of record distribution worldwide.

3. Rights: Composer hereby grants Producer rights to synchronize the Score provided to the Picture and thereafter to exploit the Picture in all media whether now known or hereafter created in perpetuity throughout the universe.

> **Hint:** *This language is the core of your agreement. Accept no less!!*

4. Credit: Provided the Music is used in the Picture, screen credit shall be accorded Composer substantially in the following form:

Music by: _____

which credit shall appear in the main titles on a separate card or frame, or its equivalent in the event of a roll. Composer shall be accorded this credit in all paid advertising, including posters, videocassette jackets and all other media, except congratulatory and team ads.

HIRING
A COMPOSER
TO WRITE
ORIGINAL
MUSIC

279

> **Hint:** *The extent of credits is always negotiable.*

• • • • •

Go to Chapter 8, Provisions Common to Most Agreements, to finish up this contract. The Indemnification paragraph is so important to the Composer Agreement that generally you cannot obtain E&O insurance if you do not include it. Use the signature block, changing "Owner" to "Composer," and the following paragraphs:
Representations and Warranties (except subparagraph c unless the composer is also a lyricist)
Indemnification
No Obligation to Exploit
Notice
Cure
Remedies
Arbitration

CHAPTER 17

FAIR USE

This chapter deals with one of the most interesting and quickly changing areas of copyright law. Every documentary filmmaker must know about Fair Use. Every filmmaker ought to be familiar with this area of the law.

FAIR USE—A SHIELD, NOT A SWORD

Fair use is not a right held by members of the public who want to poach the intellectual property of others. Rather, fair use is a defense you can use when you are sued for copyright infringement. Fair use is also a defense that can be used against you, especially when you go after somebody for using a clip from one of your films. This is the most important exception to the rights of the copyright owners. It is also the area of copyright law that is changing the most rapidly.

When you think about fair use, think good manners. They are both rooted in the same basic tenet of consideration for your fellow humankind. There are only a few rules that apply always in all situations. The overriding rule is that there are no rules that apply in every situation. Good breeding is in control here, and there are different results depending on what part of the country you are in.

Fair use has nothing to do with the law of trademark or the law surrounding the various personal rights that come into play when you are considering using the name and likeness of an individual. If you have not used someone else's copyrighted material, there is no need to address the question of fair use.

Courts recognized that it simply was not fair to say that every copying of a copyrighted work was a violation of the law. Some copying was necessary to promote the very creativity that the copyright law was designed to promote. For instance, if you are critiquing this book, a quote or two from the book might be helpful. But if I didn't like you or what you had to say about my book, I could stifle your commentary except for the fact that your use would be protected by the concept of fair use.

Fair use was never mentioned in copyright law when the law was originally passed. It is a concept that was created by the courts grounded in a great deal of common sense. Eventually, the concept of fair use was incorporated into a major copyright law overhaul known as the Copyright Act of 1976. However, the intent of the legislature was to merely restate the law as it had been handed down in court cases over the years.

Since it has been imbedded in Section 107 of the Copyright Law, fair use has been the subject of three separate cases that have gone all the way to the Supreme Court. All three cases were reversed at each level of review. Two of the cases were split decisions at the Supreme Court level (even learned appellate justices do not agree). It is hard to articulate what is fair use in objective terms. It always requires an examination of the specific facts of the case.

The language of Section 107 seems simple enough:

"The fair use of a copyrighted work . . . for purposes such as criticism, comment, news reporting, teaching . . . scholarship, or research, is not an infringement of copyright. In determining whether the use made of a work in any particular case is a fair use, the factors to be considered . . . include:

1. the purpose and character of the use, including whether such use is of a commercial nature or is for nonprofit educational purposes;

2. the nature of the copyrighted work;

3. the amount and substantiality of the portion used in relation to the copyrighted work as a whole; and

4. the effect of the use upon the potential market for, or value of, the copyrighted work."

You can see from the language of the statute that there is no list of uses that are always and under all circumstances permitted under the doctrine of fair use. The language does not give definitive guidance even to the courts, let alone the lay person. Congress merely listed the areas in which fair use is possible. The court must analyze each of the factors listed above to determine if a use is a fair use or not.

To make matters worse, the appellate courts are not consistent in their opinion about which one of the factors is most important. In a trilogy of cases decided in 2001, the federal trial courts in New York City took the position that the first factor is the most important. Most of the trial and appellate courts in the rest of the country had been taking the position that the fourth factor is the most important factor. If you are faced with fair use questions, you really need a good lawyer and a solid internal compass to mark the path between the fair use of that which was created by others and a use of someone else's creation that will require permission and compensation. As a personal rule of thumb, you should always err in favor of asking and paying, unless it simply will not do any good to ask. If the answer is surely going to be "no," it is better to never ask.

FAIR USE AND FILM CLIPS

Fair use does not automatically allow you to take a portion of another person's copyrighted film and edit it into your film without specific written permission. Even documentaries, which are usually in the public interest, do not usually incorporate uncleared footage from the films of others. Clear your film clips in advance because lawsuits are expensive. It can be even more expensive to remove a section of your film at some point in the future if a court rules against you.

The use of film clips is most commonly associated with documentaries, but many makers of feature-length fiction films use clips for dramatic effect to recreate a historical scene. *Forrest Gump* used a variety of film footage. *Apollo 13* masterfully integrated both historical footage with specially prepared live-action sequences to create an amazingly realistic film. Much of it was researched by Take Aim Research (888-TAKEAIM). Film clips are also commonly used in connection with blue-screen projections in front of which actors can perform as though they were halfway around the world.

When we were clearing clips for the Oscar®-nominated film *Smoke and Mirrors,* we faced just such a situation. The film was about the tobacco industry's use of advertising and product placement in feature films to entice the nation into an acceptance of smoking by others and the habit of smoking on an individual basis. The story could not be told effectively without the use of television commercials for tobacco. But the television commercials were bought and paid for and owned by the tobacco companies and/or their advertising agencies. What were the odds that permission would be given to make an anti-smoking documentary? We were able to convince the insurance company that this was a fair use that did not even require a request.

But, how about the clips of feature films showing major movie stars puffing away? Again, no studio would cooperate in showing how they were pulled into the campaign to turn an entire nation on to a deadly habit like smoking. They might be proud of the film, but they certainly would not be proud of the hand they had in promoting an often-fatal addiction. Here the trick was to find particularly clear and fine examples and then only use a bare minimum in order to get the idea across. Unlike the commercials, which were generously used, the feature film clips were used very sparingly in *Smoke and Mirrors* and only to the extent necessary to get the point across.

One Plaintiff, Three Cases, Same Result—The AIP cases

The New York courts seem to be much more sympathetic to a fair use argument than most courts, largely based on a trio of cases in which the holder of the underlying rights behaved so badly that the courts would have done just about anything to be sure that she did not win. They chose to hand her not one, but three defeats—all served up on the platter of fair use.

Two of the great horror meisters of all time were Sam Arkoff and James Nicholson, who had a company called American International Pictures (AIP) that literally churned these pictures out. Nicholson retained ownership of the copyright for many of the films he made. On his death, the ownership of those copyrights passed to his widow, Susan Nicholson Hofheintz. She administered the distribution rights and the occasional licensing of clips for a hefty slate of horror films.

So it was that she licensed a number of clips to AMC for use on the American Movie Classics channel for a documentary called *It Conquered the World! The Story of American International Pictures*. During post-production, the producers decided they needed one more clip to round out their narrative. They obtained the clip and sent over a clip license agreement containing the same basic terms on which they obtained all the other clips from Ms. Hofheintz. She prepared an amendment to the previous agreement, which AMC signed and returned. Nobody was in a rush for the paperwork. They had a good working relationship, and everybody knew exactly what was going on.

Oops!

After the film was locked, Hofheintz viewed the film and said "No deal." The filmmakers cried foul and went ahead and released the film. She sued.

She lost.

The court said that one could not make a documentary about the grand masters of horror films without showing a few clips, AMC didn't take more than they needed to take in order to make their point, AMC was making a documentary, not another horror film, and they didn't adversely impact the market for the underlying film. Voilá! That sounds like fair use to me. And it sounded like fair use to the court.

Note that Hofheintz's behavior hurt her when she went to court. Fair use is an equitable relief. An **equitable relief** is when the court is trying to do what is fair as between the parties, often where there are no strict statutory guidelines. When a plaintiff is asking the court for equitable relief, it is important that the plaintiff has used good faith and fair dealing throughout the transaction.

So the court already had a not-too-good impression of this particular plaintiff when she came before the same court with the same kind of lawsuit against The Learning Channel, which was making a documentary called *100 Years of Horror*. They used a variety of clips from various producers. They didn't seek permission from any of them, believing that if they used small snippets of various horror films to demonstrate the history of horror films, it would be fair use. Hofheintz was the only one who sued.

She lost . . . again.

The court said that you could not make a documentary about the history of horror films without showing a few clips, The Learning Channel didn't take more than they needed to take in order to make their point, they were making a documentary, not another horror film, and they didn't adversely impact the market for the underlying films. Sound familiar?

As though the third time might be a charm, Ms. Hofheintz sued A&E over a documentary called *Peter Graves: Mission Accomplished*. Early in his career, Graves appeared in several AIP films. A short clip from *It Conquered the World* was included without obtaining permission.

She lost . . . again.

The court said that you could not make a documentary about the career of Peter Graves without showing an early clip, A&E didn't take more than they needed to take in order to make their point, they were making a documentary, not another horror film, and they didn't adversely impact the market for the underlying films. Do you think she got the message? The court is nothing if not consistent when it comes to Ms. Hofheintz's assaults on the documentary filmmakers.

One Plaintiff, Three Cases, Different Results— The Bob Tur Cases

On the West Coast, we learn a lot about fair use from Bob and Marika Tur. They own their own helicopter and use it to gather news footage, which they then sell to various outlets. Because they do not have anyone to answer to except themselves, they are able to make decisions on their own based on when and where they think news might break. That is how they ended up being the only newscopter hovering over South Central Los Angeles when the Rodney King verdict was announced. They were the only team to capture the now infamous footage of the Reginald Denny beating that mushroomed into the L.A. Riots of 1992.

Most news outlets licensed this copyright-protected footage. Those that did not were sued with various results. KCAL-TV (Channel 9 in Los Angeles) asked for a license and was refused, so it obtained a copy of the tape from another station, slapped their logo on it, and broadcast it a number of times, without giving credit to the Turs. Not fair. And not fair use. Actually, KCAL won at trial, but the appellate court reversed the decision and sent the case back for trial because, in no small part, of KCAL's behavior of asking permission and not honoring the negative answer they received.

When Reuters New Service sent the Turs' footage out over the wires to their subscribers, it was not fair use, even though the footage related to the hottest (excuse the pun) story of the day. Reuters made no changes, just sent out the footage for their own gain and in direct competition to the Bob and Marika Tur. In that case, the court noted that forty-five seconds of the nine-minute tape constituted the "heart" of the nine-minute tape, so the inclusion of the forty-five seconds was more important than the inclusion of other segments.

However, when Court TV Channel used just a few seconds of the Tur tape of the Denny beating to promote Court TV's televising of the trial of the two men charged with Denny's beating, the court decided that was fair use. In going through the four factors, the court found that Court TV's purpose was entirely different from the fast-breaking news purpose for which the footage was originally shot. The amount used was very, very brief—no more than necessary to let the viewer know what the trial was about and did not interfere with the prime market for the footage, which was licensing to news outlets. The Turs called the few seconds that Court TV used the "heart" of the nine minutes, but the court remembered that they had previously identified the forty-five seconds that Reuter sent out as the "heart."

Get to the Heart of It

The same "heart" idea helped the owners of the character Godzilla protect their property against the use of photographs that "captured the central expressive core" of the Godzilla character. It also helped the owners of the copyright to the Laurel and Hardy films win their lawsuit against the trade paper *Hollywood Reporter* who used a single still from one of their pictures on their inside cover in order to announce a new section for placement of advertisements. You probably know the picture and would agree—it is the scene where Laurel and Hardy are balanced on the precipice of a building. The court called it the "high point" of the film and readily identifiable as being from the film. Now get this: The photo had MGM's copyright notice on the back and stated that it could only be used to promote *Laurel & Hardy's Laughing 20s*. Those reporter guys surely read that notice. They shoulda known better.

When CNN, ABC, and CBS were sued in New York for using a few seconds from *Story of G.I. Joe* in Robert Mitchum's obituary, it was held to be fair use. But when CBS was sued for using one minute and fifteen seconds from a Charlie Chaplin film in a news report on his death, CBS lost. No fair use. The court found that amount was substantial and—you guessed it—it was part of the "heart" of the film.

And when CBS was sued for putting out a video containing Martin Luther King's *I Have A Dream* speech, it was not fair use either, although CBS ultimately won the case on other (technical) grounds. CBS took too much to be fair use so that their documentary competed directly with a video being put out by King's estate. Those folks at CBS are helping to define the limits of fair use.

Enter Transformation

The Turs also sued the Court TV channel for including an even shorter clip in its montage bumper at the beginning of its show entitled *Prime Time Justice*. The clip showed up, along with clips from various trials covered by Court TV, behind the image of a clock with its hands sweeping its dial. The court held that this use was even briefer, less competitive with the original use and highly transformative. **Transformative** in the context of fair use cases means that the defendant has indeed used the plaintiff's copyrighted work, but in such a way to be quite different from the original. Think of it as meaning that the copyrighted work was a mere ingredient in something new and different. If that sounds like the creation of a derivative work, you are absolutely right, but it is the hot new toy of judges who have as hard a time as you do in understanding what is and what is not a fair use.

Today, the notion of whether the defendant's use of the plaintiff's copyright-protected work is transformative seems to be the key to the analysis. Courts spend a lot of time on this factor, even though this word does not show up anywhere in the copyright law! The transformative concept was created in a law-review article by a judge trying to make sense out of the all the fair use cases. You can see the notion in the three Hofheintz cases. In each one of those cases, the fact that the film using the clips was a documentary, not another horror film, was an important factor for the court. In the three Tur cases, discussed just above, the results changed based primarily on whether the use was new and different or the use was basically the same as and competitive with the Turs' use.

DOES FAIR USE AVOID THE NEED TO CLEAR MUSIC?

Many people who have a general notion of fair use think that there is some magic amount of a song that you can use without receiving permission or paying a fee. "Eight bars?" they ask. "Two bars?" they ask. They think that fair use dictates a specific amount of music that can be used without clearance and thus save a lot of work and some money.

Not so.

The rap group The 2 Live Crew went all the way to the Supreme Court for their parody recording of the song *Pretty Woman*. They won on the parody issue, but the Supreme Court sent the case back to the trial court because they used a bass riff from a Roy Orbison recording. It was only a single riff, yet the Supreme Court held that it was archetypical of Orbison's music and not necessarily part of the parody. Therefore, it was not automatically fair use. See the next chapter for a full discussion of parody in general and the "Pretty Woman" case in particular. Fair use is virtually no help to you in the music area. You have to clear all music. Any unauthorized use of music is a potential infringement claim if the music is recognizable. Even if the "song" is not sung, but merely spoken in the film, you must clear it.

To illustrate the importance of this point, Evan M. Greenspan, a music clearance company, encloses a button when they send out materials about their company. It reads, "USE A NOTE, GO TO JAIL."

Even background music in a documentary needs to be cleared. There is one case that has allowed a use of copyrighted music to be fair use. A television film crew was covering an Italian festival in Manhattan. The soundman picked up snippets of a copyrighted song as the cameras rolled on a band marching by. The music was replayed on the news that night. This use was held to be fair use, in part because of the transitory public interest in the news event of which the music was an integral part and the small portion of the song that could be heard on the broadcast.

In the late nineties, there was a Michigan case that found fair use of music. There were thirty-five seconds of a song used in a half-hour anti-violence episode on a series on public television targeted at teenagers. No lyrics were used, and half of the thirty-five seconds that were used were inaudible. While the court went through the four-step analysis, it feels as though the high-minded purpose of the television series had to be a factor in their favor.

The first published opinion about sampling involved the first eight bars of Gilbert O'Sullivan's hit song "Alone Again (Naturally)." The sample was continuously looped so that the same ten seconds shows up throughout the recording. The recording in question was on Biz Markie's rap album *I Need a Haircut*. The rapper's courtroom presentation wasn't the greatest. In fact, the judge was so incensed that, in his written opinion, he accused the rapper of theft and referred the entire matter to the U.S attorney to consider criminal prosecution.

The prosecutor declined to file criminal charges, but who wants to come that close? Certainly, no record company or reasonably successful recording artists want to take that kind of risk. In fact, a lot of time and energy went into clearing the sampling rights. In fact, a few specialty music-clearance houses flourished in Los Angeles and New York to obtain the rights to sample.

Along came the Beastie Boys in a case that clarified and underscored this case. In that case, the Beastie Boys had licensed a three-note, six-second musical sequence contained in a recording of jazz scholar James W. Newton's *Choir*. The exotic sounding tidbit was looped more than forty times into the Beastie Boys hit record *Pass the Mic*.

The Beastie Boys licensed the sampling rights from the owner of the master recording and thought that they had licensed the sampling rights from Newton, but the check was returned and nobody ever followed up.

The composer sued.

The composer lost.

The court correctly held that it was only the sounds taken from the sound recording that needed to be licensed in the case of that particular needle drop. The unique sound is what the Beastie Boys were after, not the composition. The court went on to add that even if the Beastie Boys were after the composition, they didn't take enough to be recognizable, let alone copyrightable all by itself. Therefore, the use of the composition was fair use and the composer lost the case.

It was a big clarification for those who want to put together a rap record based, in part, on the recordings of others. However, as this book goes to print, the composer is appealing the case. I predict that the composer will lose on appeal. This is the first case in which a judge analyzed the differences between copyrights in sound recordings and copyright in musical compositions. The conclusion in this particular situation was that the license from the owner of the master recording was enough. Had the Beastie Boys taken more, perhaps the result would have been different, but the court correctly figured out that these are two different rights' holders with different results, even for the same rap recording.

CONCLUSION

By this time you have been exposed to a variety of fairly recent court cases on fair use. Legal scholars and jurists are still casting about for a coherent way to express the basis for the various decisions. After all, court cases are supposed to give us some guidance about how to behave. About all you can draw from these cases is that courts want you to behave.

If your film is furthering some socially important purpose (news, current events, critique, education, or the like) and you behave in a socially acceptable way, you probably can use a little something from someone else's work, as long as you don't take the "heart" of the work, don't take any more than you need, and your use does not hurt the market for the original work. Mind you, this language doesn't show up in any of the cases in just that way, but I don't know a better way to distill what is in the case decisions. I have run this viewpoint by some very heavy hitters in the legal community, and they seem to think that it pretty well hits the nail on the head.

Perhaps the only enduring lesson about fair use is that for the next few years, you will have to consult with an experienced clearance attorney if you plan to rely on fair use. You will also need to have that experienced clearance attorney on your application for E&O insurance, so that the insurance company lawyer will talk to your lawyer. Talking a risk-averse insurance company lawyer into taking a plunge into the fair use pool is not something you want to do on your own. That is a job for a pro.

CHAPTER 18

PARODY

In one situation you do not have to clear the music and, in fact, it is generally useless to even ask. You won't be punished for asking; it just rarely does any good. The area is parody. The word parody does not exist in the Copyright Act. The courts created this exception and used the rationale from the fair use cases discussed in the last chapter.

DEFINITION OF PARODY

This is a very misunderstood area. You are not exempted from obtaining clearance of a copyrighted material just because the material is used in a humorous way. A parody is a very specific thing with very specific requirements. There is no humor defense for copyright infringement. There is only a parody defense.

The first time the Supreme Court ruled on the importance of parody was in what has become known as the *Gaslight Case*. It concerned a parody on television of a then-famous and serious movie. The 1985 Gaslight Case ended with four justices deciding one way, four justices deciding the other, and a ninth judge abstaining. This equally split decision did not help at all. My definition of a **parody**—drawn from an examination of the cases in this area—is the following:

1. A new, copyrightable work

2. based on a previously copyrighted work

3. to such an extent that the previous work is clearly recognizable

4. but not taking more from the copyrighted work than is necessary, and

5. that makes a social commentary which is at least in part directed to the subject matter of the previous work, usually humorously, and

6. that is not likely to hurt the value of the previous work.

Did you miss any mention of humor? Statistically speaking, most examples of parody turn out to be humorous. Certainly, commenting on an underlying work generally comes out in a way that puts a smile on the face of the listener. However, humor is absolutely not a requirement, and judges often go out of their way to say that they don't think that the parody before them is funny. Heaven forbid that the judge might have a sense of humor.

A TRUE PARODY DOES NOT HAVE TO BE CLEARED

The Supreme Court had not issued a controlling decision on parody until the 2 Live Crew case in 1994. Irving Azoff and 2 Live Crew were sent back to the trial court so that a jury could decide if a single bass riff constituted fair use. The real reason for the lawsuit, however, was the fact that the song that 2 Live Crew wrote, recorded, and released was a parody of "Pretty Woman." The Orbison estate, not surprisingly, was upset. Here are selected lyrics from Orbison's "Oh, Pretty Woman" compared to The 2 Live Crew's "Pretty Woman."

"Oh, Pretty Woman" by Orbison and Dees **vs.** "Pretty Woman" by The 2 Live Crew version

Pretty Woman, walking down the street,
Pretty Woman, the kind I like to meet,
Pretty Woman, I don't believe you,
You're not the truth,
No one could look as good as you.
Mercy.

Pretty Woman, won't you pardon me,
Pretty Woman, I couldn't help but see,
Pretty Woman, that you look lovely as can be.
Are you lonely just like me?
Pretty Woman.

Pretty woman, walkin' down the street,
Pretty woman, girl you look so sweet,
Pretty woman, you bring me down to that knee,
Pretty woman, you make me wanna beg please.
Oh, pretty woman.

Big hairy woman, you need to shave that stuff
Big hairy woman, you know I bet it's tough
Big hairy woman, all that hair it ain't legit
'Cause you look like Cousin It.
Big hairy woman.

The 2 Live Crew won their case on the parody issue. Compare the lyrics used by The 2 Live Crew's against Orbison's "Pretty Woman" and then go down the six points in the Donaldson definition set out at the top of this chapter. You'll find that the work is clearly a parody.

In fact, the first three factors in my definition fall clearly in the favor of The 2 Live Crew. These lyrics are (1) a new creation (2) that is based on Roy Orbison's "Pretty Woman" (3) to such an extent that the original "Pretty Woman" is clearly recognizable—even on the written page without the music.

The fourth factor brings in some subjective judgment as to whether The 2 Live Crew did or did not take more from Orbison's "Pretty Woman" than was necessary. Courts tend to lean toward a finding that the taking was not excessive. Perhaps The 2 Live Crew could have taken a little less, but that is basically a creative judgment. The courts try not to second guess that creative judgment if they find that all the other requirements are satisfied. I think the better reading of the fourth factor is that the taking was not unreasonable or, maybe even more accurately, that they added more than they took. As we have more litigation and therefore more decisions, this factor will be clearer. Right now, the test is whether the amount taken is "no more than necessary."

The fifth factor concerning social commentary is very broad. Almost any commentary can qualify. It does not have to be particularly intelligent or incisive, as you can see from the lyrics. The judges do not have to think it is funny. In fact, I am not aware of a single case in which the judge admitted to liking the humor of the parody. I know of many cases in which the judges made it clear that the parody was not all that funny—in the official view of the court.

Once you get this far in the analysis, it almost always follows that the new work seeks a different audience from the audience sought by the previous work. While courts spend a lot of time on this factor and most scholarly writers believe that this finding is essential, I view it as much less bothersome than the rest of the elements since it is hard to imagine a circumstance in which the parody would be seeking the same market as the previous work. To me, one result of creating a parody of a work is an appeal to a different audience.

There are two relatively recent cases from the book publishing area that really help to shed some light on the concept of parody and how the factor of social commentary on the underlying work (not humor) is the key factor in deciding whether a work qualifies as a parody and therefore does not need the permission of the owner of the copyright of the work that has been borrowed from (or pilfered from, if you are the owner of the underlying work).

Humorous Book but Not a Parody

Not too long after O. J. Simpson's murder trial and before a civil jury found him responsible for killing his ex-wife, several books came out about the case. Simon and Schuster had what they thought was a parody all printed and being shipped to stores when a court enjoined the delivery. Very few copies ever saw the light of day. The book was called *The Cat Not in the Hat* and purported to be a parody based on Dr. Suess's famous *The Cat in the Hat*.

The publisher's problem is obvious to anyone who has read the beginning of this chapter. Let's hold the book up to the six-point Donaldson test set out at the beginning of the chapter. Keep in mind that the fifth factor is the key, and that is exactly where Simon and Schuster lost their case. Although lawyers tried to argue that *The Cat Not in the Hat* was a commentary on the innocence of the Suess's book, it was crystal clear that the book was trying to take a humorous look at the murder trial. And the thing that made it humorous was the relentless, start to finish taking of the style and rhyming of Suess and even the look of the illustrations in Suess's book.

The commentary was not on the Suess book, it was on the O. J. trial. If the authors wanted to write humorously—or otherwise—on the O. J. trial, they would have to create their own work, not "borrow" someone else's work. They merely rewrote the Seuss text, preserving many of the phrases of the original in order to create a wry look at what the authors believed was a miscarriage of justice. That point of view had sufficient support to guarantee sales, but the authors needed to write their own work, not try to piggy-back someone else's creativity.

Once that factor went against the authors of *The Cat Not in the Hat*, nothing else mattered much. One could view the taking as excessive. After all, even the Suess drawings were copied into the new work. And there is a strong argument that the existence of this work would have been very confusing to the young audience of *the Cat in the Hat*. Certainly, it would have been easy for someone to grab the wrong book because of the similarity in how they looked. It would have been natural for someone to believe that there was some sort of endorsement or approval from the Suess estate for the new work. But the important reason that the copies of the new book had to be destroyed was that the social commentary was not on the underlying work, it was on a completely different subject . . . . no matter how hard the lawyers tried to twist things after the fact.

The court mentioned this case when they sided with Columbia Pictures against Miramax. Miramax made a trailer and poster for Michael Moore's documentary film *The Big One* that they intended as a parody of the highly successful *Men in Black*. The court said that Miramax's poster and trailer were not targeted at *Men in Black*, but merely incorporated features of Columbia's work to "get attention" and "avoid the drudgery in working up something fresh."

Serious Book Was a Parody

The Wind Done Gone is a small and powerful novel about the slaves who populated Tara, the cotton plantation in Margaret Mitchell's *Gone With the Wind*. In Mitchell's book, however, the only characters who came alive on Tara were white. The furniture was described in more detail than the many black people who made the place run. The Mitchell estate sued—and won an injunction at the trial court level—on the theory that this book was an unauthorized sequel. However, the estate lost on appeal and *The Wind Done Gone* was allowed to be published.

When you compare the two books using the test at the beginning of the chapter, it is easy to see why *The Wind Done Gone* is available for purchase today. It clearly makes commentary on the subject matter of *Gone With the Wind*. It takes characters right out of *Gone With the Wind* and tells their rich stories including, and maybe especially, the pain of being treated as less than human by the book's white characters who loom so large in American literary life. So the fourth factor—the key factor—is very much in favor of *The Wind Done Gone*. Having read both books, my personal opinion is that *The Wind Done Gone* could have used more material from *Gone With the Wind* than it did: the plantation name was changed, most, if not all, of the character names were changed.

This case also illustrates the massive forces who seek to broaden the fair use area. The following news organizations all joined the fight on behalf of *The Wind Done Gone:* Cox Enterprises, Cable News Network, and the owners of the New York Times and the Boston Globe, the Wall Street Journal, the Chicago Tribune, the Los Angeles Times, and the Tampa (Fla.) Tribune. They filed so-called friend-of-the-court briefs. **Friend-of-the-court briefs** are filed by someone who has an intense interest in the outcome of a case, but is not a party to the case, so they have no right to appear. These briefs are filed with the appellate court after the court gives permission to the person to file the brief. The court has to be convinced that the person has something important to say and that they have a legitimate interest in the outcome of the case.

These news organizations own a lot of copyrights, so you might think that their interests lay more closely with the Mitchell estate. However, the money they lose by expanding fair use (of which parody is a subset) pales in comparison to the money they make by having ever greater freedom in using the copyright-protected work of others as they race to gather and disseminate the news.

TRADEMARK PARODY

Yes, it is possible to parody a trademark. In fact, the courts have been increasingly tolerant of those who would make fun of a product through a parody of its trademark. At this writing, however, I was not able to find one case of a film parody of a trademark. You don't want to be the test case. Don't try this at home.

One reason that cases that defend parodies of trademarks are easier to win is that the test for trademark is a little different from the test for copyright. The test is whether the public would be confused or if the public would actually think less of product because of the parody.

One of the reasons that you don't want to tempt the holders of trademark, no matter how much confidence you have in the possibilities of breaking new legal ground, is that the holders of trademarks are very aggressive in protecting their marks. Mighty corporations go after any parody, no matter how inconsequential, out of fear that a small parody may birth a larger parody. Their complacence toward a small parody can be used against them when they are faced with a larger parody.

Another reason to be cautious is that defending this kind of litigation tends to be even more expensive than other types of litigation. That is because of the deep pockets of corporate plaintiffs and because of the need for evidence of the public's state of mind.

WHAT PARODY IS NOT

The above discussion is designed to give you a pretty good idea of what constitutes a parody. To be absolutely clear, the following items are pointed out because they are not parodies. Some people think that they are and make the mistake of not clearing the music before putting it in their film. The result is that they have to take the song out of their film or negotiate a payment under the adverse circumstance of already having it in the film or risk litigation.

- A copyrighted song presented in a funny way. A torch song sung by someone in drag or by a drunk character slurring through a song or by a singer performing a song intentionally off-key may be intended as a joke. These may (or may not) bring laughs, but they fail as parodies and therefore must be cleared. They are not parodies because they are not new works and do not make any commentary on the original lyrics. Rather, the humor is in the presentation. You must clear this music.

- Changing a song slightly to fit your purposes. Changing "Happy Birthday" to "Happy Anniversary" to make that song appropriate for the occasion or changing "Michelle" to "Miquel" to make it appropriate to a character's name may be necessary, but it is not a parody. The song must be cleared. There is no parody because it does not meet the definition. Changing just one word does not make a new work, and it certainly would not be copyrightable. The previously copyrighted work is recognizable, but there is no social commentary and the audience is essentially the same as the audience for which the song was written.

- A parody is not created when an impersonator or impressionist sings a song (without changing it) in a style of someone other than the person who made it a hit. Dana Carvey imitating President Bush singing "The Party's Over" is not a parody. If the words and music remain the same and the humor is derived from the notion of former President Bush singing that song, there is no parody. The song has to be cleared.

PARODY IN A FILM SCORE

Note that one of the reasons that true parody is allowed without permission from (or payments to) the original copyright holder is that to do otherwise would eliminate the art form. If someone creates a serious work, they do not want someone else to take the heart of the work and poke fun at or belittle its core message.

Your problem as a filmmaker is that a music soundtrack is not like a single record, which can be pulled from the market. No producer wants to be in a position of losing the rights to a song after it is recorded into a film production. Be sure to check in with a copyright specialist if you want to proceed without permission to use a particular song on the theory that you are using a parody of the song. Remember that parody is one of those rare clearance areas where there is no harm in asking. You are almost always denied permission, but since it does not take a great amount of time, you might just be surprised.

CHAPTER 19

CLEARING FILM CLIPS

The same family of myths swirl around film clips as shroud the use of music in films. Many filmmakers believe that there is some magic length of film that can be used without having to clear the clip. "Two minutes?" they ask hopefully. "It is two minutes, isn't it? I can use up to two minutes of a film clip without getting permission, can't I? It's called fair use."

The simple answer to that question, is "NO!"

CLEARING CLIPS WITHOUT ACTORS OR MUSIC—STOCK FOOTAGE

Many independent filmmakers have saved a bundle on a chase scene or an explosion or a sunrise or crashing waves or a running deer by using stock footage. **Stock footage** is pre-existing film that you can license for use in your film. It is usually obtained from a stock footage house, a business that owns the rights to license clips. The various stock footage houses have collections that are small to very large, a broad selection to highly specialized and collections that are difficult to sift through or very well curated and organized. Most stock footage houses have their own written forms, which are quite adequate but give you no protection.

However, if anything goes wrong, the fact that you "thought" that you had cleared all the rights is of little help. Such good intentions can protect you from punitive damages in the event of litigation, but you still have to pay for your mistakes. The solution: When you license a film clip, be sure to establish the ownership of rights held by the person you are getting the film clip from. That person or business entity cannot grant you any more rights than they possess. If they don't hold all the rights you need, either go elsewhere for your clip or do your own investigation to locate and license the rights you need.

The film-clip release at the end of this chapter adequately covers all the points you need. Remember that these releases only cover the exact clip you described, for the exact length you requested, and only in the film you described. Any different or more extensive use has to be cleared. You might want to wait to finalize your contract until you are sure of the exact use you are going to make of the clip.

Usually, if you have the opportunity to use stock footage, you want to check out the resources of a stock footage house. They have remarkable choices available to you. The following is a sampling of some of the reputable stock footage houses:

Fabulous Footage
www.fabfootage.com
inquiry@fabfootage.com

Penn State Media Sales–Stock Footage
(800) 770-2111
www.mediasales.psu.edu
Penn State has an extensive collection of footage dating back to 1932. Categories include agriculture, anthropology, education, health, science, wildlife, classic psychology, and primates.

Silverman Stock Footage
www.silvermanstockfootage.com
info@silvermanstockfootage.com
Specializes in aerial time-lapse scenes plus "wild and wacky glimpses" of Americana.

Producers Library Service, Inc.

(818) 752-9097

(800) 944-2135

www.filmfootage.com

research@filmfootage.com

More than 10 million feet of film and an extensive collection of B&W and color photographs covering motion picture subjects, vaudeville, radio and television, and Hollywood history. Founded in 1957. One of the country's oldest and largest independent stock footage houses providing 16mm and 35mm stock footage and photographs.

UCLA Film and Television Archive

(323) 466-8559

www.cinema.ucla.edu/footage

footage@ucla.edu

Internationally renowned for its pioneering efforts to preserve and showcase not only classic but current and innovative film and television.

Footage Hollywood Stock Footage Library

(818) 760-1500

www.footagehollywood.com

info@footagehollywood.com

Specializes in hard-to-get film and television footage from the silent movie era up to the present day.

Historic Films Stock Footage Library

1 (800) 249-1940

(631) 477-9700

www.historicfilms.com

info@historicfilms.com

Owns or represents more than 45,000 hours of 1895-1990 vintage television programs, musical performances, feature films, newsreels, industrial films, silent films, educational films, sales films, TV commercials, celebrity interviews, TV news, home movies, and travel films.

Air Power Stock Library
(516) 869-3082
1 (888) 247-4420
www.airpowerstock.com
forflying@aol.com

Extensive collection of military, civilian, and archival footage. Features fighter planes, bombers, attack helicopters, aircraft carriers, tanks, troops, artillery, missiles, and ground support equipment and personnel. Non-military footage includes: explosions, plane crashes, special effects, firefighting, and police operations. All footage is edited and catalogued for your convenience.

BBC Library Sales
New York: (212) 705-9466
Los Angeles: (818) 840-9770
Toronto: (416) 362-3223
www.bbcfootage.com
lals@bbcfootage.com

A division of BBC Worldwide. Offers comprehensive footage and sound library for film and television production, commercials, and interactive media. Includes more than 500 million feet of film, 300,000 hours of video, and 500,000 sound recordings.

F.I.L.M. Archives
(212) 696-2616
www.fastimages.com
info@fastimages.com

Contemporary and vintage images. Includes more than 100 years of film images, nearly two decades of news video (1986 to present) from News 12 Long Island, and exclusive representation of the British government film library.

NBC News Archives
New York: (212) 664-8558
Burbank: (818) 840-4249
www.nbcnewsarchives.com
footage@nbc.com

Since introducing the first radio network and the first television network, NBC has been capturing the sights and sounds of our times for more than seventy years.

Jazz on Film–The Chertok Archives

(845) 639-4238

jazzfilm@mail.com

Specializes in music and also covers the entertainment industry in general, including vintage television. An important source of African American images.

Action Sports–Scott Dittrich Films

(212) 681-6565

(310) 459-2526

www.sdfilms.com

Action sports footage produced by Scott Dittrich Films since 1972, plus nearly every sport and many of the world's top cinematographers.

Airboss Military Stock Footage

(502) 595-8177

www.airbossfootage.com

airbossfootage@aol.com

Historical and military stock footage with more than 6,000 hours of naval, aviation, and ground forces footage available. Coverage includes U.S. and foreign footage from the Spanish-American War of 1898 to the latest "hot spots" around the globe.

All Stock

1 (800) 323-0079

www.all-stock.com

info@all-stock.com

A sister company to Action Sports/Scott Dittrich Films for an ever-expanding list of subjects.

Archive Films by Getty Images

(800) 876-5115

www.gettyimages.com/motion

sales.archivefilms@gettyimages.com

More than 15,000 hours of archival black & white and color footage.

Kesser Stock Library

(305) 358-7900

1 (800) STK-FTGE

www.kesser.com

kesser@ix.netcom.com

Founded in 1984. Contains extensive archival, sun and fun, aerials, travel, underwater, sports, animal footage and more.

Streamline Stock Footage

New York: (212) 925-2547

Los Angeles: (323) 660-5868

www.streamlinefilms.com

Footage Central

(800) 510-5595

(212) 265-9558

info@clipcafe.com

35mm exclusive collections of Hollywood gems, gladiators, kung fu and monsters, educational and TV, newsreels, shorts, and cartoons.

National Geographic Film Library

(877) 730-2022

London: (44) 0207-632-5970

www.natgeostock.com

sabbott@ngs.org

Outstanding programming since 1968.

When you license stock footage, be sure that you understand what you are getting. If you rely on the stock footage houses for more than the visual images on the film stock, make sure that you obtain specific representations and warranties. When you license a piece of stock footage, there is usually no sound or effects on the film—a film-clip license does not usually grant any rights to music that may be on the film.

WRITERS AND DIRECTORS

Both the Writers Guild of America and the Directors Guild of America have specific agreements covering the "reuse" of material. **Reuse** under the union agreements refers to taking footage shot for one film and using it in another film. Clips from films produced under the Minimum Basic Agreement for either of these unions may require additional payments to the union members who helped create the film from which you want to use a clip. The theory for these provisions is that if you were not using the clip, you would have to create your own footage, and for that you would employ a writer and director. To the unions, it is a jobs issue. Even though the payment would be the obligation of the person who sold you the clip and not your specific obligation, you need to check this out, because if the unions do not get paid, they go after everybody—including you.

CLIPS WITH ACTORS

It is common, even in fictional films, to have scenes in which a television set is on. If the screen is visible and playing a program, you have two choices: You can create your own video and play it on the television set, or you can clear an existing clip. Such a clip usually has actors in it.

This process can be confusing to a filmmaker who licenses a clip from a television show or another feature. The owner of the copyright of the film or television program can grant you the right to use the actual film, but usually cannot grant you permission to use an actor who appears in the film clip.

If the person appearing on the screen is a member of either of the actors' unions (SAG or AFTRA), there are specific provisions in the Basic Agreement for each of the unions that cover reuse. In the case of reuse, the actor is due a payment, which must be negotiated separately from the agreement under which the actor originally rendered services and must be at least equal to one day's minimum wages under the union contract.

WHEN THERE IS NO UNION AGREEMENT

The situation is different when the creator of the original film is not a signatory to any of the union agreements or the footage being used was news or candid footage, so that the persons appearing are not union members. The argument that the use of this footage throws another actor out of work no longer applies. Your use of the film might well be lending reality to the film you are making as opposed to ripping someone off.

For example, legendary singer James Brown sued 20th Century Fox because the film *The Commitments* used twenty-seven seconds of Brown's performance on a 1965 television show without his permission. Defendant's summary judgment motion was granted. The twenty-seven seconds consisted of seven different cuts from *The T.A.M.I. Show* where James Brown is performing on a television set. Brown's name is not mentioned at all during this brief scene. Later in the film, Brown's name is simply mentioned in a laudatory fashion. In this case, pursuant to their agreement with the rights holders of the television clip, the producers did in fact secure the rights to use the lyrics and the musical composition from the music publishing company holding the copyright in those works.

Why did the court find for the defendant? Because the use was perceived by the court as building reality. It was much like a verbal reference to any living public figure. They did not use Brown's face to sell or promote the film. It was just there in the background. Because of the age of the film, no union agreement protected Brown.

Do not rely on the logic of the above case without checking with an experienced lawyer. Not all courts would agree with that case. California courts tend to be particularly protective of the value of celebrityhood. Even if you are right, you do not want to be sued. Remember the golden rule of filmmaking: When in Doubt, Clear. There is a letter at the end of this chapter that you can use to obtain permission to use a name and likeness in most situations.

CLIPS WITH MUSIC

By this time, it should be no surprise to you that you have the responsibility to clear the music playing at any time in your film, including the clips you use from other films. You either have to replace the music in a clip with new, cleared music or go through the music clearance procedure for the music that is already there. This is true even for the theme music in television programs. In that case, the music may well be owned by the studio that owns the program itself, but established composers can reserve rights in their music as part of the negotiation of their employment contracts. One of the more commonly reserved rights is the right to authorize producers other than the studio to use the music in connection with new motion pictures. These rights are held by the publishers of the music. See Chapter 15 for the details about music clearance. Because this music was often created especially for filmed entertainment, you may also have to make payments under the AFM agreement. The **AFM** is the American Federation of Musicians. Almost all studio musicians belong to it. The AFM's contracts—like those of the other unions discussed above—have special provisions to cover the reuse of music.

On a related topic, beware of the music video. For some reason, independent filmmakers are sometimes lulled into a belief that receiving a music video from a performer or a public relations company who wants you to use the video in your film serves to clear the music for your film. It is *not* the same. You receive the video to whet your appetite. If you want to use it in your film, you must go through all the steps that were outlined in Chapter 15 to clear music, even if the video comes to you from the record company.

19.01   **FILM CLIP RELEASE**

This is an agreement between _____ located at _____ ("Owner") and _____ located at _____ ("Producer") with regard to the use of a film clip owned by Owner to be used in a film being produced by Producer by the name of _____ ("Motion Picture").

1.   The Film Clip to be used by Producer is as follows:

Name of Source Film: _____

Maximum length of clip to be used: _____

Description of Motion Picture: _____

Approximate time of Motion Picture: _____

Description of how the clip fits into the Motion Picture: _____

_____

Black and white: _____   Color: _____

Fiction: _____   Non-fiction: _____

Describe the intended distribution: _____

Are distribution contracts in place? Yes _____ No _____

If so, with whom? _____

> **Note:** Be very specific and accurate and as complete as possible so that the permission you obtain covers your needs.

2.   Producer may use the above-referenced clip in perpetuity, throughout the universe.

3.   Producer shall pay Owner the sum of _____ ($____), to be paid upon execution and delivery of this letter. Owner hereby grants Producer a non-exclusive, irrevocable license to include the specified Film Clip in the specified way and to advertise or exhibit such Motion Picture in every country of the world, to make copies of the Motion Picture and to otherwise exploit such Motion Picture in all media and by all devices, whether now

existing or hereafter invented, including, without limitation, video-cassettes, videodiscs and other audio-visual devices.

4. This license does not authorize or permit any use of the Clip not expressly set forth herein and does not include the right to alter the fundamental character of the music of the Clip, to use the title or subtitle of the Clip as the title of a motion picture, to use the story of the Clip or to make any other use of the Clip not expressly authorized hereunder.

5. The rights hereinabove granted include such rights for screen, video and television trailers for the advertising and exploitation of the Motion Picture.

> **Hint:** *Owners sometimes want extra money if you use their clips in advertising. If so, you have to decide if it is worth it. Generally, it isn't, in which case you would eliminate this paragraph.*

6. The rights hereinabove granted shall endure for the periods of all copyrights in each country of the territory in and to the Film Clip, and any and all renewals or extensions thereof in each country of the territory that Owner may now own or control or hereafter own or control without Producer having to pay any additional consideration therefor.

7. This agreement grants the use of the Clip as described herein and does not authorize or guarantee the right to use the name or likeness of anybody appearing in the Clip or to use any music in the Clip, the clearance of which is the sole and separate responsibility of Producer. Producer also has the sole and separate responsibility of complying with any obligations by any applicable union, included but not limited to, the Writers Guild of America, the Directors Guild of America, the Screen Actors Guild and the Association of the American Federation of Television and Recording Artists.

• • • • •

Go to Chapter 8, Provisions Common to Most Agreements, to finish up this contract. Use the signature block and the following paragraphs:
    Representations and Warranties
    (use b and d only; omit a and c)
    Indemnification
    No Obligation to Produce
    Remedies
    Arbitration

19.02   **ACTOR'S RELEASE FOR FILM CLIP USE**

[date]

To: [your name]
    [your address]

312

This letter shall confirm that the undersigned person ("Actor"), for good and valuable consideration, the receipt and sufficienty of which is hereby acknowledged, has granted permission to _____ ("Producer") and its successors, assignees and licensees to use Actor's name and/or likeness as such name and/or likeness appears in _____ ("Name of Clip Source") in the motion picture tentatively entitled _____ ("Picture") and in connection with advertising, publicizing, exhibiting and exploiting the Picture and other motion pictures, in whole or in part, by any and all means, media, devices, processes and technology now or hereafter known or devised in perpetuity throughout the universe. Actor hereby acknowledges that Producer shall have no obligation to utilize Actor's Name and/or Likeness in the Picture or in any other motion picture.

> **Comment:** *Most actors will not authorize the use of their likeness in your advertising without substantial extra payment. It is generally not worth it, so you may have to take out that permission.*

Producer's exercise of such rights shall not violate or infringe any rights of any third party. Actor understands that Producer has been induced to proceed with the production, distribution and exploitation of the Picture in reliance upon this agreement.

Actor hereby releases Producer, its successors, assignees and licensees from any and all claims and demands arising out of or in connection with such use, including, without limitation, any and all claims for invasion of privacy, infringement of Actor's right of publicity, defamation (including libel and slander), false light and any other personal and/or property rights.

Very Truly Yours,

[Actor's signature]
[Actor's name]
[Actor's address]
[Actor's Social Security number]

> **Note:** *You need the actor's social security number so that you can fill out a W-2 tax form.*

PART V

YOUR FILM IS COMPLETE

After you have finished making your film, you have to register it with the copyright office. That's right—it ain't over just because your film is in the can. And you still have to sell your film to the public, if not to a distributor. Unfortunately, you also often have to fight off claims of copyright infringement.

CHAPTER 20

REGISTERING COPYRIGHT FOR YOUR COMPLETED FILM

Copyright in a motion picture is automatically secured when the work is created and "fixed" on film or video. Each element is absorbed into the final film and covered by one copyright. The script, music, photography, effects, design, and performances all merge into the film. Even though some elements such as the script and music, standing alone, may also carry their own copyright, for numerous legal and industry reasons, you still must register the completed film with the copyright office.

WHEN TO REGISTER COPYRIGHT IN YOUR FILM

You should register the copyright in your film as soon as your film is locked. **Locked** means that the film is in its final form and ready to have prints struck. There is actually a statutory requirement that you register your film within ninety days of this event.

The most practical reason for registering the copyright in your film at the earliest possible time is that you have to lodge the two copies of your film in the "best format" with the Library of Congress. If you do it immediately, you can usually get away with supplying a tape as opposed to a print, so early registration can save you money. See more on the deposit requirement later in this chapter.

IN WHOSE NAME DO YOU REGISTER THE FILM?

The author of the film and the copyright claimant are the same in almost all studio-film circumstances when it comes to a completed film. They both are the production company that produced the film. Everyone who worked on the film should have signed work-for-hire agreements, making the production company the author of the film. The various contracts in this book (and every other book on filmmaking) provide work-for-hire language to insure that there is no confusion on this point.

FORM OF NOTICE FOR MOTION PICTURES

The use of a copyright notice is even more important for a finished film than for your script. It informs the public that your work is protected by copyright, identifies the copyright owner, and shows the first year of completion. It also should indicate the country of origin.

Today, use of the copyright notice on new films is optional under U.S. law, though it is still highly recommended. People are so used to seeing the notice that its absence might cause someone to jump to a wrong conclusion. Below is a notice that meets the copyright laws of every country in the world, including the small nation that still requires, as of this writing, "All Rights Reserved." (The notice usually is the last item in the credits.)

REGISTERING
COPYRIGHT
FOR YOUR
COMPLETED
FILM

317

**Copyright 1996, _____ [copyright owner's name].
All Rights Reserved.**

**The United States is considered the first country of
publication for purposes of the Berne Convention.**

APPLYING FOR REGISTRATION OF YOUR COMPLETED FILM

To register a motion picture, send the following to the Copyright Office:

1. A SIGNED APPLICATION on Form PA. See Chapter 9 on how to obtain forms from the Copyright Office

2. ONE COMPLETE COPY of the motion picture being registered

3. A SEPARATE WRITTEN DESCRIPTION of the contents of the motion picture—this is called a **Continuity**.

4. A NON-REFUNDABLE FILING FEE (which, at the time of this writing, is $30) in the form of a check, money order, or bank draft payable to: Register of Copyrights. Do not send cash.

Send the application, copy, description, and fee in the same package, along with a cover letter (like the one at the end of this chapter) describing all of the enclosed elements to:

Register of Copyrights
Library of Congress
Washington, DC 20559

It is not absolutely necessary, but our office always take two additional steps to create a record of sending. We send these letters by certified mail, return receipt requested. It is a little more trouble, but it provides a positive record for your files. We back this up with a postcard that the Copyright Office will date-stamp and return very quickly showing that they have received your packet and its contents. A sample of the postcard is at the end of the chapter with the cover letter.

FILLING OUT FORM PA FOR YOUR COMPLETED FILM

The following comments supplement the information provided in Chapter 9. (Check out Chapter 9 to be sure that you don't miss anything, especially where you are referred to Chapter 9 in the text below.)

SPACE 1: NATURE OF THIS WORK

"Motion picture" is generally the appropriate term. It covers documentary and fictional films, feature-length and shorts, and color and black-and-white. There is no need to elaborate. If the motion picture is part of a multimedia kit or other larger work and you are claiming copyright in the entire work, you should indicate that in this space. For example, you could state "multimedia kit, including motion picture and workbook," if applicable.

SPACE 2: NAME OF AUTHOR, "WORK MADE FOR HIRE," AND "NATURE OF AUTHORSHIP"

Ordinarily, a number of individuals contribute authorship to a motion picture, including the writer, the director, the producer, the camera operator, the editor, and others. These individuals are hardly ever considered "authors," however, because a motion picture is almost always a "work made for hire." Chapter 5 explains why you should use the work for hire approach for your film. In the case of a work made for hire, the employer—not the individuals who actually created the work—is considered the author for copyright purposes. Without work for hire agreements, most of the above-the-line talent have a potential claim on your film.

1. If the entire work was made for hire, name the employer as author and answer "yes" to the work-made-

for-hire question. The employer can be you or you and your investor(s), but would generally be a single picture production company that you create. Under "Nature of Authorship," state "entire motion picture." You should always be sure that everyone working on a film has signed a work for hire agreement.

2. If no part of the work was made for hire, name all of the individuals who made the motion picture as authors and answer "no" to the work made for hire questions. Under "Nature of Authorship," briefly describe what each person did: for example, "director," "producer," or "writer." This is not a good idea, but some people buy this book after things have begun to unravel with cast and crew and it is difficult to obtain signatures.

SPACE 3a: Year in Which Creation of This Work Was Completed

Give the year in which the final cut of the motion picture was completed. If the motion picture is a new version of an older film, give the year of completion of the version being registered.

SPACE 3b: What Is Publication?

Publication of a motion picture is one of the most confusing areas of copyright law. To avoid a mistake in this murky area, you should register your film as soon as possible after it is completed.

Publication of a motion picture takes place when one or more copies are distributed to the public by sale, rental, lease, or lending, or when *an offering* is made to distribute copies to a group of persons (wholesalers, retailers, broadcasters, motion picture distributors, and the like) for purposes of further distribution or public performance. Offering to distribute a copy of a motion picture for exhibition during a film festival may be considered a publication of that work. For such an offering to constitute a publication, copies must be made and be ready for distribution. Bear in mind that whether a film is old or new is not the relevant question. The issue is whether your film has been published in a legal sense. Sending a limited number of copies of the film to a select group of individuals to see if they want to distribute it does not publish the film for copyright purposes. Publication occurs when your film is shown to the public at large or prints are made for a public release, even a small release.

Publication of a motion picture publishes all of the components embodied in it, including the music, the script, and the sounds. Thus, if a motion picture made from a screenplay is published, the screenplay is published to the extent that it is contained in the published film.

Date of First Publication

If the work is published, give a complete date (month, day, year) and nation of first publication. You should register your film as soon as it is completed before publication, to reduce the deposit requirements. If the work is not published at the time the application is submitted, leave the publication lines blank.

SPACE 4: COPYRIGHT CLAIMANT(S)

This should be a single film production company that you created for this film alone.

SPACE 5: PREVIOUS REGISTRATION

This is rarely necessary with a motion picture.

SPACE 6: DERIVATIVE WORK OR COMPILATION

A motion picture is a derivative work of the screenplay. Therefore, at (a) say, "The movie was based on the script by the same name written by _____ and _____." At (b) say, "All cinematic elements including scenery, music, photography, and all other cinematic elements."

SPACE 7: DEPOSIT ACCOUNT

Leave blank. You will pay by check.

SPACE 8: CERTIFICATION

See Chapter 9 for a detailed explanation of this space.

SPACE 9: ADDRESS FOR RETURN OF CERTIFICATE

Complete legibly. This will show through the window envelope used by the Copyright Office to mail back your completed form.

REGISTERING
COPYRIGHT
FOR YOUR
COMPLETED
FILM

321

DEPOSITING ONE COMPLETED COPY OF YOUR FILM WITH THE COPYRIGHT OFFICE

To register a completed motion picture, you will be required to deposit both a written copy of the contents of the motion picture and a copy of the film or video or DVD itself.

In addition to the separate, written description of the motion picture, the Copyright Office also requires, for an unpublished work, deposit of one complete copy of the motion picture, containing all of the visual and aural elements that the registration covers. This can be on tape or on film. Publication of the film makes the process potentially more expensive.

For a published motion picture, the Copyright Office requires deposit of one complete copy of the "best" edition of the work. For motion pictures first published abroad, deposit one complete copy of the film as it was first published abroad.

The following is a list, in descending order, of the Library's current preference for what constitutes the "best edition":

1. Film rather than another medium

2. Videotape

3. Videodisc

To be complete, the deposit copy of the motion picture should be clean, undamaged, undeteriorated, and free from any defects that would interfere with showing the film or that would cause mechanical, visual, or audible defects or distortions.

The Examining Division of the Copyright Office does not have equipment to view motion pictures in certain formats, including 2-inch and 1-inch tapes, PAL and SECAM $^3/_4$-inch videocassette, Betacam, or 8mm videocassette. Therefore, these are highly disfavored and you must receive special permission to deposit one of these instead of a more accessible print or video.

EXCEPTIONS TO THE NORMAL DEPOSIT REQUIREMENT FOR FILM

Where it is unusually difficult or impossible to comply with the deposit requirement for a particular motion picture (usually because of the expense of striking an extra print of a published film), you may submit a written request for special relief from the normal requirement. The request should be addressed to the Chief of the Examining Division, U.S. Copyright Office, Library of Congress, Washington, DC 20559. It must state why you cannot provide the required copy and describe the nature of the substitute copy being deposited. This letter should be included with the registration material. Always put it on your own letterhead. The Copyright Office has the attitude that if you can afford a lawyer, you can afford to give them a pristine print.

The Copyright Office may or may not grant special relief in a particular case. They consider the difficulty of providing a required copy, the acquisitions policies and archival considerations of the Library of Congress, and the examining requirements for registration.

If relief is granted, you are usually required to sign a Motion Picture Agreement provided to you by the Copyright Office. Its terms are non-negotiable. The Motion Picture Agreement establishes several alternative deposit procedures for published motion pictures. If they do grant relief, they still require that you send a print after you are through using it.

All activities related to the Motion Picture Agreement are under the Motion Picture, Broadcasting, and Recorded Sound Division of the Library of Congress. For a copy of the Agreement, call the Motion Picture, Broadcasting, and Recorded Sound Division (MBRS) at (202) 707-5604, or write to:

REGISTERING
COPYRIGHT
FOR YOUR
COMPLETED
FILM

323

ATTN: Reference Assistant
MBRS
Library of Congress
Washington, DC 20540-4805

In general, whether the motion picture is published or unpublished, the deposited material should present a full, complete, and detailed description of the work, including its running time. It may be a detailed synopsis or continuity. A **continuity** is the actual dialogue script annotated with timing code taken from a tape or work print of the feature film. I recommend a continuity because you have to prepare one anyway for sale to non-English-speaking territories, and it provides you with a more complete and accurate description of your film than a synopsis.

Mailing

Everything for a single registration must go in the same envelope or box. Be sure that your application is signed, your check or money order is in the correct amount, and that you have enclosed either one or two deposits of the work you are registering. You should list all of this in a cover letter.

Mail the entire package to:

Register of Copyrights
Library of Congress
Washington, DC 20559-6000

SPEEDING UP THINGS AT THE COPYRIGHT OFFICE

There is little you can do or need to do to speed up the copyright process. Remember that having the registration certificate in hand does not change any of your ownership rights. Copyright attaches to your work the moment you fix your creation in some permanent form for the first time. Your registration is effective as of the date your application is received by the Copyright Office. That's why the forms in this book give you proof of receipt.

However, there are some circumstances for which you just have to have that little piece of paper quickly. Here are the most common circumstances:

1. You are going to sue for infringement of copyright, and you have to have the copyright registration number. Therefore, you need expedited service from the Copyright Office, since you only know the copyright registration number when your registration form is returned to you.

2. You have signed a distribution contract requiring that you have the actual registration certificate in hand. You can usually negotiate that a copy of the completed Form PA is sufficient if you can also show proof of receipt by the copyright office. You then promise to supply the certificate as soon as you receive it. If you cannot negotiate around this requirement, you may need expedited service from the Copyright Office.

3. You have asked customs to confiscate bootleg films coming into the country. They will not do this without a copyright certificate. Proof of receipt Form PA by the Copyright Office is not enough because of the disruptive, if not draconian, consequences of confiscation.

These are about the only reasons recognized by the Copyright Office to expedite an application. Obtain a Request for Special Handling, a sample of which is supplied on the next page, and fill it out. Note the detail needed if you claim you need speedy action because of litigation. Even with this form, it still takes at least a week and usually longer to receive the Form PA back with your registration number.

Note the "remarks" section at the bottom of the form. This is not for you to use to make a plea. Put your sob story in a cover letter instead. It doesn't belong here.

There are certain services located in Washington, DC, that "walk through" applications for speedy handling. Some claim that they can obtain one-day results. This is not always the case. If you want to try this approach, Thomson & Thomson in Washington, DC, (800) 356-8630 is one very reliable, well established company that offers this service.

request for
special handling

1

SPECIAL HANDLING IS NOT FOR CONVENIENCE ONLY !

NOTE: The special handling of a registration application or other fee service severely disrupts the entire registration process and workflow of the Copyright Office. It is granted only in the most urgent of cases. A request for special handling is subject to the approval of the Chief of the Receiving and Processing Division, who takes into account the workload situation of the office at the time the request is made. A minimum period of five working days is required to process a registration application under special handling procedures.

Why is there an urgent need for special handling?

☐ Litigation   ☐ Contractual/Publishing Deadlines

☐ Customs Matter   ☐ Other, Specify

2

If you must have the requested action to go forward with the litigation, please answer the following questions.

a. Is the litigation actual or prospective?

Unless all blanks are completed your request cannot be processed.

b. Are you (or your client) the plaintiff or defendant in the action? Please specify.

c. What are the names of the parties and what is the name of the court where the action is pending or expected?

I certify that the statements made above are correct to the best of my knowledge.

(Signature)

(Address)

(Phone)   (Date)

FOR COPYRIGHT OFFICE USE ONLY

Information Specialist handling matter

remarks

20.02 SAMPLE COVER LETTER FOR MOTION PICTURE REGISTRATION

REGISTERING
COPYRIGHT
FOR YOUR
COMPLETED
FILM

327

Date: _____

Certified
Return Receipt Requested

Register of Copyrights
Library of Congress
Washington, DC 20559-6000

Dear Register:

Enclosed please find the following:

1. Check in the amount of thirty dollars ($30.00) for the Copyright Registration

2. Completed PA Form

3. Continuity

4. Videocassette of film

5. Return postcard

Please register the above film immediately.

We understand that the stamped original Form PA will be returned to this office.

Thank you.

Very truly yours,

_____

Enclosures: as listed

You should type this letter on your letterhead.

20.03   RETURN POSTCARD FOR MOTION PICTURE
REGISTRATION

The copyright office will date-stamp and sign and return to you a self-addressed, stamped postcard (not a letter, a postcard). That is your proof of receipt. Use the following language on the back part of the postcard when you want to register the copyright in your film. The returned postcard will have your proof.

BACK

This postcard shall act as a receipt for the following items:

Form PA to register the motion picture entitled:

_____

Together with a check in amount of $30.00 and a copy of the Continuity of the motion picture and the motion picture itself for Registration of Copyright.

FRONT

Your Name
Address

Your Name
Address

CHAPTER 21

COPYRIGHT INFRINGEMENT

Oh happy day! Your film is opening in a week. You have overcome all the obstacles. All your troubles are behind you. All you have to do is go to the premiere, travel the talk-show circuit, and pick out an outfit for the Oscars. Oops! Think again.

WHAT IS INFRINGEMENT?

All too often, you will receive a letter claiming copyright infringement. **Copyright infringement** occurs when your film was based in whole or in part on the copyrighted work of another to such an extent that the court will say, "You took too much." These claims arise when somebody thinks they were ripped off.

These claims are very, very common. As the court said in denying a claim by a playwright against the creators of the film *E.T.*, there is an "obsessive conviction, so common among authors and composers, that all similarities between their works and any others that appear later must inevitably be ascribed to plagiarism."

Plagiarism is the lay term for taking someone else's writing and calling it your own.

The frustration and pressure in getting a project off the ground are so great that when one sees a film that generally resembles a script or a treatment or even an idea that one was not able to get made, one immediately feels ripped off. The hurt, anger, and frustration send that person on a diligent search for a lawyer. Due to the over-population of lawyers in America, it is not difficult to find attorneys to take a case, even when they don't know that area of law particularly well.

You, of course, have protected yourself from such a frustrated reaction with E&O insurance, as discussed in Chapter 12. You want to give maximum help to the attorney whom your insurance company assigns to defend you. The following is a general discussion of the area of law known as copyright infringement. It is very hard to prove that a film infringes a previous work, whether the claimant is the copyright holder of a script, a treatment, or a book.

When reading the actual language in the cases, one gets the impression that this kind of lawsuit is disfavored by the courts. There is a strong public interest in promoting creativity among authors. There is also the inherent difficulty of assessing infringement claims.

The process of establishing copyright infringement involves four steps. The first two steps seldom involve serious problems, but nevertheless must be proved. The court will not just assume them to be true.

1. The person making the claim must own the copyright to the work being infringed.

2. The work must have been "copied."

3. The defendant must have had *access* to the pre-existing work.

4. There must be *substantial similarity* between the two works.

Ownership is generally proved by copyright registration, but even that is subject to attack if work for hire agreements have not been signed with the various people who helped to create your film. See the crew deal memo in Chapter 10 for a discussion of work for hire.

"Copied" carries a special meaning in the law of copyright. Being photographed in a film is not a copyright infringement for many copyrighted items because the form is so different. The item has not been "copied" in the sense that that word is used in copyright law. Making a movie from a script, book, or another film is exactly the kind of copying that the copyright law protects.

Access has a very special meaning in copyright infringement. The courts have defined and refined it through case law over the years. **Access** means the reasonable opportunity to review the copyrighted work. It is not necessary for the plaintiff to prove that the defendant actually read the copyrighted work, only that they had the reasonable opportunity to do so. Therefore, submission of a script to a studio could establish access for virtually everyone who was working in acquisitions at the studio at the time. In a case involving *Peter Pan*, the fame and frequency of the productions of this play was enough to establish access by the general public to that work. The court basically said, "C'mon, everybody knows the story of Peter Pan."

The courts rarely say so, but practitioners in the field know that the stronger the similarities, the less access needs to be shown. There is a seesaw relationship between access and substantial similarity. If you were to find a scene lifted in its entirety, word for word, from another script, that would itself be proof of access.

Substantial similarity is the courts' phrase to describe the situation in which two works are so similar that a jury could determine that the second work was copied from the first. If there is no substantial similarity, the case is dismissed. When one considers the plain-English meaning of the words "substantial similarity," one might think that plaintiffs would win most of these summary judgment motions. Surely, if the plaintiff and plaintiff's lawyer (and the plaintiff's circle of friends) all see substantial similarity, then the judge would at least let the case go to the jury.

Wrong!

Remember that substantial similarity, as a concept, has a legal meaning that has nothing to do with how you or I might define that term if it were up to us. Substantial similarity has been very narrowly defined by many courts over the years. It is very difficult to establish.

The first problem is that the law, as it has developed, is not really set up to deal with copyright infringement by films of a book or story. The early infringement cases dealt with one written work compared with another written work. Judges began the comparisons of written work to film with woefully inadequate case guidelines. You are stuck (as a plaintiff seeking redress) or benefited (as a defendant filmmaker fighting off a claim) by the state of law as it is today. Typically, copyright ownership and access to the work are conceded for the purpose of the summary judgment motion. The court just considers the issue of substantial similarity. There are four steps in determining substantial similarity:

1. The plaintiff gets to dissect the work into its component parts to show the court all the areas that the plaintiff believes are substantially similar.

2. The court then decides which of the elements are protected by copyright law and which are not protected because they are facts or ideas or are otherwise in the public domain. As the cases discussed below show, this process often leaves very little to compare.

3. The court compares the protected elements in both works.

4. The court decides if there is substantial similarity between the protected elements as a result of the defendant's copying the plaintiff's work. If the substantial similarity came from the copying of unprotected material (e.g., public domain material), there is no infringement.

Some elements may be copied exactly and not be protected under copyright law. In such cases, there would be no copyright infringement. Three cases help illustrate the hurdles that have to be overcome to establish substantial similarity as it is used by the courts.

E.T. filmmaker Steven Spielberg was sued by a playwright who had submitted her play *Lokey from Maldemar* to Spielberg with the hope that a motion picture would be made out of her work. The court held that the two works were not substantially similar, even though both stories dealt with aliens from other worlds who are stranded on Earth. The court stated that the plaintiff cannot simply rely on a list of similarities. Such lists are inherently unreliable and should be approached with caution. Anyone can make a list of similarities between two films. Try it yourself as a game. List the comparisons between *Pocahontas* and *Gone With the Wind*. The court felt that no lay observer would recognize *E.T.* as *Lokey*, and that any similarity existed only at the most general level. The opening scenes with an alien coming to Earth may be similar. In fact, the court said that these scenes were more similar than stock scenes, but this did not constitute substantial similarity. The reason is that the events that flow from this general idea—an alien landing on Earth—are limited in the way that they could proceed. In fact, there are only three obvious possibilities: The aliens could be warmly welcomed, the aliens could be feared, or the aliens could arrive unnoticed. Each of these three possibilities carries its own set of subpossibilities, but there are finite choices. The courts call these scenes a faire. **Scenes a faire** is a fancy legal term that means that the scenes flow naturally from the general premise, so they are not protected by the law of copyright and copyright infringement.

Scenes a faire contain certain elements that come with the territory, so to speak. They are removed from the plot (at Step 2 above) before the court commences the substantial-similarity analysis. Scenes a faire are not protectable because they necessarily result from the choice of setting or situation. The film has copyright protection. The scenes a faire within the film are not protected, just as any facts contained in the film because facts are in the public domain and therefore cannot be protected. Both scenes a faire and public domain material can be used as elements of other films.

So, in the *E.T.* case, the plaintiffs lost. The same reasoning failed the plaintiffs in the next case, which was based on fact instead of fiction.

It is even harder to establish substantial similarity when the works are based on true events. The author of the book *Fort Apache* brought a suit alleging copyright infringement against the producers and screenwriter of the motion picture *Fort Apache: The Bronx*. Both stories take place in the early 1970s at the 41st Precinct, in the borough of the Bronx, New York City. Nicknamed "Fort Apache" by officers who worked there, the 41st Precinct had a reputation for a high incidence of violent crime since the late 1960s, and had attracted the attention of the press and other news media. The book's author was a New York City police officer who worked in the 41st Precinct in 1971 and 1972 and based his 1976 book on his experiences on the job.

Both the book and the movie begin with a prostitute shooting two police officers in their squad car with a handgun at close range; both depict cockfights, drunks, stripped cars, prostitutes, and rats; both feature, as central characters, third- or fourth-generation Irish policemen who live in Queens and frequently drink; both show disgruntled, demoralized police officers and unsuccessful foot chases of fleeing criminals.

However, the court felt that these similarities relate to uncopyrightable material. The killing of the two police officers actually occurred and was reported in the news media, which placed the historical fact of the murders in the public domain and beyond the scope of copyright protection. The court held that the filmmakers, who had also reviewed the newspaper articles, had not infringed on the book's story. Foot chases, prostitutes, shoot-outs, and the vermin associated with a story based on factual events in an urban police situation are scenes a faire that are not protected by copyright.

The author of *Fort Apache* had a separate story in each chapter so that, as a whole, the work was disconnected. In contrast, the movie *Fort Apache: The Bronx* linked many of the incidents together. For example, a prostitute who has murdered some police officers earlier in the film returns later to encounter other police officers, who kill her. A fact-based movie can still be protected by copyright because those facts are put in a particular order and arranged and depicted in a certain way. The facts, however, remain in the public domain.

Let's now examine a case in which the plaintiff won. The case is unusual because it is one of the rare cases that involves a comparison of film against film. The defendant filmmakers seemed to go out of their way to underscore the links between their film and the film that was being ripped off.

It concerned Universal's legendary movie *Jaws*. In an attempt to ride *Jaws'* wave of success, a low-budget movie production called *Great White* surfaced to catch some of the financial spillover. Both *Jaws* (released June, 1975) and *Great White* (released March, 1982) are fictional stories about a great white shark that terrorizes inhabitants of a town on the Atlantic seaboard.

The court stopped the release of *Great White* and dismissed the defendant's motion for summary judgment. This case shows that when a person uses many of the specific details of someone else's film, this is copyright infringement. The extent of similarity was overwhelming. The plot, the main characters, the development of major story points, and the sequence of incidents were so substantial that a copying of the work obviously had taken place.

- Both movies opened with teenagers playing on the beach and underwater shots of a swimmer (*Jaws*) or a windsurfer (*Great White*) that are accompanied by bass tones that build up tension to indicate the shark approaching its first victim.

- Both movies end with the skipper being eaten by the shark and the police chief (*Jaws*) or shark expert (*Great White*) killing the shark, which swallows an explosive device.

- For each major character in *Jaws,* there is a similar character in *Great White*, including skippers with English accents, a shark, a shark expert, and a politician.

- The action and theme of both films are similar: The shark expert and skipper, with motives of financial gain, try to kill the shark and characters try to bait the shark with raw meat at the end of a pier, but part of the pier breaks off and they fall in the water. The political figure attempts to downplay the shark attacks.

The court pointed out that *Great White*'s main character was Peter Benton, and the name of the author of *Jaws* was Peter Benchley. Even though titles are not protected by copyright, the opinion considered that *Great White* was made from a screenplay originally titled *The Last Jaws*. Neither of these two facts have anything to do with substantial similarity, but it is just this kind of brazen attitude that causes defendants to lose their lawsuits. Here, the defendant's film was enjoined from further exhibition. It was ordered off the market. It has no more economic value.

WHAT IF THE COPYRIGHT
TO YOUR FILM IS INFRINGED?

As an independent filmmaker, you might find yourself on the plaintiff's side of such a contest. You might be hard at work on a project or you may have a fully developed script that you have been shopping around Hollywood for years. Suddenly you begin receiving congratulatory calls from friends who saw in the trades that a film that sounds like your movie is being made or saw a trailer for what they were sure was your film.

The first thing you feel is a stab to your heart. The upset and disappointment are hard to describe. You check it out. It is true. Your dreams are dashed by a bad imitation of what you were going to make. Then, you spring into action. You sue.

On whichever side you land, be sure to obtain an expert litigator familiar with this particular area of the law. Your lawyer must be conversant with the cases and principles discussed above.

Before you ever go in to see the attorney, make a list of similarities between the two works. Analyze them based on character, theme, setting, point of view (who's telling the story), plot, mood/tone, and type (drama, comedy, mystery). If you find dialogue similarities, be sure to note them. Matters that are identical are particularly important. However, as noted above, the courts do not look with a great deal of favor on lists of random similarities when they make the threshold decision of substantial similarity.

As you make this list, be mindful of which similarities are your creations and which flow naturally from the situation. Remember that when an alien comes to Earth, there are only three language choices: It learns the language quickly and easily, it never learns the language, or something in between.

Write a separate memo on access. Exactly why do you think that the filmmaker had a chance to view your work? Add in any other little tidbits concerning the possibility of access, such as an executive moving from one studio to another. Often, it is an internal studio memo that provides the smoking gun.

Finally, and perhaps most importantly, make a list of the differences. Eventually, this bridge must be crossed. A lawyer is more likely to take your case if you are being realistic and helpful. No one likes surprises, especially in a litigation situation. So look at the differences as thoroughly (if not as passionately) as you look at the similarities.

Substantial similarity is a very difficult concept to sell to a judge. Judges tend to lean toward finding works to be not substantially similar, even when experts are brought in to crystallize the similarities. Be aware that you will have to spend time and money to file the case and fight the defendant's motion for summary judgment. Studios and their insurance companies have an army of lawyers to fight off such attacks and a stack of summary judgment motions to be filed. They do not quickly offer settlements.

CHAPTER 22

COPYRIGHT ON THE INTERNET

For this second edition, my editor wanted a chapter about copyright on the Internet. "It's the big, new thing," he said. "It's the cutting edge," he said. "Sure, sure," I said, but what I meant was, "Nobody knows anything. The landscape is changing so fast that all I can do is point out a few issues." But it is probably a good idea to include such a chapter, so that no one thinks that they now know everything there is to know about copyright. Here goes. We will cover a few things that we know, some of the things we don't know, and then how come this is all so unpredictable.

THE INTERNET:
A NEW AND DIFFERENT MEDIUM

When we say **Internet**, we mean that collection of new gee-whizzes that include broadband, private secure networks, and the traditional Internet. To distribute a work on the Internet requires separate and specific authority to do so, in the same way that separate and specific authority is needed to distribute your film on television or through videocassettes.

This may seem so basic and obvious that it doesn't need to be said, but a lot of people have forgotten a fundamental fact: The Internet is a new and separately licensed medium. They thought they could throw your movie on the Internet, just because they had some sort of distribution rights.

Don't feel bad if you were among the folks gazing into a picture of the Internet future without stopping to think of this fundamental truth. Even *The New York Times*, which hires many freelance writers, became seduced by this vision. In its old freelance agreement, *The New York Times* had the right to print an article in the newspaper, but the author retained the copyright and the right to any exploitation of the material other than the newspaper. When *The New York Times* launched an Internet edition of its newspaper, it reprinted the entire newspaper on the Internet without asking freelance authors for permission, without paying those authors, and without remorse. *The Times* never looked back.

Great for readers addicted to the Internet. The freelance writers who worked laboriously on their articles were not so happy. They owned the copyrights, so they felt entitled to extra compensation or at least the right to say "yea" or "nay" to the Internet idea.

The writers sued.

The writers won . . . in court.

The New York Times got the last laugh, however. They said, "Fine, give us a free license for the additional Internet use of your material or you won't ever write for this newspaper again. We'll strip your articles off the Internet, apologize for that oversight, and not print another word of yours until you come around to our way of looking at things." Pretty powerful stuff. As near as I can tell, pretty effective, also.

YOUR LESSON: When you acquire the right to any element of your film, including all materials, performances, effects, clips, pieces of music, and underlying property, you want to be sure to acquire the right to retain the clip, music, or underlying property no matter how it is exploited, even if it is exploited over the

Internet. The forms in this book accomplish that purpose. Many old contracts cover this exploitation possibility of a film with a fairly common phrase that has brought a smile to many a non-lawyer. The phrase is "by any means, whether now known or hereafter created." Somebody was thinking ahead.

THE INTERNET IS FREE, NOT THE STUFF THAT IS ON IT

Many folks also thought they could just take anything off the Internet and use it any way they felt like. It was on the Internet. That meant that it was free for the taking . . . and the using . . . and whatever . . . without having to pay anything to anyone.

Wrong.

You still need the same old licenses that you always needed from the copyright holder in order to incorporate what you saw or heard into your film. You can't use something in your film just because it is on the Internet. The old copyright laws still apply.

In a nutshell, you can only take things off the Internet for your own personal use, including research for your film, viewing on your big screen, or listening in the comfort of your home or car. There is even some question about this personal-use right under the Digital Millennium Copyright Act that we will discuss below. That act has a lot of restrictions about bypassing copy protection technology to reach public domain material or to make fair use of copyright protected material. Most people polled at this writing think that the courts and the legislature will not let the law go as far as the preventing of personal use of materials on the Internet. But remember, this is America. Anything can happen here.

If you have any doubt about this, consider the $3,740,000 award Playboy won against a San Diego-based company for distributing almost 7,500 photographs owned by Playboy over the Internet. Some of the photos were obtained from other Internet user groups that traded the digital photographs. The judge arrived at the figure by valuing each photograph at $500. That should make you think twice before entering into such a scheme.

Napster, eBay, TiVo, and Others that Provide Cool Things Through the Internet

Many people wonder why the file-swapping services of Napster put them out of business, while eBay prospers even though copyrights and personal rights are sometimes violated by the sale of stuff over the eBay system. The Digital Millennium Copyright Act provides a safe harbor for the likes of eBay because eBay has a system in place for investigating and knocking off vendors once eBay receives notice of problems with the products being sold. Such a notice must be in writing from the legitimate owner of the violated rights. Then the vendor is given a limited time to respond. This system allows eBay to stay in business even though some of its vendors are occasionally shut down.

Napster, on the other hand, refused to recognize the rights of copyright holders, held copyrighted songs on its master server, and, therefore, was found to be actively aiding in the unauthorized swapping of copyrighted songs among its subscribers. The court said that was a "no-no." So Napster shut down under the burden of a $200,000,000-plus judgment against it. Almost immediately, other services grew up that facilitated the same result without storing the songs on a master server and without even knowing who was giving what to whom. It is the law of the technological jungle that as soon as one perceived dragon is slain, one or two other dragons will pop up that do just about the same thing. Innovation happens.

TiVo and SONICblue let viewers record programs without knowing anything more than the name of the program. The devices capture programs whenever they air, extend the recording time if a program runs over, and tells you about similar programs, just in case you are interested. SONICblue is in litigation with all the major studios and the networks because it added features that automatically skip over the commercials and allow its customers to send programs to other customers. TiVo wisely sat back and let the fireworks occur. They will find out soon enough whether these features are allowable without spending time and energy in the courthouse. In the meantime, the expense of the litigation contributed to Sonicblue having to file protection with the bankruptcy court.

Telephone companies and folk who inadvertently help people get to a site where they can obtain infringing materials have avoided liability under the copyright laws because of rules protecting common carriers and the requirement for *substantial participation* in infringement before one is liable. This situation probably will not change, because the accused parties are essentially innocent participants in a process that only leads to infringing activity in a tiny percentage of the traffic on their systems.

INTERNET RESOURCES FOR THE FILMMAKER

The Internet can help you realize your film in four primary ways: Research, Licensing, Communicating with the Copyright Office, and Advertising.

Research on Your Film's Subject and Potential Cast and Crew

For this purpose, you can think of the Internet as the biggest library in the world. If you know how to do it, you can browse to your heart's content. As with any other research tool, you can use all of the facts you gather to create your own original work. Remember to make a note of your sources. You may need them for the script annotation that is required by many studios for fact-based films, and you may need to know the sources of your facts in your discussions with the insurance company.

Several resources are available for the seeking out information about film-industry types. The best source for credits is IMDb.com (Internet Movie Database). This is an advertiser-supported service that is incredibly complete, though occasionally inaccurate. You can type in almost anyone's name and find out the films they were in and the credits they received. Beware of someone who says that they really produced a picture, but their credit was as an associate producer. A whole lot of people didn't earn the producer credit that they were awarded. Few receive a credit that is less than what they actually did on the picture.

Another fine resource is iFilm.com. It offers information similar to IMDb but not as broad a range or as complete.

Licensing Artwork and/or Film Clips

Almost every business in the country has a website today. Even lawyers have websites. Some of them, like mine, can be pretty feeble, but there they are to be accessed by anyone with nothing better to do. Most, if not all, of the various services from which you can license artwork and film clips have websites. On most of those websites you can view materials and then, usually, order and pay for the materials over the Internet. I have tried to include e-mail addresses for each of the resources listed in this book. Use them.

Interfacing with the Copyright Office

This process is fully explained in the chapter on registering your script with the Copyright Office. Once you use it, you may never go back to the old way of ordering the forms through the mail or—worse yet—running to the post office to pick up the forms if their supplies are stocked for you. You can go to www.copyright.gov/forms to pull up all the forms that you need. For more general information, go to www.loc.gov/copyright. It has an enormous amount of helpful information about the copyright law and about the Copyright Office and its procedures.

You can also use the website of the Copyright Office to find out who owns what. This process is a big boon to strapped and time-pressed filmmakers. You can very quickly find out who owns a property if it is a matter of public record. Chapter 2 refers you to

Thomson and Thomson. They still have a role to play in tracking such rights because they have a huge library of information. Note: People with an interest in a property often will issue a press release before they file anything with the Copyright Office.

A cool website called GigaLaw.com started up in January 2000. It's dedicated to high-tech law discussed in a surprisingly straightforward way. Born as the dot-com bubble was about to burst, this site has grown into a significant resource, with hundreds of articles, continuing discussions, and much more. The site was originally intended solely for nonlawyers, but its audience has expanded to include a number of lawyers.

Advertising and Marketing Your Film Project

No savvy filmmaker overlooks the Internet as an effective medium for promoting a film. The classic example of this is *The Blair Witch Project.* The long lead-up and the mystique that were built on the Internet were phenomenal. When the filmmakers came to me, I wasn't very Internet savvy. I took a look at their project and made an old-fashioned judgment to pass on it because it looked like a mess to me. Well, maybe it was a mess, but everybody involved in the film became wealthy. This film, produced for a few hundred thousand dollars, grossed over $150,000,000 in worldwide box office receipts. Those numbers make *Blair Witch* the best return on investment of any film ever made. And it is all because of the filmmmakers' promotional efforts on the Internet.

When you set up your website and select a domain name, make your selection based on a legitimate connection to your project— usually the title of your movie. The law surrounding domain names is still developing, but it is clear that you cannot trade off someone else's name for commercial gain. You cannot mislead or confuse the public. The good thing is that in order to resolve disputes, registrants must use speedy and relatively inexpensive arbitration procedures that have been set up through the World Intellectual Property Organization Arbitration and Mediation Center. This arbitration is not binding unless you fail to file a court case to confirm the award within ten days of receiving your decision from the arbitrator.

BE CAREFUL ABOUT GRANTING
INTERNET DISTRIBUTION RIGHTS

Because of the pervasiveness of the Internet, most distributors are pushing hard for the right to include Internet distribution along with all the rights they want to acquire. There are a lot of reasons for this, but the main reason is that there has got to be money in them thar hills. Even if not a buck is made today, there surely will be many bucks to be made sometime in the future. Specifically, the promise of video-on-demand will certainly be fulfilled before this book is revised again.

Video-on-demand is a phrase that covers several different technological developments that will make it possible for you and I to select our motion pictures for the evening from hundreds of thousands of titles and order them and receive them instantly in the comfort of our homes. MGM, Paramount, Sony, Universal, and Warner Bros. have formed a joint venture called Movielink to offer an almost unlimited selection of films over the Internet. Other enterprises will pop up either over the traditional Internet or satellite broadcast or private, secure systems or broadband or something that has not yet been created.

In selling your film to a distributor, you will often split the foreign and domestic rights. You can give television rights to a foreign sales agent and a domestic distributor because the territories are different. The Internet crosses all these political boundaries. That is part of the beauty of it. For you, it makes it imperative that you give the Internet distribution rights to only one entity. You may want to wait on assigning Internet rights until Internet delivery systems are a reality, and then grant those rights directly to the organization that will be actually distributing your film over the Internet. Today, every distributor wants to grab these rights from you at the earliest possible time.

You do not want to give Internet distribution rights to any company without checking out its security provisions. The ease with which things can be downloaded and traded is amazing. My office fights hard for the right to approve the specific technology used for any Internet distribution when my clients want to grant Internet rights to a distributor or foreign sales agent.

Finally, many distributors will tell you truthfully that they send trailers and sometimes the entire film to potential buyers around the world using secure Internet lines. This is true. This, however, does not require that you give them Internet distribution rights. It only requires that you give them permission, in writing (as part of the contract) to send the entire film, the trailer, or selected clips to their clients around the world through the Internet for the limited purpose of selling those clients the rights to further distribute the film in their territories. That permission is a lot narrower than the unfettered right to distribute your film on the Internet.

THE NEW COPYRIGHT LAWS RESPONSIVE TO THE INTERNET

Of course, no self-respecting legislative body can sit by while the people develop a widget without passing widget laws. So that is just what Congress did. They passed the Digital Millennium Copyright Act. That is mouthful, so in this section I am going to refer to it as DMCA like most everybody else does. It was so long and complicated and counter-intuitive that when I first sat down to read it, I gave up. Quit! I couldn't understand it, didn't believe what I thought I understood, and generally felt inadequate. If I couldn't understand the text of this important piece of legislation, how could I call myself a copyright expert?

I reviewed that legislation more carefully for this book and for a scholarly article. I was right the first time. The DMCA is too long. It is internally inconsistent. It is counter-intuitive. It is the product of the powerful forces that have grown up around the multi-billion-dollar businesses that control copyright in creative works, such as movie studios and large record labels. Congress listens carefully to advocates of copyright holders. If you think traditional copyright holders are going to yield anything to the new playground called the Internet, you are in for a major surprise.

This new playground has movie studios terrified. Ordinary citizens can make perfect copies of their movies. Ordinary citizens can send these copies far and wide for very little money. Ordinary citizens can edit their movies using readily available, low-cost programs and devices. All of this is very scary to these behemoth corporations that are behemoths because they own and control a myriad of copyright-protected properties.

The chief purpose of the DMCA is to protect copyrights on the Internet any way the copyright holders want, including making properties inaccessible even for legitimate fair use purposes, such as writing a critique or to educate. DMCA then goes on to make illegal anything you try to do to get around the copyright protection, even if your purpose in getting around the protection is to exercise one of your fair use rights, such as criticism or private viewing. Under this law, asking your sister for her password in order to enter a file could be considered a criminal act. Obviously, the law will not be enforced so vigorously against individual citizens, but the law is on the books, and it is—at this writing—a mess, in my opinion.

Oops. I had no sooner written those words than the record industry filed a lawsuit against an Internet service provider to obtain the name of one of its customers who was using a peer-to-peer program to obtain free music. It is a test case. A **test case** means that the case's main purpose is to obtain a judicial ruling about people's rights. The major record labels want to expand their fight against online piracy by going after people who use file-sharing networks to copy songs for free. The problem is, they don't know who those people are. And Internet service providers, who do know, don't want to tell. As we went to press, the judge ordered the Internet service provider to turn over the name of its customer.

So I scratched around some more and discovered that, indeed, the criminal provisions of the DMCA were being used. So far, the criminal provisions have only been used against folks who made a lot of bootlegged copies of videotapes, which is a totally appropriate use of the criminal law system. A California man was the first to be convicted in that state in the Spring of 2002. The U.S. attorney in Nebraska had already obtained a conviction earlier that year. But there are those who fear the DMCA noose will tighten to include less egregious cases.

The far-reaching right to try to control access to copyright-protected materials, as opposed to controlling the copying of protected works, is new and mind-boggling to those among us who enjoy dabbling around with copyright-protected materials on their own for their own use. The major studios have gone a step further and tried to control efforts to circumvent fair use protections for even the most legitimate reasons, such as education, critiques, and comment. However, such controls and regulations could help you as an independent filmmaker because you are a potential owner of the copyright in the films that you produce. As such, you may benefit from harsh laws that protect your rights.

FUTURE TRENDS IN COPYRIGHT LAW
FOR THE INTERNET

It's helpful to understand how copyright law grows and changes. With copyright law, the process has become a negotiation among interested businesses (with their many lobbyists) and Congress. The public has not had much in the way of input or even the opportunity for input. It is the copyright lawyers for the studios and publishers and related businesses who work out the legislation. No wonder the law is so convoluted and often counter-intuitive. No wonder these businesses can get passed such laws as the 3% royalty on every blank tape and the $1.00-$8.00 royalty on every tape machine, no matter how you or I are going to make use of these items.

However, a feeling is spreading that the recent amendments to the copyright law are not fair, not workable, and are not right. It is quite possible that individual citizens, who have never participated in the process before, may very well try to find a place at the bargaining table where legislation is crafted. Whether this will produce better legislation or just protracted wrangling is not foreseeable at this point.

Whether copyright protections will be strengthened and whether the new copyright law modification will make it clear that individual downloading and copying for the purpose of private viewing is acceptable is uncertain at this writing. It seems clear to me that criminalizing individual conduct, which most people think is a birthright, will never work. Such laws won't be obeyed. They won't be enforced. So some loosening of the DMCA restrictions on trying to move around copy protection devices is sure to be sought after by consumer groups.

The lobbying strength of the studios is not what it used to be. In the old days the studios made movies. When television came along, they also made television programs. When they went to Washington under the coordinated leadership of Jack Valenti, they had a very, very high success rate in getting what they wanted from the United States Congress. In fact, Congress generally limited its work to being sure that all the studios agreed.

Today the studios are part of international conglomerates. Their interests are not always so clearly aligned. Occasionally, they are on opposite sides of a legislative issue. For instance, the most recent copyright battle was embodied in a piece of legislation introduced by Senator Ernest Hollings (Democrat of South Carolina), the Chairman of the powerful Senate Commerce Committee. His legislation would help block the unauthorized downloading of movies and music. Great for Warner Bros. Studio, bad for AOL. Both companies are part of the same international conglomerate, which also is one of the country's largest print media and cable operators.

With Internet legislation, the public begins to experience copyright law first hand and for the first time, and the public is forming opinions about what should and should not be in the copyright law. The public, for the first time, is forming reactions to fundamental questions of copyright law, such as the extent to which one can make copies of the creative work of another and the extent to which one can pass along copies of the creative work of another. That is why this area is so vulnerable to change in the future.

There are stirrings in the land that this esoteric area of the law is no longer the exclusive domain of the copyright experts employed by large corporations. The intense press interest in the Supreme Court hearings about the copyright extension bear this out. The editor of the American Bar Association's Entertainment and Sports Lawyer newsletter recently wrote: "A protection racket is defined as money extorted by racketeers posing as a protective association. A racketeer obtains money by an illegal enterprise usually involving intimidation. With the advent of digital file sharing over the Internet, hard-hitting tactics by copyright owners and their lawyers are beginning to look a lot like intimidation." Pretty heavy stuff!

The prospect of readers of this book and other individuals rising up and expressing their personal views on the copyright law is exciting to me. It will create a balance in the law that has not been there in the past (and has not been sought in the past). What a great note on which to end this book. Good luck to you in all your copyright encounters.

CHAPTER 23

LEGAL REFERRAL SERVICES

Certainly, you will have many legal questions down the road. Your concerns may be personal to your situation and fall beyond the scope of this book. The following list of Bar Association and non-profit referral services can help point you in the right direction. The role of the referral services is simply to refer you to a lawyer competent to assist you, not to give out legal advice. They usually charge a small fee for that service. Generally, the initial consultation with the lawyer will be free or at a highly reduced rate.

Bear in mind that the time you have to speak to the attorney to whom you are referred may be limited. It is in the best interests of both parties for you to realize that this is a preliminary stage of consultation. Therefore, a good approach is to think, develop, and write down your questions ahead of time. Perhaps you will be able to answer them yourself, especially after referring to this book. In the event that new questions arise in your conversation, there will be time for the attorney to address them, provided that you have prepared well prior to the conversation.

Your thorough preparation insures the most valuable communication between you and your attorney in the shortest time. By knowing what you want to ask, you are more likely to gain credibility and respect from any lawyer you contact through a referral service.

Los Angeles is the entertainment center of the world. As a result, there are more legitimate entertainment attorneys practicing there than in other major cities. Therefore, you may want to call the Beverly Hills Bar Association Lawyer Referral and Information Service at (310) 553-4022. In providing a referral, the Beverly Hills Bar Association reviews many attorneys who practice in the area of entertainment law. The Beverly Hills Bar Association requires a referral fee of $25, which entitles you to two referrals and a half-hour consultation with an attorney. You are under no obligation to retain the attorney. (In fact, you should question the attorney about his or her experiences with problems that are similar to yours.)

In addition to Los Angeles, several other cities have groups that provide helpful legal information to filmmakers. The executive directors of the various services listed below tell me that the clear majority of people who call these services do not need an attorney for their problem. Some of these organizations provide workshops on various topics of interest to the independent filmmaker. Be precise when you call such services. For instance, if you feel that you have been ripped off, ask for a plaintiff's attorney for a copyright infringement case. If you are being sued, ask for a defense attorney. For any contract preparation or interpretation, ask for a transactional lawyer. Always, always employ a lawyer to look over contracts as complicated as film distribution and/or sales agreements.

AMERICAN BAR ASSOCIATION (HQ in Chicago)

(312) 988-5000

www.abanet.org

service@abanet.org

The ABA does not have a referral service. But, it does sell a nationwide lawyer referral list.

California

Beverly Hills Bar Association
(310) 553-4022
www.bhba.org
submit@bhba.org

Los Angeles County Bar Association
(213) 243-1525
www.lacba.org
webmaster@lacba.org

California Bar Association
(213) 765-1000
www.calbar.ca.gov
barrcomm@calbar.ca.gov

California Lawyers for the Arts (Los Angeles)
(310) 998-5590
www.calawyersforthearts.org
userCLA@aol.com

California Lawyers for the Arts (San Francisco)
(415) 775-7200
www.calawyersforthearts.org
cla@calawyersforthearts.org
A nonprofit, tax-exempt service organization founded in 1974 that provides both lawyer referrals and dispute resolution services.

Colorado

Colorado Lawyers for the Arts
(303) 722-7994
www.coloradoartslawyers.org
info@coloradoartslawyers.org
The organization provides pro bono legal services, mediation, and legal education. **Pro bono** is Latin, meaning "for free." I guess the only way lawyers can give it away is to say it in Latin. Be sure to *always* verify the fee arrangement before you start your meeting.

Georgia

Georgia Volunteer Lawyers for the Arts (Atlanta)
(404) 837-3911

www.glarts.org

gla@glarts.org

Illinois

Lawyers for the Creative Arts
(312) 944-ARTS

www.law-arts.org

wrattner@law-arts.org

This not-for-profit, tax-exempt organization provides pro bono legal services to qualifying individuals.

Louisiana

New Orleans Film, Video Society

(504) 523-3818

www.neworleansfilmfest.com

admin@neworleansfilmfest.com

Arts Council of New Orleans

(504) 523-1465

www.ArtsCouncilOfNewOrleans.org

mail@ArtsCouncilOfNewOrleans.org

Maryland

Maryland Lawyers for the Arts

(410) 752-1633

imani2@msn.com

Massachusetts

Volunteer Lawyers for the Arts of Massachusetts, Inc.

(617) 350-7600

www.vlama.org

mail@vlama.org

Volunteer Lawyers for the Arts of Massachusetts, Inc. (VLA) is a non-profit organization established to meet the legal needs of the state's artistic community.

Minnesota

Resources and Counseling for the Arts (St. Paul)

    (612) 292-4381

    Chris@rc4arts.org

    www.rc4arts.org

Missouri

St. Louis Volunteer Lawyers & Accountants for the Arts

    (314) 652-2410

    www.vlaa.org

    vlaa@stlrac.org

    They provide free legal and accounting assistance and sponsor a wide range of affordable educational programs.

New York

New York Bar Association

    (518) 463-3200 x2700 (statewide)

    www.nysba.org

    foundation@nysba.org

    The official statewide organization of the legal profession.

Volunteer Lawyers for the Arts

    (212) 319-ARTS

    www.vlany.org

    vlany@busy.net

    vlany@vlany.org

    VLA provides pro bono legal services, education, and advocacy to the New York arts community.

Ohio

Cleveland Bar Assoc. Volunteer Lawyers for the Arts

    (216) 696-3525

    www.clevelandbar.org

    lchenault@clevelandbar.org

    They have legal education programs for both attorneys and the public and provide a lawyer referral service for those who need to find an attorney.

Oregon

Northwest Lawyers and Artists, Inc.
(503) 295-2787
Artcop@aol.com

Pennsylvania

Philadelphia Volunteer Lawyers for the Arts
(215) 545-3385
www.libertynet.org/pvla
pvla@libertynet.org
Provides pro bono legal assistance and basic business
counseling to area artists and cultural organizations.

Rhode Island

Ocean State Lawyers for the Arts
(401) 789-5686
www.artslaw.org
dspatt@artslaw.org
Dedicated to providing legal assistance regarding contracts,
copyrights, trademarks, tax-exempt status, collection of
accounts, and any other arts-related problems.

Texas

Texas Accountants and Lawyers for the Arts–Houston
(713) 526-4876
(800) 526-TALA
www.talarts.org
info@talarts.org
Provides pro bono legal and accounting services to
artists and arts organizations.

In step with the current legal trends for conflict resolution, referral services and volunteer lawyers for the arts organizations often offer mediation. **Mediation** is a formalized settlement meeting with all disputing parties and a trained professional who runs the meeting. The purpose is to reach a settlement, but you do not have to agree to anything unless you think that it is in your best interests to do so. You have nothing to lose by pursuing such mediation.

Mediation is never binding. It is designed to have the parties reach a voluntary settlement agreement. An Interstate Mediation Network has been established among several of these organizations. Parties to a conflict often wish to settle disputes quickly and cost-effectively without the hassle of going through tedious litigation and the court system. A mediator acts as a neutral third party to help the disputing parties reach a settlement. Experienced mediators are usually successful in finding a remedy for your problem. Fees range from modest to very substantial, so be sure to shop. Some of the organizations listed above purport to arrange for pro bono mediators.

Before you close this book in amazement at the amount of space spent on selecting a lawyer, reflect on the cases in this book. They all grew out of oh-so-typical situations. There was not one exotic situation in the bunch. The cases involved properties or people of sufficient notoriety to make them interesting, but the real situations that gave rise to these lawsuits were very common. You may or may not find yourself in these situations. These cases are expensive. All of the cases mentioned in this book went through the trial courts. Most went on to the appellate courts, and sometimes to the Supreme Court of the United States. Choose your lawyer carefully. You are not searching for bravado. You are searching for experience, integrity, and unflinching honesty in all communications you have with your attorney.

Good luck! If you carry the lessons of this book with you, you have significantly reduced your chances of being embroiled in legal entanglements. If you back away from doing business with those you don't trust, with whom you don't connect on a human level, you have reduced the odds of unhappy encounters even more. Choose your friends and your business associates with uncompromising care. You won't have to spend so much time with lawyers.

APPENDIX A

GLOSSARY

Above-the-line. Personnel who are the key creative elements of a picture and the key financiers. This designation generally includes all producers, lead actors, the director, and the writer.

Access. The reasonable opportunity to review a copyrighted work. Proof of access is the first requirement of persuing copyright infringement.

Actual Damages. The actual provable dollars you lost or the defendant gained on account of copyright infringement.

Adaptation rights. The rights to change or add to the music or lyrics of a piece of music or literature.

American Federation of Musicians (AFM). The union that represents professional musicians.

AFM. The new name for the American Film Market, which is held each February in Santa Monica, California.

AFMA. The new name for the American Film Marketing Association, which is made up mostly of foreign sales agents and sponsors the AFM (formerly American Film Market).

Annotated script. A script that contains references to the various sources the writer relied on when writing it. A script is annotated by placing handwritten numbers, which refer to a key list of factual sources, directly on the script's factual assertions.

Anonymous author. An author whose name is not given on copies of a script at the Copyright Office, but who still retains significant rights under copyright law.

"As is" document. Used when a document is incomplete or when the person filing the document with the Copyright Office cannot or does not want to vouch for it.

Audio-visual rights. The same as film rights, but, as a descriptive phrase, better anticipates the possible development and use of future technologies.

Below-the-line. All personnel who aren't above-the-line personnel; this includes the crew, non-star actors, suppliers, and licensors.

Bible. Primarily a television term for a detailed story, more detailed than the typical script treatment.

Blanket license. A license obtained by the periodic payment of a flat fee for the right to perform various pieces of copyright-protected music.

Captions. The titles of contract paragraphs.

Case citation. The exact book and page number where a case summary and court's opinion may be found in a law library's legal reference works.

Ceiling. The maximum price to be paid.

Chain of title. A collection of the contracts and other documents that show any change in ownership of a film project from its inception. The documents are a trail of transfers from the original author of a work through the final film (or whatever stage the project is at at the time).

Cite. *See* "Case citation."

Clear. To obtain written permission from the proper individual to use a certain item in your film or to obtain a legal opinion that permission is not necessary.

Compilation. A work formed by the collection and assembling of pre-existing materials.

Consideration. Legalese shorthand for whatever is of value that you give up for what you get. Money is the "consideration" that most people think of. Your promises can also be consideration.

Continuity. The actual dialogue script annotated with timing code taken from a tape or workprint of the feature film.

Copyright infringement. The situation in which a work is based in whole or in part on a copyrighted work to such an extent that a court will enjoin it.

Copyright report. A detailed history of a work's copyright ownership and related registered items.

Damages. The money a court awards the winning party at the end of a lawsuit.

Defamation. The publication of anything false that is injurious to the reputation of another or which tends to bring them disrepute.

Defined term. A term that is capitalized throughout a contract because it is defined somewhere in a contract and has a special meaning throughout that contract.

de minimus. The injury is too trivial for the court to bother with.

Derivative work. A work based on one or more pre-existing works, such as a script based on a book or a magazine article.

Double source. To have two separate and independent sources for each factual assertion in a script.

Double vested. In control of two production or development entities, one of which is a signatory of a union agreement and the other of which is not.

Drawn characters. *See* "Visual characters."

Droit moral. *See* "Moral rights."

Enjoin. To restrain someone from a certain activity by means of a court order.

Equitable relief. The court trying to do what is fair between parties when no strict statutory guidelines exist.

Errors and omissions (E&O) insurance. Insurance to compensate others for damage caused by negligent mistakes.

Express contract. A contract in which the parties have agreed to specific terms in specific words, either orally or in writing.

Fair use. This concept recognizes that it simply is not fair to say that every copying is a violation of the law, and that some copying of a copyrighted work is necessary to promote the creativity that the law was designed to promote. Fair use is a defense that can be used when one is sued for copyright infringement.

False light. Statements that fall short of being defamatory yet cause some discomfort to the party they address simply because they are not accurate.

Film rights. A film-industry term for a collection of different rights. Those rights include the right to make a film for initial exhibition on television or in theaters, the right to make sequels and remakes of that film, the right to distribute the film on videocassettes and other media, even those that aren't invented yet. Sometimes referred to as motion picture rights.

Floor. The minimum price to be paid.

Franchise. A character, concept, or title that is supposed to guarantee a good opening weekend for a film. James Bond is the best example in film history.

Good title. Ownership of that which one claims to own, free and clear of any encumbrances or liens.

Grand performing right. Performance of a song or other piece of music as part of the story of a play or a film. *See* "Small performing right."

Holdback period. A period during which certain rights that are possessed are not used.

"Hot" news exception. An exception that protects hard-to-gather factual information for a short period of time even though it is in the public domain.

Implied contract. An agreement that arises without any party specifically stating the terms.

Independent contractor. An employee or independent business entity who controls the time, the place, and the manner in which their tasks are performed.

Injunction. The court says you can't do something. In our world, that usually means you can't distribute a film.

Internet. That collection of electronic communications methods that include broadband, private secure networks, and the traditional Internet.

Judgment on the Pleading. A court ruling that finds that the plaintiff could not state a good complaint, so the defendant wins without even filing an answer to the lawsuit.

Knock-off. A slang term for something that has been especially created to appear or sound very similar to something or someone else, often a notable person or thing.

Laches. You sat on your rights too long before suing, so you lose.

Lanham Act. A Federal Law covering various business practices. It is the source of protection for the title of a film or script.

Leading Case. Refers to the first case to clearly state a certain conclusion of law.

Libel. A defamation in print.

Library. A group of films whose copyright is owned by one entity.

Limited Liability Corporation. A hybrid business entity that provides the shared responsibilities of a partnership with the protection from personal liability of a corporation.

Locked. A film's final edited form that is ready to have prints struck from it.

Lookalike. Someone who looks so much like a celebrity that they pass as the same person.

Master use license. License to use a specific recording. This name refers to the fact that you are licensing the master recording of a song.

Mechanical rights. The rights to reproduce a piece of music on audio records, CDs, or tapes.

Mediation. A formalized settlement meeting with all disputing parties and a trained professional who runs the meeting.

Moral rights (droit moral). A group of rights that protect a work from being changed without permission of the person who, by the act of creating that work, holds moral rights.

Mortgage of copyright. A document signed in order to give someone a security interest in your film.

Motion picture rights. *See* "Film rights."

Music clearance. Obtaining the permissions necessary to use specific pre-existing pieces of music in a film.

Music cue sheet. A document that lists each song or portion of a song used in a film, along with the composers, publishers, performing rights affiliation (ASCAP or BMI or SESAC), usage, and timing of each song. (Music cue sheets also list the composers, performing rights affiliations, usage, and timing of each underscore cue.)

Music publisher. An entity that manages a song and collects money for the writer from the royalties derived from its exploitation.

Music supervisor. The person who helps select music, supervise the clearing of music, hire a composer, and supervise the recording of the score.

Non-disclosure agreement. An agreement that states that a producer will not disclose to others a pitched idea unless he or she buys it.

Off air. A film or video copied directly off a television as the program is coming across the cable or over the airwaves.

Off the top. A reimbursement made before the agreed split of proceeds.

Out-of-Context Rights. The right to use the music from your film in a trailer advertising the film.

Option. The exclusive right to purchase something in the future, on fixed terms and conditions.

Oral contract. A non-written contract.

Package agreement (music). An agreement between a composer and a producing entity that specifies that the composer composes all the music, hires the musicians, records the music, and delivers all the fully recorded music to the producer for a fixed fee.

Pan and scan. Refers to the process by which motion pictures are adapted from the wide screen theater format to a narrower format fitting on the old-style television screens.

Parody. A new, copyrightable work based on a previously copyrighted work to such an extent that the previous work is clearly recognizable, but not taking more from the copyrighted work than is necessary, and that makes a social commentary which is at least in part directed to the subject matter of the previous work, usually humorously, and that is not likely to hurt the value of the previous work.

Per diem. A specific amount paid to cover all expenses without any need to provide receipts or an accounting.

Performing rights society. An organization that monitors the performance of music and collects royalties due the songwriter from performances on radio and television, in restaurants, lounges, bars, hotels, and retail stores playing music on a radio, and workout/dance studios playing music for aerobics classes.

Plagiarism. The lay term for taking someone else's writing and calling it your own. The legal term for this is copyright infringement.

Pre-sales. Sales of the right to distribute a film in a certain territory made before the film is complete—usually before filming has even started.

Prequel. Something of a slang term to describe a sequel that is set earlier in time than the original.

Pro bono. Latin. It means "for free." I guess the only way lawyers can give it away is to say it in Latin. Be sure to *always* verify the fee arrangement before you start your meeting.

Product placement. The practice of receiving some consideration from the company that owns the trademark for a product that is clearly used or displayed in a film.

Pseudonymous. The author of a script identified by a fictitious name.

Public domain. Literally, "owned by the public." A property to which no individual or corporation owns the copyright.

Public performance rights. The right to perform a piece of music in public. Licensing this right allows the music in a film to be "performed," which is what happens every time the film is projected.

Publishing company (music). The company that administers the various rights that flow from ownership of the copyright to a song or other piece of music.

Publishing income (music). The income flowing to the copyright holder of music, such as performance royalties when the film is played on TV or in theaters outside the U.S., or when the music is played apart from the film—on radio, for example.

Quote. The price that a writer (or other artist) received (or is purported to have received) for past work.

Remake. A movie in which the script that formed the basis for another film is recast and reshot.

Reproduction Rights. The rights to reproduce a piece of music (these include synchronization rights and mechanical rights).

Reuse. Taking a piece of film or video that was shot for one project and using it for another project (e.g. a television show playing on a television set that is included in a scene of a movie or a clip cut from one film and used in another film). Union agreements for writers, directors, and actors require a separate negotiation for reuse.

Residuals. Additional payments to artists when the work they created is exploited in a medium other than the medium for which it was primarily created (e.g. a theatrical film moving to video). These payments are pre-set within union contracts.

Right coupled with an interest. A situation in which your representative also has an interest in the thing being represented. This makes it difficult to terminate the relationship.

Right of privacy. An individual's right to be left alone.

Right of publicity. The inherent right of everyone to control the commercial use of his/her identity.

Scenes a faire. A legal term that means that the scenes flow naturally from the general premise, so they are not protected by the law of copyright and copyright infringement. (Scenes a faire are not protectable because they necessarily result from the choice of setting or situation.)

Script clearance report. This document identifies potential script problems and researches whether names and locations used in the script exist in the real world.

Script clearance. The process of identifying all the potential problems contained in a script and then obtaining either written permission from the proper person or a legal opinion that such permission is not necessary.

Secondary meaning. A shorthand phrase that describes the existence of a condition from which public confusion will flow if the defendant is permitted to pursue his deceptive scheme.

Section 205 documents. These include almost all of the documents you will record as a filmmaker. Examples of Section 205 documents include transfers of copyright ownerships and other documents pertaining to a copyright such as exclusive and non-exclusive licenses, contracts, mortgages, powers of attorney, certificates of change of corporate name or title, wills, and decrees of distribution. (Section 205 refers to that specific section of the Federal Copyright Law that provides for the recording of these important documents.)

Security agreement. An agreement issued by a film's lender or financier to secure the repayment of their money by the producer.

Sequel. A story that uses some or all of the same characters in a different story, set in a different time.

Settled. A court ruling that a law is not likely to change because of the number of courts that have issued decisions in the area over a long period of time.

Single-purpose production company. A production company that is formed solely and exclusively for the purpose of producing a film and has not performed any other business before producing the film.

Slander. An oral defamation.

Small performing right. The right to perform a song or other piece of music by itself, apart from a play or a film. *See* "Grand performing right."

Soundalike. One performer or group of performers recording a song in the manner and style of another performer or group of performers.

Source material credit. The credit that acknowledges the original, pre-existing material upon which the script was based.

Spec script. A script written on speculation—the speculation that a producer will want to option and/or purchase the script and make it into a movie.

Spotting. Picking the points in a film where music will be heard. The company and director and music team do this together.

Statutory damages. Damage awards granted by a court when a copyright owner's work has been infringed but the owner cannot prove the actual losses or the losses are quite small.

Stock footage. Pre-existing film, usually without sound, that can be licensed for use in another film.

Story characters. Characters originating in works of literature, such as Frankenstein and James Bond. Dialogue, plot, and interaction with other characters define these characters.

Submission agreement. An agreement that provides that if a prospective producer reads a script, the script's writer will not bring a claim against the producer for copyright infringement if he or she produces a similar movie without the writer's participation.

Substantial similarity. The situation in which two works are so similar that a jury could determine that the second work was copied from the first.

Summary judgment motion. A motion heard by a judge who determines whether there are issues of fact that should be tried by a jury.

Superintendence. For writers, it means that they can accept or reject suggestions without giving any reason.

Synchronization rights (or synch rights). The rights to record music to be heard as part of a film.

Target defendant. Anyone who looks as though they have the capacity to pay big bucks to avoid being sued.

Test case. The main purpose of a test case is to obtain a judicial ruling about people's rights.

Title report. A list of all the titles of films, books, songs, and plays together with press mentions of these titles.

Title search. Traces the ownership records from an initial land grant through transfers from owner to owner by way of sale, death, subdivisions, marriages, divorces, and on and on, up to your ownership.

Trade libel. Falsely assigning a bad attribute to a trademark. One does not have the right to hold a product up to ridicule or do anything that harms the reputation of a product.

Trademark. A name or symbol used by a manufacturer to identify the source of products: Coca-Cola, Infinity, IBM, and so on.

Transformative. In the context of fair use cases, this term designates that the defendant's work has indeed used the plaintiff's copyrighted work, but in such a way to be so different from the original use that it is not a copyright infringement.

Treatment. A script story in abbreviated form. It can be a few paragraphs, a few pages, or more than twenty pages.

Turnaround provision. A contractual provision that allows a screenwriter to purchase a script back from a production entity.

Underlying property. The source material used as the basis for a script that is not wholly original with the author.

Underlying rights. The foundational rights that you must control to have the right to make and distribute a film based on an underlying property.

Underscore. Background music that accompanies (and often comments on what is happening in) a film.

Underwriters. The people who assess risk and decide whether to issue an insurance policy and what it should cost.

Video on demand. A phrase that covers several different technological developments that will make it possible to select a motion picture from hundreds of thousands of titles and order it and receive it instantly in the comfort of one's home.

Visual character. A character based on a drawing. It is not so much a character as a copyrighted drawing, figure, or image, such as a cartoon character that would be recognizable in any context.

Work for hire. Defined in U.S. Copyright Law as either (1) a work prepared by an employee within the scope of employment; or (2) a work specially ordered or commissioned for use as one of a very limited number of specified works.

APPENDIX B

TABLE OF FORMS

372

APPENDIX C

TABLE OF CASES

LIST OF LAW CASES MENTIONED IN THIS BOOK

Many law cases are mentioned in this book. You can read the original case by going to a law library or accessing the case through one of the online services. You will need the official case name and the official cite (**cite** is shorthand for citation). The **case citation** tells you the exact book and page where you can find the case. Most librarians are happy to get you started.

Most cases in the book are from appellate courts, which means that the case has been through the trial court. That represents a lot of legal fees and a lot of time and energy from the filmmakers involved in these lawsuits. When you first read a law case, skip over all the introductory stuff and go right to the summary of facts that the courts use to start an opinion. As you get into the opinion itself, skip over all the case cites within the opinion; they will only distract you. Good luck!

Chapter 1
* Blaustein v. Burton, 9 Cal.App. 3d 161, 88 Cal.Rptr. 319 (1970)
* Desny v. Wilder, 46 Cal. 2d 715, 299 P.2d 257 (1956)
* Mann v. Columbia Pictures, Inc., 128 CalApp. 8d 628, 180 Cal.Rptr. 522 (1982)

Chapter 2
* Stewert v. Abend, 495 US. 207, 110 S.Ct. 1750 (1990)
* Konigsberg Int'l, Inc. v. Rice, 16 F. 3d 355 (qtrCir. 1994)

Chapter 4
* Midler v. Ford Motor Co., 849 F. 2d 460 (qtr.Cir. 1988) cert denied, 112 S.Ct. U.S. 1513 (1990)
* Eastwood v. Superior Court of Los Angeles County, 198 Cal.Rptr. 342 (Cal.Ct.App. 1983)
* Stecco v. Moore

Chapter 12
* Lutz v. De Laurentiis (1989) 211 Cal.App.3d 1317 [260 Cal.Rptr. 106]

Chapter 14

- Maura v. Columbia Broadcast Syst., Inc., 245 F.Supp. 587 (S.D.N.Y. 1965)
- Shapiro, Bernstein & Co. v. P. F. Collier & Sons, 26 U.S.P.Q. 40 (S.D.N.Y. 1934)
- Amsnick v. Columbia Pictures Indust., Inc., 862 F.Supp. 1044 (S.D.N.Y. 1994)
- Dallas Cowboy Cheerleaders, Inc. v. Pussycat Cinema, Ltd. 467 F.Supp 366 (S.D.N.Y.) eff'd   604 F.2d200 (2d CIR. 1979)
- Ringgold v. Black Entertainment Television, Inc. 126 F.3d 70 (2d Cir. 1997) Producer had to clear a decorative quilt used as set decoration in TV show, visible a total of 26.75 seconds spread over 9 shots. Money damages.
- Producer did not have to clear statue used in *Bat Man* because it was really an architectural feature. Artist ent. LL
- Producer had to clear a relief made to strongly resemble a religious piece of art. Visible 20 minutes. Injunction issued while film was in release.

Chapter 17

- Hofheinz v. AMC Productions, Inc., 147 F. Supp. 2d 127 (E.D.N.Y. 1/11/2001)
- Hofheinz v. A&E Television Networks 1467. Supp. 2d 442 (S.D.N.Y. 6/27/2001)

Chapter 18

- Campbell v. Acuff-Rose Music, Inc. 114 S.Ct. 1164 (1994)
- Loew's v. Columbia Boradcasting Co., Inc., 131 F.Supp. 165 (S.D.Cal. 1955) app'd sub nom.
- Benny v. Loew's Inc., 239 F.2d. 532 (9th Cir. 1956) off'd by an equally divided court, 356   U.S. 43 (1958)

Chapter 19

- Brown v. 20th Century Fox Film Corp., 799 F.Supp. 166 (D.D.C. 1992). Court approved use of clip without payment.

Chapter 21

- Litchfield v. Spielberg, MCA, Inc. 736 F. 2d. 1352 (1984)
- Walker v. Time Life Films, Inc., 784 F. 2d. 44 (1986)
- Universal City Studios, Inc. v. Film Ventures International, Inc., 543 F.Supp. 1134 (1982)
- The Hospital for Sick Children v. Melody Fare Dinner Theatre, 516 F.Supp 67 (1980)

APPENDIX D

FILMS AND TELEVISION SHOWS MENTIONED IN THIS BOOK

Ace in the Hole

Chapter 1
Idea protection case that found a writer (Desney) who shared his story idea with director Billy Wilder had an implied oral contract.

Amityville Horror, The

Chapter 12
One of six movies using similar titles that were approved by the court on the theory that the public was not confused.

Amityville 3-D

Chapter 12
One of six movies using similar titles that were approved by the court on the theory that the public was not confused.

Amityville II: The Possession

Chapter 12
One of six movies using similar titles that were approved by the court on the theory that the public was not confused.

Amy Fisher, My Story

Chapter 3
This TV movies is mentioned with reference to purchasing life rights related to a public domain news story.

Apollo 13

Chapter 19
This film integrated actual historical film clips into its story.

Asphalt Jungle

Chapter 11
The estate of John Huston asserted his moral rights in France to enjoin exhibition of the colorized version of his famous black-and-white film.

Batman Forever

Chapter 14
The statue that formed the basis of this film's advertising campaign did not have to be cleared because it was an architectural element of the office building location used in the film.

FILMS
& TV SHOWS
MENTIONED
IN THIS
BOOK

377

Frances

Chapter 3
In a suit involving this film, the court found that a published biography's fictionalized elements that are presented as true are public domain "facts."

Frankenstein (Universal, 1931)

Chapter 2
This film helps illustrate the difference between copyrightable cinematic characters created by a studio and public domain story characters.

French Kiss

Chapter 12
Originally titled *Paris Match*, this film's release was scheduled for around the same time as the film *Forget Paris*. Reviewing the possible competition and confusion of these films' titles, MPAA arbitrators denied the use of the title *Paris Match*, which was changed to *French Kiss*.

Great White

Chapter 21
This film was enjoined by the court from further distribution because it infringed the film *Jaws*.

Harper Valley P.T.A.

Chapter 2
An example of a song used as the basis of a television series.

Highway to Heaven

Chapter 12
As this TV show's pilot episode was about to be aired, the producers found out that a book by the same name was about to be published. Both parties decided that they could live with the competing titles.

Hook

Chapters 3 and 21
Peter Pan, the J.M. Barrie play on which *Hook* is based, is public domain in the United States, but an act of Parliament granted it a special copyright protection in perpetuity in Great Britain. *Hook*'s producers had to make special arrangements to show the film in the U.K.

FILMS
& TV SHOWS
MENTIONED
IN THIS
BOOK

379

Immediate Family	Chapter 14 This film shows a particular mobile that hangs over a child's crib. Although the mobile was prominently displayed and copyright protected, it did not have to be cleared.
It Conquered Hollywood! The Story of American International Pictures	Chapter 12 This documentary used film clips without paying, the producers were sued, and won on a Fair Use defense.
It's a Wonderful Life	Chapters 3 and 15 A copyright-like protection for the re-release of this film, which had fallen into public domain, was achieved through the film's music, which carried separate and still enforceable copyrights.
Jaws	Chapter 21 The producers of *Jaws* sued and won their copyright infringement case against the producers of *Great White*. (Comparing these two films will give you an excellent grasp of just what it takes to win an infringement action.)
Lawnmower Man	Chapter 11 Stephen King won an injunction against the use of his name beyond that specifically allowed in the contract because the film was such a departure from his short story.
Long Kiss Goodnight, The	Chapter 3 New Line did not have to pay the Three Stooges for use of their name and likeness in a clip from a public domain film.
Mary Shelley's Frankenstein	Chapter 3 This film held close to Shelley's book, and thus was protected from any claims by Universal Studios involving the cinematic character created for Universal's classic *Frankenstein*.
Malcolm X	Chapter 6 A contributor to this film's script sued Spike Lee and Warner Bros. for screenwriting credit and profit shares, but failed to win his suit.

McLintock!

Chapter 3
Copyright-like protection for this film
was achieved through its music.

My Big Fat Greek Wedding

Chapter 2
This film illustrates the need to obtain
underlying rights.

Night In Casablanca

Chapter 12
Marx Brothers answered a lawyer's
letter to cease and desist using a title
containing the word "Casablanca."

9$^1\!/_2$ Weeks

Chapter 15
A song and a particular performance
of that song were licensed for use in
this film. However, a different
performance of the song was
inadvertently inserted into the film.
The filmmakers had to license this
other performance, too.

100 Years of Horror

Chapter 17
This documentary used film clips
without paying, the producers were
sued, and won on a fair use defense.

*Peter Graves:
Mission Accomplished*

Chapter 17
This documentary used film clips
without paying, so the producers
were sued, but won on a fair use
defense.

Peter Pan

Chapters 3 and 21
Peter Pan, the play and character
created by J. M. Barrie, received
special copyright protection in
perpetuity in Great Britain only due
to a special act of Parliament.

*Positively True Adventures of
the Alleged Texas Cheerleader-
Murdering Mom, The*

Chapter 3
This TV movie is mentioned with
regard to film stories based on public
domain materials.

Prime Time Justice

Chapter 17
Producers of this series used a
privately owned and copyrighted film
clip in a montage bumper.

Quincy

Chapter 3
The case involving this television series successfully relied on the public domain status of stories that the author of a fictional book represented as true.

Rear Window

Chapter 2
This 1954 Hitchcock film was based on Cornell Woolrich's short story of the same name (published in 1944). For the film's 1962 re-release, Universal had to pay for the rights to the story again because of the unique copyright renewal provisions provided by the copyright laws of the time.

Roc

Chapter 14
Producers of this series were sued when an episode's set displayed a poster depicting a noted artwork.

Roger & Me

Chapter 4
Filmmaker Michael Moore was sued by a man who felt this documentary portrayed him in a false light. The jury agreed with the plaintiff.

Shampoo

Chapter 1
In a case similar to the one regarding the film *Ace in the Hole* (see above), a writer sued Warren Beatty, Columbia Pictures, and Robert Towne over the authorship of the idea for the film *Shampoo*. This case helped spell out the specific requirements for a writer to achieve idea protection.

Smoke and Mirrors

Chapter 17
Major use of clips of television commercials for cigarettes were cleared without obtaining permission from the tobacco companies because the documentary was about the history of cigarette advertising.

Snow White and the Seven Dwarfs

Chapter 3
This film helps illustrate the difference between copyrightable cinematic characters created by a studio and public domain story characters.

Story of G.I. Joe, The	Chapter 17 Three networks were sued for their use of clips from this film in their news programs' obituaries of actor Robert Mitchum. The court held this to be fair use.
Switchblade Sisters	Chapter 11 Quentin Tarantino's affection for this B-film by Jack Hill led him to organize its re-release, making the original independent filmmaker very happy because he still owned the copyright.
Taming of the Shrew, The	Chapter 1 Case involved the concept of idea protection: A noted producer, Julian Blaustein, pitched to the agents representing Elizabeth Taylor and Richard Burton the *idea* of combining the couple in a film of this Shakespeare play.
Thunderball and other Bond films	Chapter 6 Highlighting the importance of a good collaboration agreement, the co-author of the film *Thunderball* and other Bond films was in litigation for years with Ian Fleming and his successors after creating a cinematic James Bond that was quite different from the literary character in Fleming's novels.
Titicut Follies	Chapter 4 Written permission to use film of asylum patients failed because it was not signed by the patients' guardians.
12 Monkeys	Chapter 14 The producers of this film were sued because one of its sets closely resembled a noted architect's drawing.
Yellow Submarine	Chapter 2 An example of a song used as the basis of a movie.

INDEX

ABOUT THE AUTHOR

Michael C. Donaldson is a founding partner of Donaldson & Hart, a Los Angeles, California, firm specializing in entertainment and copyright law with an emphasis in the representation of independent film producers. He is the author of *Do It Yourself! Trademarks & Copyrights,* which was released in June, 1995. He co-wrote *Negotiating for Dummies*, which was published in September, 1996. He also wrote the introduction to *Conversations with Michael Landon* and is a contributor to the book *Movie Secrets.* He writes and lectures extensively.

Donaldson earned his law degree in 1967 at the University of California at Berkeley. He is a member of the Los Angeles Copyright Society, the Beverly Hills Bar Association (where he was formerly co-chairman of the Entertainment Section), the Los Angeles County Bar Association, the State Bar of California, and the American Bar Association. He is listed in the current edition of *Who's Who in American Law.* He served in the United States Marine Corps and competed in the 1998 Senior Olympics on the men's gymnastics team.

You may contact Donaldson at 1 (310) 273-8394, ext 23, or MCD@donaldsonhart.com.